MEDIUM ÆVUM MONOGRAPHS

EDITORIAL COMMITTEE

K. P. Clarke, A. J. Lappin,
N. F. Palmer, P. Russell, C. Saunders

MEDIUM ÆVUM MONOGRAPHS
XXXI

MISERA HISPANIA:

JEWS AND *CONVERSOS* IN ALONSO DE ESPINA'S *FORTALITIUM FIDEI*

ROSA VIDAL DOVAL

The Society for the Study of Medieval Languages and Literature

OXFORD · MMXIII

THE SOCIETY FOR THE STUDY OF
MEDIEVAL LANGUAGES AND LITERATURE
http://mediumaevum.modhist.ox.ac.uk

© Rosa Vidal Doval, 2013

British Library Cataloguing Publication Data

A catalogue record for this book is
available from the British Library

ISBN-13: 978-0-907570-50-9 (pb)

First published, in hardback, 2013
This paperback reprint first issued 2015

Para mis padres

CONTENTS

Preface ix
Abbreviations xi
1: The Origins of the *Converso* Debate 1
2: The Contours of the *Converso* Debate 33
3: The Fortress of Faith: Unity and Enmity 67
4: Jews and Judaism: Carnality and Criminality 87
5: From Converts to Judaizers 119
Conclusion 147
Bibliography 151
Index 177

PREFACE

I began work on Alonso de Espina's *Fortalitium fidei* in 2000 for the doctoral thesis on the *converso* problem in Castile that partly underlies this book. In the years since the completion of that thesis, the field of *converso* studies has grown wider, providing new insights into the contributions of New Christians to political, economic and cultural aspects of late medieval and early modern life in the Iberian Peninsula and beyond. Although responding to and drawing on this new work, my own research has remained focused on the origins of the *converso* problem and the role played therein by polemical texts and treatises. This book explores one of the main contributions to the *converso* debate, Alonso de Espina's *Fortalitium fidei*. It provides a close study of the work itself, particularly with regard to its presentation of Jews and *conversos*, and seeks to contextualize *Fortalitium fidei* through comparison with contemporary pro-*converso* texts and by reference to Espina's career as an Observant Franciscan.

The first chapter explores the emergence of the *converso* problem and outlines existing historiographical approaches before providing a biography of Espina himself and setting out what is known of the immediate context of *Fortalitium fidei*. Chapter Two studies three pro-*converso* works: Alonso de Cartagena's *Defensorium unitatis christianae*, Juan de Torquemada's *Tractatus contra madianitas et ismaelitas*, and Alonso de Oropesa's *Lumen ad revelationem gentium*. It does so through the exploration of three interrelated themes that were central to discussions about New Christians: the unity of the faithful, the issue of judaizing, and the relationship between Judaism and Christianity. Chapter Three examines the central image of the fortress to review how Espina arranged his work overall, what his broad aims and intentions were, and what the logic of his argument was. Chapter Four provides a close reading of Espina's treatment of Jews and Judaism across Books I and III, while Chapter Five offers the same for his treatment of *conversos* in Book II.

My debts to institutions and individuals are many. I thank for support of my research the Arts and Humanities Research Board (now Council), the Departments of History, and Spanish,

Portuguese and Latin American Studies at the University of Manchester, the Anne Helen Leyland Fund, and the Cañada Blanch Centre for Advanced Research in Hispanic Studies, the Department of History at Johns Hopkins University, and the School of Languages, Linguistics and Film at Queen Mary, University of London.

Over the years I have received advice and encouragement on this project from numerous individuals and my particular thanks go to: Andy Beresford, Carlos Conde Solares, Edward Cooper, Trevor Dadson, Alan Deyermond, John Edwards, Roger Highfield, Julia Hillner, Richard Kagan, Jordi Larios, Rosemary Morris, Parvati Nair, Tom Nickson, David Nirenberg, David Pattison, Hilary Pearson, Chris Pountain, María del Pilar Rábade Obradó, Miri Rubin, Rebeca Sanmartín Bastida, Barry Taylor, Jonathan Thacker, and Hannah Williams. I am grateful to my colleagues in the department of Iberian and Latin American Studies at Queen Mary, University of London who provide a most congenial environment for academic work. To the anonymous reader of this volume, I offer sincere thanks for good advice.

I have a special debt of gratitude to my PhD supervisors: Jeremy Lawrance, who kindled my interest in *conversos* when I was still an undergraduate, and Conrad Leyser, who helped me broaden my historical horizons. Anthony Lappin, editor for the Society for the Study of Medieval Languages and Literature, has offered encouragement, advice, and much patience. My greatest thanks go to my family without whose love, support, and companionship I could have never completed this project: my grandmother, Ángela; my brother, Agustín; my husband, Martin, for 'spending warm summer days indoors' with me; and my parents, Carmela and Alberto, to whom I dedicate this book.

RVD,
Hove, August 2013

ABBREVIATIONS

AIA	*Archivo Ibero-Americano*
BHS	*Bulletin of Hispanic Studies*
CCSL	Corpus Christianorum Series Latina
CSIC	Consejo Superior de Investigaciones Científicas
Defensorium	Alonso de Cartagena, *Defensorium unitatis christianae (Tratado en favor de los judíos conversos)*, ed. by Manuel Alonso (Madrid: CSIC, Instituto Arias Montano, Escuela de Estudios Hebraicos, 1943).
FIRC	Fontes Iudaeorum Regni Castellae
Fortalitium	[Alonso de Espina], *Fortalitium fidei* [Strasbourg: Jean Mentelin, 1471].
Lumen	Alonso de Oropesa, *Luz para conocimiento de los gentiles*, ed. and trans. by Luis A. Díaz y Díaz (Madrid: Universidad Pontificia de Salamanca, Fundación Universitaria Española, 1979).
Memorial	*Memorial contra los conversos*, in *De la 'Sentencia-Estatuto' de Pero Sarmiento a la 'Instrucción' del Relator: estudio introductorio, edición crítica y notas de los textos contrarios y favorables a los judeoconversos a raíz de la rebelión de Toledo de 1449*, ed. by Tomás González Rolán and Pilar Saquero Suárez-Somonte (Madrid: Aben Ezra Ediciones, 2012), pp. 193–242.
P&P	*Past and Present*
PL	*Patrologiae cursus completus: series latina*, ed. by J-P. Migne, 221 volumes (Paris: by the editor, 1844–65).
Sentencia	*'Sentencia-Estatuto' de Pero Sarmiento*, in *De la 'Sentencia-Estatuto' de Pero Sarmiento a la 'Instrucción' del Relator: estudio introductorio, edición crítica y notas de los textos contrarios y favorables a los judeoconversos a raíz de la rebelión de Toledo de 1449*,

	ed. by Tomás González Rolán and Pilar Saquero Suárez-Somonte (Madrid: Aben Ezra Ediciones, 2012), pp. 20–31.
Tractatus	*Tratado contra los madianitas e ismaelitas, de Juan de Torquemada (Contra la discriminación conversa)*, ed. by Carlos del Valle R. (Madrid: Aben Ezra Ediciones, 2002).

All quotations of *Fortalitium fidei* are from its *editio princeps* (Strasbourg: Jean Mentelin, 1471). I transcribe the text, regularizing its punctuation and capitalization and adding folio numbers. To allow comparison with other printings, all references are given by book and section as well as folio number. Books are referred to by roman numerals in small capitals with further subdivisions referred to by section name and number in lowercase.

THE ORIGINS OF THE *CONVERSO* DEBATE

Late Medieval Castile witnessed a radical and far-reaching change in the treatment of religious minorities. Out of a long history of religious coexistence unparalleled elsewhere in Europe arose a new polity where national identity became associated with religious uniformity and orthodoxy. The arrangement of *convivencia* – the toleration under strict legal conditions of Jewish and Muslim minorities within Christian society – was dismantled.[1] At the same time, the Castilian Church and monarchy were concerned increasingly with the extirpation of heresy and religious dissidence, hitherto rare problems.[2] By the end of the fifteenth century a series of measures had been put into place that cemented these changes. The Spanish Inquisition was established in 1480; in 1492 Jews were given the choice between conversion and expulsion; the same year the Kingdom of Granada was conquered, ending the seven-century long presence of an Islamic polity in the Iberian Peninsula.

The key catalyst for these changes was the development of what historians have termed the *converso* problem.[3] Difficulties in

---

[1] There is a survey of the concept in Maya Soifer, 'Beyond *Convivencia*: Critical Reflections on the Historiography of Interfaith Relations in Christian Spain', *Journal of Medieval Iberian Studies*, 1 (2009), 19–35.

[2] The papal Inquisition had never operated in Castile, while in the Crown of Aragon it had been in place since 1232 but by the fifteenth century it was nearly inactive, Henry Kamen, *The Spanish Inquisition: An Historical Revision* (London: Weidenfeld & Nicolson, 1997), p. 43.

[3] The expression comes from Eloy Benito Ruano, *Los orígenes del problema converso*, Clave Historial, 31, rev. edn (Madrid: Real Academia de la Historia, 2001). The bibliography on the subject is vast and is best approached through two recent bibliographical essays: Isabel Montes Romero-Camacho, 'El *problema converso*: una aproximación historiográfica (1998–2008)', *Medievalismo*, 18 (2008), 109–247; Óscar Perea Rodríguez, 'Minorías en la España de los Trastámara (II): judíos y conversos', *eHumanista*, 10 (2008), 353–468. Important studies published since 2008 include: *The Conversos and Moriscos of Late Medieval Spain and Beyond*, I: *Departures and Change*, ed. by Kevin Ingram, Studies in Medieval and Reformation Traditions, 141 (Leiden: Brill, 2009); *Late Medieval Jewish Identities: Iberia and Beyond*, ed. by Carmen Caballero-Navas and Esperanza Alonso (New York: Palgrave Macmillan, 2010); *Marginal Voices: Studies in Converso Literature of Medieval and Golden Age Spain*, ed. by Amy Aronson-Friedman and Gregory B.

accommodating the descendants of converts from Judaism in late medieval and early modern society ultimately resulted in the wholesale suppression of all religious difference and dissent. Such repression has long been regarded as a characteristically Spanish phenomenon, arising from the distinct religious conditions in medieval Iberia and influencing directly the configuration of the emerging absolutist state. Modern Spain would pursue these essentially religious values through repressive institutions and mechanisms such as the Inquisition and the doctrine of purity of blood.[4]

The *Converso* Problem

The origins of those changes can be traced to the pogroms that spread throughout Castile and Aragon in 1391, where Jews were given the choice of death or conversion. Many Jewish communities suffered numerous losses, some almost disappeared entirely. Faced with such violence, large numbers of Jews, perhaps even the majority, chose instead to accept baptism and enter the Christian

---

Kaplan, The Medieval and Early Modern Iberian World, 46 (Leiden: Brill, 2012).

[4] On the Inquisition see, Francisco Bethencourt, *The Inquisition: A Global History, 1478–1834* (Cambridge: Cambridge University Press, 2009), and bibliography therein. On purity of blood the essential work remains, Albert A. Sicroff, *Los estatutos de limpieza de sangre: controversias entre los siglos XV y XVII*, Juan de la Cuesta Hispanic Monographs: Estudios Judeo-Españoles 'Samuel Armistead y Joseph Silverman', 6, 2nd edn (Newark, DE: Juan de la Cuesta, 2010); and now see, Juan Hernández Franco, *Sangre limpia, sangre española: el debate sobre los estatutos de limpieza (siglos XV–XVII)* (Madrid: Cátedra, 2011); and Gregory B. Kaplan, 'The Inception of *Limpieza de Sangre* (Purity of Blood) and Its Impact in Medieval and Golden Age Spain', in *Marginal Voices: Studies in Converso Literature of Medieval and Golden Age Spain*, ed. by Amy I. Aronson-Friedman and Gregory B. Kaplan, The Medieval and Early Modern Iberian World, 46 (Leiden: Brill, 2012), pp. 19–41. On the social and cultural consequences of the Inquisition and *limpieza* see, for example, Francisco Márquez Villanueva, 'El problema de los conversos: cuatro puntos cardinales', in *De la España judeoconversa: doce estudios*, Serie General Universitaria, 57 (Barcelona: Edicions Bellaterra, 2006), pp. 43–74 (first pub. as 'The Converso Problem: An Assessment', in *Collected Studies in Honour of Américo Castro's Eightieth Year*, ed. M. P. Hornick (Oxford: Lincombe Lodge Research Library, 1965), pp. 317–333); and a revisionist interpretation of these phenomena in Henry Kamen, 'Limpieza and the Ghost of Américo Castro: Racism as a Tool of Literary Analysis', *Hispanic Review*, 64 (1996), 19–29.

community.⁵ The second decade of the fifteenth century saw another wave of mass conversions. The preaching campaign of Vincent Ferrer, sponsored by Pope Benedict XIII and the regents of Castile, sought to bring about the conversion of those Jews still remaining in the kingdom. Ferrer's preaching created a climate of fear and menace and inspired the passing of legislation – the *Leyes de Ayllón* – that placed severe restrictions on the economic activities and social standing of the Jews, and on the autonomy of their communities. The resulting severe deterioration of their social, economic and religious conditions drove many Jews into accepting Christianity.⁶ Although the situation of Jewish communities would improve again before their expulsion from Spain in 1492, the mass conversions had already altered radically the religious demographic in Castile. Furthermore, they had raised the possibility of a kingdom without Jews and revealed a tendency among rulers and ruled alike to consider the separation and elimination of Judaism to be 'structurally necessary for the improvement of the Christian community.'⁷

Baptism conferred full rights upon the newly converted. Enjoying the privileges of Christians, *conversos* had access to trades forbidden to Jews, to universities, and to careers in civil administration and the Church. Although very many among them did not benefit from such opportunities and remained poor, nonetheless they saw their social standing improved. Significant numbers of *conversos* did, however, enter the Church, gain employment in local government and royal administration, and establish

---

⁵ The most comprehensive account of these events is Emilio Mitre Fernández, *Los judíos de Castilla en tiempo de Enrique III: el pogrom de 1391*, Estudios de Historia Medieval, 3 (Valladolid: Universidad de Valladolid, 1994). There are narrative overviews of the development of the *converso* problem in Gregory B. Kaplan, *The Evolution of 'Converso' Literature: The Writings of the Converted Jews of Medieval Spain* (Gainesville: University Press of Florida, 2002), pp. 16–31; and, taking into account developments in the Crown of Aragon, David Nirenberg, *Anti-Judaism: The Western Tradition* (New York: Norton, 2013), pp. 218–45.

⁶ Rosa Vidal Doval, 'Predicación y persuasión: Vicente Ferrer en Castilla, 1411–1412', in *Hacia una poética del sermón*, ed. by Rebeca Sanmartín Bastida, Barry Taylor and Rosa Vidal Doval (= *Revista de Poética Medieval*, 24 (2010)), pp. 225–43, and bibliography therein.

⁷ Nirenberg, *Anti-Judaism*, p. 221.

marriage alliances with noble families.⁸ During the reigns of Juan II (r. 1406–54) and Enrique IV (r. 1454–74) a small but conspicuous elite rose to the very highest echelons of ecclesiastical and royal administration. This included figures such as Pablo de Santamaría (1353–1435), Bishop of Burgos, and his son Alonso de Cartagena (1385–1456), also Bishop of Burgos, Cardinal Juan de Torquemada (1388–1468), Lope de Barrientos (1382–1469), Bishop of Cuenca, the Relator Fernán Díaz de Toledo (d. 1457), and Diego Arias Dávila (1405–66).⁹

From an early stage, the arrival of New Christians into the main fold of society was problematic. Sources for the first half of the fifteenth century are scarce but point to tensions between *conversos* and their old and new coreligionists. At a local level, the rapid ascent of *conversos* led to rivalries among the professional classes and urban oligarchies. Old Christians justified their attempts to bar these newcomers from access to lucrative positions through appeal to their *converso* status. Likewise, some Old Christians refused to marry New Christians in an effort to impede their access to local networks of power, which were arranged around kinship groups.¹⁰

---

⁸ David Nirenberg, 'Enmity and Assimilation: Jews, Christians, and Converts in Medieval Spain', *Common Knowledge*, 9 (2003), 137–55 (p. 153). For an overview of participation in local government, a case paradigmatic of *converso* success, see, Francisco Márquez Villanueva, 'Conversos y cargos concejiles en el siglo XV', in *De la España judeoconversa: doce estudios*, Serie General Universitaria, 57 (Barcelona: Edicions Bellaterra, 2006), pp. 137–74 (first pub. in *Revista de Archivos, Bibliotecas y Museos*, 63 (1957), 503–540).

⁹ A general treatment of the careers of these figures may be found in Luciano Serrano, *Los conversos don Pablo de Santa María y don Alfonso de Cartagena, obispos de Burgos, gobernantes, diplomáticos y escritores* (Madrid: CSIC, 1942); Luis Fernández Gallardo, *Alonso de Cartagena (1385–1456): una biografía política en la Castilla del siglo XV* (Valladolid: Junta de Castilla y León, Consejería de Educación y Cultura, 2002); Juan José Llamedo González, 'Juan de Torquemada: apuntes sobre su vida, su obra y su pensamiento', in *Tratado contra los madianitas e ismaelitas, de Juan de Torquemada (Contra la discriminación conversa)*, ed. by Carlos del Valle R. (Madrid: Aben Ezra Ediciones, 2002), pp. 87–118; Ángel Martínez Casado, *Lope de Barrientos: un intelectual en la corte de Juan II* (Salamanca: Editorial San Esteban, 1994); Nicholas G. Round, 'Politics, Style and Group Attitudes in the *Instrucción del Relator*', *BHS*, 46 (1969), 289–319; María Eugenia Contreras Jiménez, 'Diego Arias Dávila en la tradición y en la historia', *Anuario de Estudios Medievales*, 15 (1985), 475–95.

¹⁰ B. Netanyahu, *The Origins of the Inquisition in Fifteenth Century Spain*, 2nd edn (New York: The New York Review of Books, 2001), pp. 266–95; David Nirenberg, 'Was There Race before Modernity? The Example of "Jewish" Blood in Late Medieval Spain', in *The Origins of Racism in the West*, ed. by

Attempts at discrimination were, however, 'sporadic' and do not suggest 'an organized popular movement to impede *conversos*' social advancement'.[11] Thus, despite tensions, *conversos* assimilated, at least apparently, into Christian society, their rights protected by a crown and Church that had regarded the mass conversions as eminently positive events.[12]

This situation changed dramatically in the middle of the fifteenth century. Voices arose claiming that mass conversions had had deleterious and dangerous effects. The focus of these complaints was the religious observances of *conversos*: they were accused of practising Judaism in secret – judaizing. This heresy, it was claimed, was accompanied by moral corruption and enmity towards the Old Christian majority. New Christians were an alien, self-interested group whose usurping of power was the cause of Castile's decline.[13]

In 1449, the citizens of Toledo rose up against King Juan II of Castile and his favourite Álvaro de Luna.[14] As the revolt took hold,

---

Miriam Eliav-Feldon, Benjamin Isaac and Joseph Ziegler (Cambridge: Cambridge University Press, 2009), pp. 232–64 (pp. 252–54).

[11] Kaplan, 'The Inception', in *Marginal Voices*, ed. by Aronson-Friedman and Kaplan, p. 27. Though see Carlos del Valle R., 'En los orígenes del problema converso', in *Tratado contra los madianitas e ismaelitas, de Juan de Torquemada (Contra la discriminación conversa)*, ed. by Carlos del Valle R., (Madrid: Aben Ezra Ediciones, 2002), pp. 29–74 (pp. 54–57) who claims that the *converso* problem already existed in the first half of the century and brings forward Pablo de Santamaría's *Scruptinium scripturarum* as evidence of attempts to tackle the issue from a theological perspective.

[12] José María Monsalvo Antón, *Teoría y evolución de un conflicto social: el antisemitismo en la Corona de Castilla en la Baja Edad Media* (Madrid: Siglo Veintiuno de España Editores, 1985), pp. 283–85. In response to the situation in Castile, the Council of Basle (1434) had restated the Church's longstanding position that new converts ought to enjoy full legal rights, Netanyahu, *The Origins*, p. 276. For the text of the decree, see Joannes Dominicus Mansi, *Sacrorum conciliorum nova et amplissima collectio*, 31 vols (Florence: Antonium Zatta, 1759–98), XIX: 100.

[13] There is an overview of the main themes of the debate in María del Pilar Rábade Obradó, 'Judeoconversos e inquisición', in *Orígenes de la monarquía hispánica: propaganda y legitimación, ca. 1400–1520*, ed. by José Manuel Nieto Soria (Madrid: Dykinson, 1999), pp. 239–72 (pp. 246–49).

[14] There are detailed accounts of the events of the rebellion in Eloy Benito Ruano, *Toledo en el siglo XV: vida política*, Escuela de Estudios Medievales: Estudios, 35 (Madrid: CSIC, Escuela de Estudios Medievales, 1961), pp. 35–76; B. Netanyahu, *The Origins*, pp. 296–350; and Tomás González Rolán, and Pilar Saquero Suárez-Somonte, 'Introducción', in *De la 'Sentencia-*

Toledo's ruling rebel council sought to purge the city of its enemies. A group of Christians of Jewish descent were singled out and subjected to a set of unprecedented measures of legal and religious persecution that would have far-reaching consequences and long-lasting repercussions. What had started as a popular uprising against Álvaro de Luna's demand for an extraordinary tax, morphed into an open rebellion that that led to the city removing itself from royal and episcopal obedience for over a year. *Conversos* were from the beginning the victims of violence. The property of the city's chief tax gatherer, the *converso* Alonso Cota, had been looted and burned as retribution for his involvement in the levying of the tax.[15] Once the rebels set themselves as the government of the city, persecution of *conversos* became systematic. Suspicions about apostasy and political and socio-economic tensions led to inquisitorial proceedings and executions, and to the passing of restrictive legislation, the *Sentencia-Estatuto* of Pero Sarmiento, barring New Christians and their descendants from access to office and ecclesiastical benefice.[16]

This document claimed that an inquest or *pesquisa* conducted by the cathedral authorities had shown the majority of *conversos* to be

---

Estatuto' de Pero Sarmiento a la 'Instrucción' del Relator: estudio introductorio, edición crítica y notas de los textos contrarios y favorables a los judeoconversos a raíz de la rebelión de Toledo de 1449, ed. by Tomás González Rolán and Pilar Saquero Suárez-Somonte (Madrid: Aben Ezra Ediciones, 2012), pp. xvii–cxvii. See also Rosa Vidal Doval, '"Nos soli sumus christiani": *Conversos* in the Texts of the Toledo Rebellion of 1449', in *Medieval Hispanic Studies in Memory of Alan Deyermond*, ed. by Andrew M. Beresford, Louise M. Haywood and Julian Weiss (Woodbridge: Tamesis, 2013), pp. 215–36; and eadem, 'La matriz medieval de la disidencia en Castilla: la herejía judaizante y la controversia sobre los conversos', in *Disidencia religiosa en Castilla la Nueva en el siglo XVI*, ed. by Ignacio J. García Pinilla (Ciudad Real: Almud, 2013).

[15] The attack on Cota's property on 26 January 1449 sparked off the Toledo revolt. Álvaro de Luna had required of the city a loan of a million *maravedíes*, an amount so large it required the imposition of an extraordinary tax on even the poorest neighbours. The rebels suspected that Cota 'habia seydo movedor deste empréstido' and accused him of excessive zeal in the collection of the tax, *Crónica del serenísimo rey don Juan el Segundo deste nombre*, in *Crónicas de los reyes de Castilla desde don Alfonso el Sabio hasta los Católicos don Fernando y doña Isabel*, ed. by Cayetano Rosell, 3 vols, Biblioteca de Autores Españoles, 66, 68, 70 (Madrid: M. Rivadeneyra, 1875–78), II, 273–695 (p. 662).

[16] Benito Ruano, *Toledo*, pp. 35–76.

suspect in their faith and guilty of judaizing.[17] On the basis of such findings and the allegedly ample evidence that *conversos* were the political enemies of Old Christians, allied with Álvaro de Luna, and were responsible for mismanagement of the city while holding official posts, they were banned from holding office and ecclesiastical benefit in Toledo.[18] The exact terms of exclusion conflated Jewish ancestry with charges of heresy and hatred of Old Christians.[19] Although the *Sentencia* was not a statute of purity of blood *avant la lettre*, it inaugurated the legal discrimination of *conversos* and the development of a genealogical model of exclusion based on Jewish descent.[20]

The attempt to enshrine the discrimination of *conversos* in law largely on the basis of their Jewish inheritance had grave implications for the lives of New Christians, the fabric of Castilian society,

---

[17] 'E por quanto contra muy gran parte de conversos de esta çibdad, desçendientes del linaje de los judíos de ella, se prueba, e pareçió e pareçe evidentemente ser personas muy sospechosas en la sancta fe católica de tener e creer grandíssimos herrores contra los artículos de la sancta fe católica, guardando los ritos e çeremonias de la ley vieja [...] según más largamente se contiene en la pesquisa sobre esta razón fecha por los vicarios de la sancta iglesia de Toledo', *Sentencia*, pp. 24–25.

[18] 'otrosí han mostrado e muestran ser enemigos de la dicha çibdad e vezinos christianos viejos de ella y que notoriamente a su instançia y prosecuçión e solicitaçión estuvo puesto real sobre la dicha çibdad contra nosotros por el condestable Don Álbaro de Luna [...]. E otrosí por quanto durante el tiempo que ellos han tenido los ofiçios públicos de esta çibdad e regimiento e governaçión de ella, mucha e la mayor parte de los lugares de la dicha çibdad son despoblados y destruidos', *Sentencia*, pp. 25–27.

[19] 'todos los dichos conversos desçendientes del perverso linaje de los judíos, en qualquier guisa que sea, así por virtud del derecho canónico y civil [...] como por razón de las heregías e otros delitos, insultos, sediçiones e crímenes por ellos fasta oy cometidos e perpetrados, [...] sean avidos e tenidos [...] por infames, inhábiles, incapaçes e indignos para aver todo ofiçio e benefiçio público y privado', *Sentencia*, pp. 27–28. For a discussion of the legal elements adduced by the *Sentencia* to justify this exclusion, see Vidal Doval, 'Nos soli sumus christiani', in *Medieval Hispanic Studies*, ed. by Beresford, Haywood and Weiss, pp. 221–25.

[20] Michel Jonin, 'De la pureté de foi vers la pureté de sang: les ambiguïtés orthodoxes d'un plaidoyer *pro converso*', in *L'hérédité entre Moyen Âge et époque moderne: perspectives historiques*, ed. by Maaike van der Lugt and Charles de Miramon, Micrologus' Library, 27 (Florence: SISMEL/Edizioni del Galluzzo per la Fondazione Ezio Franceschini, 2008), pp. 83–102 (pp. 86–87). For a discussion of the role of heredity in the *Sentencia*, see Vidal Doval, 'Nos soli sumus christiani', in *Medieval Hispanic Studies*, ed. by Beresford, Haywood and Weiss, pp. 226–27.

and the very nature of the Church. Such legal discrimination threatened to split the Christian community along ethnic lines, while seeming to deny the efficacy of baptism. Thus, the *Sentencia* was met by a determined legislative and polemical response, aiming to curb the rebellion itself and to defeat the ideology that underpinned it.[21] Juan II sought advice from lawyers and theologians and had prepared a number of memoranda – no longer extant – that aimed to enlist papal support against the rebels. In September 1449, Pope Nicholas V issued three bulls – *Humani generis inimicus*, *Si ad reprimendas*, *Nuper siquidem ad aures* – that insisted on the full rights of converts and their descendants to access secular and ecclesiastical office and excommunicated the rebels.[22]

The claims of the *Sentencia* were also challenged in a series of pro-*converso* texts produced over the summer and early autumn of 1449. The sequence opened with Alonso de Cartagena's *Defensorium unitatis christianae*, followed by Fernán Díaz de Toledo's *Instrucción del Relator para el obispo de Cuenca, a favor de la nación Hebrea*, and Lope de Barrientos' *Contra algunos zizañadores de la nación de los convertidos del pueblo de Israel*.[23] The rebels responded to the papal condemnation and these polemics with a further work, the *Memorial contra los conversos* (or *Apelaçión y suplicaçión*) written by the ideologue of the rebellion Marcos García de Mora. This hastily written polemic defended and justified the rebels' treatment of New Christians and, although it fell short of formulating a full and coherent doctrine of purity of blood, nonetheless it intensified the anti-*converso* rhetoric.[24] There were further replies to the rebels: Juan de Torquemada's *Tractatus contra madianitas et ismaelitas*

---

[21] Sicroff notes that 'fue la pluma más bien que la espada la que les [*conversos*] proporcionó su arma de defensa', in Sicroff, *Los estatutos de limpieza de sangre*, p. 53.

[22] González Rolán and Saquero Suárez-Somonte, 'Introducción', pp. xxviii–xxxiv. See also V. Beltrán de Heredia, 'Las bulas de Nicolás V acerca de los conversos de Castilla', *Sefarad*, 21 (1961), 22–47.

[23] There is a discussion of pro-*converso* texts in Benito Ruano, *Los orígenes*, pp. 47–70 and, more extensively, Sicroff, *Los estatutos de limpieza de sangre*, pp. 53–88.

[24] For instance, the *Memorial* refered to *conversos* as 'judíos baptiçados' and labelled their Jewish ancestry 'línea dañada', p. 200. Nicholas G. Round linked the rebels' ideology, as put forward in the *Memorial*, with millenarist heresies: 'La rebelión toledana de 1449: aspectos ideológicos', *Archivum*, 16 (1966), 385–446.

completed in 1450, and Alonso Díaz de Montalvo's *Tratado sobre los conversos*, composed in 1449 but published in the 1480s.[25]

Though the Toledo revolt was not the beginning of the *converso* problem, it was the stimulus for its textualization.[26] By the 1460s, the flurry of works produced in the aftermath of the revolt was joined by two of the longest and most detailed works on the *converso* problem – Alonso de Espina's *Fortalitium fidei* (1458–64), and Alonso de Oropesa's *Lumen ad revelationem gentium* (1466). Though both texts were greatly influenced by the events in Toledo they moved beyond the immediate context of the 1449 revolt. Espina presented *conversos* as part of the wider assault of the enemies of the Christian faith in Castile – heretics, Jews, Muslims, and demons and witches. Oropesa, by contrast, offered a detailed defence of the rights of New Christians as part of a sustained ecclesiological meditation.

The development of the *converso* problem across the second half of the fifteenth century was, thus, driven by texts. The revolt in Toledo had ended with the return of the city to royal obedience and the revocation of the *Sentencia* in 1450 but this did not end the dispute. Political considerations meant that the following year Juan II pardoned the rebels and reinstated much of their anti-*converso* legislation. The following years saw further episodes of violence against *conversos* throughout the kingdom, with revolts in Toledo in 1467 and Córdoba in 1473 and outbreaks of disorder in other cities.[27] The *converso* problem was no longer primarily a religious issue but rather one of public order, becoming a feature of political propaganda within a kingdom plagued by political anarchy and

---

[25] Díaz de Montalvo's treatise appeared as a gloss to the word *tornadizo* within the first edition of the *Fuero Real*, González Rolán and Saquero Suárez-Somonte, 'Introducción', pp. xciii–xciv. There is a modern edition: Alonso Díaz de Montalvo, *La causa conversa*, ed. by Matilde Conde Salazar and others (Madrid: Aben Ezra Ediciones, 2008).

[26] John Edwards, 'The *Conversos*: A Theological Approach', *BHS*, 62 (1985), 39–49 (p. 40).

[27] On Toledo, see Benito Ruano, *Los Orígenes*, pp. 141–75. On Córdoba, see John Edwards, 'The *Judeoconversos* in the Urban Life of Córdoba', in *Villes et sociétés urbaines au Moyen Âge: hommage à M. le professeur Jacques Heers*, Cultures et civilisations médiévales, 11 (Paris: Presses de l'Université de Paris-Sorbonne, 1994), pp. 287–97. For an account of other violent episodes, see Angus MacKay, 'Popular Movements and Pogroms in Fifteenth-Century Castile', *P&P*, 55 (1972), 33–67.

civil war.²⁸ With New Christians increasingly presented as an unassimilated and problematic minority, resolving the *converso* problem became a central concern for the crown. In 1480, the Catholic Monarchs, Isabel and Fernando, established the Spanish Inquisition, an institution independent from the Castilian episcopate and charged with eradicating judaizing heresy. A decade later, the remaining Jews were expelled from Castile and Aragon, their continued presence in the kingdoms portrayed as the main impediment to the successful integration of *conversos*.²⁹ Far from solving the *converso* problem, the measures taken by the Catholic Monarchs lent further visibility to the difference of New Christians and obsession with lineage and fear of judaizing remained central features of Castilian life during the Early Modern period.³⁰

Approaching the *Converso* Problem

Because of its central place within a series of key historical narratives the *converso* problem is one of the best-studied phenomena of late medieval Spanish history. The mechanisms put in place to scrutinize and to correct the judaizing heresy of New Christians – the Spanish Inquisition – and to curtail their social advancement – statutes of purity of blood – became central elements in Early Modern Spain. In the case of the Inquisition it was, from the outset, one of the most powerful institutions of the new unified state. If historians in the nineteenth century had relatively little to say about the *conversos* themselves, nevertheless they saw the repressive religious measures put in place in the later Middle Ages as fundamental to the development of Imperial Spain. For Marcelino Menéndez Pelayo, the Inquisition had been almost entirely positive in effects: 'I understand, and I applaud, and I even bless the *Inquisition* as a prescription of the philosophy of *unity* that has ruled and governed national life through centuries, as the daughter of the genuine Spirit of the Spanish people, and not as an oppressor of it except in a few individuals and on very rare

---

[28] Stefania Pastore, *Il vangelo e la spada: l'inquisizione di Castiglia e i suoi critici (1460–1598)*, Temi e Testi, 46 (Rome: Edizioni di storia e letteratura, 2003), p. 54.

[29] There is a summary of these arguments and of scholarly interpretations of these events in Monsalvo Antón, *Teoría y evolución*, pp. 317–36.

[30] 'Mass Conversion and Genealogical Mentalities: Jews and Christians in Fifteenth-Century Spain', *P&P*, 174 (2002), 3–41 (pp. 3–4).

occasions.'³¹ Others, many under the influence of Krausism, were less sure. The obsession with honour and the imposition of religious unity and orthodoxy were presented as incompatible with outlooks that resulted elsewhere in the rise of the forces of modernity. The Inquisition had retarded the intellectual and cultural growth of Spain, the expulsion of Jews had affected deleteriously the development of science and industry.³²

Though such debates would continue well into the twentieth century – being replayed in parts in the acrimonious disputes between Américo Castro and Claudio Sánchez-Albornoz about *convivencia* and the nature of Spanish identity – by the 1920s other voices were increasingly being heard.³³ Historians of Judaism were presenting the persecution of New Christians and the expulsion of the Jews from Spain as the culmination of medieval anti-Semitism. In the late-fourteenth century the progressive deterioration of conditions for the Jews throughout Western Europe – the massacres, the forced conversions, and the expulsions – finally reached the Iberian Peninsula. The long-flourishing Sephardic communities, who had previously enjoyed unparalleled toleration, were eliminated. Within this schema, the Lachrymose school of thought, epitomized by Yitzak Baer, regarded all New Christians as victims of forced conversion, who continued to identify fully with Judaism, practicing it within their households, and maintaining networks of social and religious solidarity through many generations. Accusations of judaizing thus reflected an observable religious reality and the Inquisition turned New Christians into Jewish martyrs.³⁴ Baer's student Benzion Netanyahu, though extending and amplifying his teleological vision of Jewish persecution, proposed the opposite view.³⁵ In Netanyahu's model,

---

³¹ For citation and discussion see Carolyn P. Boyd, *Historia Patria: Politics, History, and National Identity in Spain, 1875–1975* (Princeton: Princeton University Press, 1997), pp. 101–2.

³² Boyd, p. 123.

³³ For a discussion of the disputes between Castro and Sánchez-Albornoz see Boyd, pp. 284–85.

³⁴ Yitzhak Baer, *A History of the Jews in Christian Spain*, trans. by Louis Schoffman, 2nd edn, 2 vols (Philadelphia: Jewish Publication Society, 1992), see especially II, 270–99, 324–423.

³⁵ The most explicit statement of such views appears in Netanyahu, *The Origins*, pp. 1141–46 where he plots the relationship between the development of racism in fifteenth century Spain and nineteenth century Germany. There is a critique of this emphasis on continuity of hatred and persecution

the majority of neophytes embraced their new religion fully and sincerely and their descendants regarded themselves and were, overwhelmingly, good Christians. Accusations of judaizing were little more than slanders designed to offer a rationale for the discrimination and destruction of an entire group on the basis of their perceived racial origin.[36]

Although confessional voices dominated scholarship in the nineteenth and early twentieth century, there was nevertheless a current of liberal history. Such scholarship took a more circumspect view of polemical texts, seeing them less as sources of genuine information about religious practices and identities and more as the product of competing ideologies and factions. Accusations of judaizing were often self-interested and the product of religious or racial tensions.[37] By the second half of the twentieth century, these views were in the ascendancy, particularly in Anglophone scholarship. At the same time, historians were increasingly exploring the non-religious elements of the *converso* problem, seeing it primarily as the product of social, economic and political forces, and employing hitherto untapped sources such as economic data.[38] The root of Old Christian hostility towards *conversos* was a failure of assimilation: Castilian Christian society had been unwilling or unable to absorb the large influx of converts.[39] Old Christians found themselves in competition with New Christians, some of whom rose rapidly through the ranks to positions of significant power and prestige. Presenting *conversos* as heretics and accusing them of sharing the supposed shortcomings of their Jewish forebears was an attempt to exclude them permanently. The development of a genealogical model of discrimination – the doctrine of purity of blood – not only denied individual *conversos* their full Christian rights but also closed off competition from whole lineages. Such approaches continue to dominate scholarship, though historians disagree about

in David Nirenberg, *Communities of Violence: Persecution of Minorities in the Middle Ages* (Princeton: Princeton University Press, 1996), pp. 3–17.

[36] Netanyahu, *The Origins*, especially pp. 927–32.

[37] See, among others, José Amador de los Ríos, *Historia social, política y religiosa de los judíos de España y Portugal*, 3 vols (Madrid: Imprenta de T. Fortanet, 1876); Henry Charles Lea, *A History of the Inquisition of Spain*, 4 vols (London: Macmillan, 1906–07).

[38] Angus MacKay, 'The Hispanic-*Converso* Predicament', *Transactions of the Royal Historical Society*, 35 (1985), 159–79.

[39] See, for instance, Nirenberg, 'Mass Conversion'; idem, 'Enmity'.

the levels and prevalence of anti-*converso* feeling in Castilian society during the fifteenth century.⁴⁰

Over the last few decades, approaches to the *converso* problem have expanded radically. Alongside the abandonment of overtly confessional positions, the adoption of insights from the field of literary criticism as well new trends in historical practice have opened up fresh avenues for enquiry, particularly with regard to *converso* identity and the dynamics of the formation of public opinion.⁴¹ Most significant has been the rejection of essentialist conceptions of *converso* identity and the concomitant highlighting of the multiplicity of *converso* experiences and the emphasizing of the range of possible religious outlooks among New Christians.⁴² At the same time there has been the recognition that the religious identity and attitudes of many *conversos* changed from generation to generation and were shaped by and responded to increasing persecution and rejection by mainstream society.⁴³ Overall, this has led to the placing of far greater value on the experiences of *conversos* as individuals and, by contrast, interpretations that speak of New Christians as a coherent social group have been viewed with increasing distrust.⁴⁴

These assertions of the multiple possible *converso* identities have raised again the question of why New Christians would come to be persecuted in the later fifteenth century. Or, rather, they have

---

⁴⁰ For divergent positions see Dayle Seidenspinner-Nuñez, 'Prelude to the Inquisition: The Discourse of Persecution, the Toledan Rebellion of 1449, and the Contest for Orthodoxy', in *Strategies of Medieval Communal Identity: Judaism, Christianity and Islam*, ed. by Wout J. van Bekkum and Paul M. Cobb, Mediaevalia Groningana New Series, 5 (Paris: Peeters, 2004), pp. 47–74, and Kaplan, 'The Inception', in *Marginal Voices*, ed. by Aronson-Friedman and Kaplan.

⁴¹ There is a good summary of these positions in the essays in *Inflecting the Converso Voice: Critical Cluster*, ed. by Gregory S. Hutcheson, *La Corónica*, 25 (Fall, 1996), 3–68.

⁴² David M. Gitlitz, 'Forum: Letter on "Inflecting the *Converso* Voice"', *La Corónica*, 25 (Spring, 1997), 163–66.

⁴³ See, for example, Renée Levine Melammed, 'Identities in Flux: Iberian *Conversos* at Home and Abroad', in *Late Medieval Jewish Identities: Iberia and Beyond*, ed. by Carmen Caballero-Navas and Esperanza Alonso (New York: Palgrave Macmillan, 2010), pp. 43–53.

⁴⁴ E. Michael Gerli, 'The *Converso* Condition: New Approaches to an Old Question', in *Medieval Iberia: Changing Societies and Cultures in Contact and Transition*, ed. by Ivy A. Corfis and Ray Harris-Northall, Colección Támesis, A247 (Woodbridge: Tamesis, 2007), pp. 3–15.

focused attention on the processes by which *conversos* came to be identified with Jews. As David Nirenberg saw, the existence of a tradition of anti-Semitism is not sufficient in and of itself to explain its activation in any given historical situation; the essential Jewishness of the *conversos* had to be constructed and 'the transformation of the convert from Christian back into "Jew" required a century of vast sociological and theological change'.[45] If such was achieved through a variety of methods and mechanisms, scholarship has emphasized in particular the importance of polemical texts in such processes in medieval Iberia and beyond. These sources are now understood to have been central elements in the construction of minority groups and, very often, their creation and dissemination bore a direct relationship to episodes of religious persecution.[46] Moreover, rather than seeing such texts as simply reflecting or shaping public opinion, scholars are increasingly viewing these works as in dialogue and discussion. Texts can be simultaneously repositories of values and shapers of opinion; records of past activity and programmes for future action, polemical and dialogic.

Recent work has also exposed the teleology underlying much of the earlier scholarship.[47] Pastore has challenged the notion that the establishment of the Inquisition was necessarily a foregone conclusion in the 1460s, showing this to be a construction of historians writing over a century later. There existed in the mid-fifteenth century genuine debate about the religious future of Castile; and the rise of a persecuting society, or at least one that persecuted New Christians, was by no means certain. The triumph of anti-*converso* texts, the establishment of the Inquisition, and the enactment of statutes of purity of blood have all overshadowed this debate. Authors and texts proposing different models of Christian society or different means of dealing with the religious problems that faced

---

[45] David Nirenberg, 'Figures of Thought and Figures of Flesh: "Jews" and "Judaism" in Late-Medieval Spanish Poetry and Politics', *Speculum*, 81 (2006), 398–426 (p. 417).

[46] The now classic study of these phenomena in the Middle Ages is R. I. Moore, *The Formation of a Persecuting Society: Power and Deviance in Western Europe, 950–1250* (Oxford: Basil Blackwell, 1987). Seidenspinner-Nuñez, 'Prelude', in *Strategies of Medieval Communal Identity*, ed. by van Bekkum and Cobb, has applied Moore's model to the study of the *converso* problem.

[47] For general comments see Mark D. Meyerson, 'Forum: Letter on "Inflecting the *Converso* Voice"', *La Corónica*, 25 (Spring, 1997), 179–182 (particularly p. 181).

Castile have been relegated to the margins.⁴⁸ Whether viewing it as positive or retrograde, justified or persecutory, historians who have charted the end of *convivencia* in Spain have tended to see it as inevitable and as the genuine expression of a majority opinion. As is argued below, the texts of the mid-fifteenth century may be better understood if such assumptions are jettisoned.

The *converso* problem has long been understood as a uniquely Iberian phenomenon, arising from the very particular religious and cultural circumstances that existed in the Peninsula. As such, it has tended to be treated in isolation by historians, separated off from wider European developments and trends. Yet the *converso* problem had an international dimension almost from the outset – it was discussed at a session of the Council of Basle in 1434. Moreover, the cultural and intellectual frameworks that shaped discussions of *conversos* and other religious minorities, even the very terms in which such debates could be conducted, were international. Theology and canon law were, by their very nature, supra-national and were deployed throughout Western Christendom to address very different contexts and realities. Likewise, the religious orders transcended national boundaries and had their own distinctive identities, intellectual approaches, and agendas. If anxieties about New Christians were particular to the Iberian context, nevertheless questions about the nature of the Church and the Christian community, about the role of the secular powers in enforcing religious orthodoxy, and about the status of non-believers and dissidents were universal. Likewise although statutes of purity of blood were a uniquely Spanish phenomenon, the Bible contained numerous examples of 'the transformation of an individual's lineage by moral lapses' and concerns about nobility and descent were ubiquitous in medieval Europe.⁴⁹

---

⁴⁸ Pastore, *Il vangelo*; eadem, *Una herejía española: conversos, alumbrados e inquisición (1449–1559)*, introd. by Ricardo García Cárcel and Adriano Prosperi (Madrid: Marcial Pons, 2010).

⁴⁹ Jorge Cañizares-Esguerra, 'Demons, Stars, and the Imagination: The Early Modern Body in the Tropics', in *The Origins of Racism in the West*, ed. by Miriam Eliav-Feldon, Benjamin Isaac and Joseph Ziegler (Cambridge: Cambridge University Press, 2009), pp. 313–25 (p. 316). For example, on interpretations of of the moral lapse of Ham that affected his lineage by condemning Canaan's descendants to eternal slavery, see David M. Goldenberg, *The Curse of Ham: Race and Slavery in Early Judaism, Christianity, and Islam* (Princeton: Princeton University Press, 2003), pp. 167–68. More generally, on medieval notions of descent and heredity see the essays in *L'hérédité entre*

The clearest example of such wider influences operating on the *converso* problem is that of medieval traditions of anti-Semitism and toleration. In their discussion of Judaism and the Jews, writers on the *converso* problem were heirs to an intellectual tradition that stretched back to the earliest days of Christianity.[50] That Christ was the Son of God and the Messiah prophesized in the Old Testament was the foundational tenet of mainstream Christianity, yet almost all other aspects of the relationship between Judaism and Christianity were debated and contested.[51] Such debates had both theological aspects – asking such questions as what was the status of the Mosaic Law after the Incarnation, why had the Jews not accepted Christ as their Messiah, and would any of the Jews be saved – and practical ones – primarily, what was the place of Jews within Christian society, should they be tolerated or persecuted, permitted to remain or driven out.[52]

Moyen Âge et époque moderne: perspectives historiques, ed. by Maaike van der Lugt and Charles de Miramon, Micrologus' Library, 27 (Florence: SISMEL/Edizioni del Galluzzo per la Fondazione Ezio Franceschini, 2008). On cultural precedents to the notion of purity of blood, see John Edwards, 'La prehistoria de los estatutos de "limpieza de sangre"', in *Xudeus e conversos na historia: actas do congreso internacional, Ribadavia 14–17 de outubro de 1991*, ed. by Carlos Barros, 2 vols (Santiago de Compostela: Editorial de la Historia, 1994), I, 351–57

[50] Steven J. McMichael, 'The End of the World, Antichrist, and the Final Conversion of the Jews in the *Fortalitium fidei* of Friar Alonso de Espina (d. 1464)', *Medieval Encounters*, 12 (2006), 224–73 (pp. 227–28), thus observes that *Fortalitium fidei* is the heir to a long intellectual tradition. 'Alonso assembled one of the most copious apologetic texts in Christian history and one of the most encyclopedic texts within the Christian anti-Jewish literary tradition. In fact, there is no other work as comprehensive in its argumentation against the Jews.'

[51] On those branches of early Christianity that rejected the Old Testament and the Jewish roots of Christianity, see Bart D. Ehrman, *Lost Christianities: The Battles for Scripture and the Faiths We Never Knew* (New York: Oxford University Press, 2003), particularly pp. 95–112.

[52] The bibliography on attitudes towards Jews in the Middle Ages and on *adversus Judeos* literature is vast. See, among others, Anna Sapir Abulafia, *Christians and Jews in the Twelfth-Century Renaissance* (New York: Routledge, 1995); *Religious Violence between Christians and Jews: Medieval Roots, Modern Perspectives*, ed. by Anna Sapir Abulafia (Basingstoke: Palgrave, 2002); Robert Chazan, *Daggers of Faith: Thirteenth-Century Christian Missionizing and Jewish Response* (Berkeley: University of California Press, 1989); idem, *Fashioning Jewish Identity in Medieval Western Christendom* (Cambridge: Cambridge University Press, 2004); idem, *Reassessing Jewish Life in Medieval Europe* (Cambridge: Cambridge University Press, 2010); *Christian Attitudes*

Discussion of these questions had coalesced around the interpretation of a relatively restricted set of Biblical passages, drawn principally from the letters of Paul, the Gospels, and from a number of Old Testament prophets, such as Isaiah.[53] What, for example, had the Apostle meant by his words in the Letter to the Romans (11.25–26) that 'all Israel should be saved' or that the blindness of Israel would persist 'until the fullness of the Gentiles should come in'?[54] How should Christ's statement, 'Do not think that I am come to destroy the law, or the prophets', be understood and what did it mean for the ritual life of Christians?[55] What was the significance of the statement in Isaiah 10.21 that of Israel 'The remnant shall be converted, the remnant, I say, of Jacob, to the mighty God'? Again, though certain interpretations were almost universally accepted – the idea that the Jews, or a remnant thereof, would convert to Christianity at the end of time was well-established in the Middle Ages – much else remained open.

Medieval debate about the place of Jews within Christian societies tended to draw on ideas and concepts first outlined by Augustine of Hippo (d. 430). Though Augustine's pronouncements on such issues were far from systematic and were never intended to acquire the value of 'juridical injunction', they became the basis for a doctrine of limited toleration of Jews in Medieval Christendom.[56] The continuing presence of Jews, exiled from Israel

---

toward the Jews in the Middle Ages: A Casebook, ed. by Michael Frasetto (New York: Routledge, 2007); Jeremy Cohen, *The Friars and the Jews: The Evolution of Medieval Anti-Judaism* (Ithaca: Cornell University Press, 1982); idem, *Living Letters of the Law: Ideas of the Jew in Medieval Christianity* (Berkeley: University of California Press, 1999); Mark R. Cohen, *Under Crescent and Cross: The Jews in the Middle Ages* (Princeton: Princeton University Press, 1994); Gilbert Dahan, *Les Intellectuels chrétiens et les juifs au Moyen Âge* (Paris: Cerf, 1999).

[53] For a more comprehensive list of Scriptural passages employed in Christian anti-Jewish writings, see Cohen, *Living Letters*, p. 6 and, more extensively, Nirenberg, *Anti-Judaism*, pp. 66–86.

[54] For a detailed exploration of the use of Romans 11.25–26 in this tradition, see Jeremy Cohen, 'The Mystery of Israel's Salvation: Romans 11.25–26 in Patristic and Medieval Exegesis', *Harvard Theological Review*, 98 (2005), 247–81.

[55] Matthew 5.17

[56] Paula Fredricksen, *Augustine and the Jews: A Christian Defense of Jews and Judaism* (New York: Doubleday, 2008), p. 364. For a discussion of Augustine's doctrine of Jewish witness, see also Cohen, *Living Letters*, pp. 23–65.

and in servitude as punishment for their rejection of Christ, bore witness to the truth of Christianity and confirmed Christians as the new Chosen People of God. The Jews were the involuntary helpers of Christianity because they acted as the guardians of texts that contained the prophecies that had been fulfilled in Christ and the words of the Psalmist 'slay them not' were understood as an injunction to permit the Jews to practice their own religion.[57] This position of the Jews as a tolerated underclass was given legal weight by the papal bull *Sicut Judaeis*, first issued by Calixtus II in the 1120s. This asserted the right of Jews to live freely within Christian society and to practice their religion without hindrance or persecution, provided they did not conspire against Christianity.[58]

Despite the existence of this tradition of limited toleration, there was in practice considerable freedom of movement. The general ideas that underpinned it were repeatedly reinterpreted across the Middle Ages, often with radical consequences for the Jews. From the thirteenth century onwards, stimulated by the work of mendicant scholars, there was a progressive move away from toleration towards persecution and expulsion, as the idea of a Jewish threat to Christianity gained traction and the very meaning of Judaism itself was redefined.[59] Jews were depicted by friars as 'an ever-present danger to the faith, and which all but excluded the

---

[57] Psalm 59.12 (Vulgate 58.12). See also Cohen, *Living Letters*, pp. 35–37

[58] On *Sicut Judeis*, see Leonard B. Glick, *Abraham's Heirs: Jews and Christians in Medieval Europe* (Syracuse: Syracuse University Press, 1999), pp. 119–20; and also Solomon Grayzel, 'The Papal Bull *Sicut Judeis*', in *Studies and Essays in Honor of Abraham A. Neuman*, ed. by Meir Ben-Horin, Bernard D. Weinryb and Solomon Zeitlin (Leiden: Brill, 1962), pp. 243–80. On the legal status of Jews in Medieval Europe in general, see Shlomo Simonsohn, *The Apostolic See and the Jews: History*, Studies and Texts, 109 (Toronto: Pontifical Institute of Mediaeval Studies, 1991), Kenneth Stow, *Alienated Minority: The Jews of Medieval Latin Europe* (Cambridge, MA: Harvard University Press, 1992) and, more specifically, Yosef Hayim Yerushalmi, '"Serviteurs des rois et non serviteurs des serviteurs": sur quelques aspects de l'histoire politique des Juifs', *Raisons politiques*, 7 (2002), 19–52 <DOI: 10.3917/rai.007.0019>.

[59] See, for example, Cohen, *The Friars and the Jews*, and Robert Chazan, 'Medieval Anti-Semitism', in *History and Hate: The Dimensions of Anti-Semitism*, ed. by David Berger (Philadelphia: Jewish Publication Society, 1986), pp. 49–65. For specific case studies, see the esssays in *Friars and Jews in the Middle Ages and Renaissance*, ed. by Steven J. McMichael and Susan Myers, The Medieval Franciscans, 2 (Leiden: Brill, 2004).

chance of conversion and incorporation'.⁶⁰ The potential impact of such ideas on the *converso* problem is clear. Alongside these large-scale transformations and reinterpretations, there was also latitude for individual authors to establish their own distinctive positions by emphasizing or underplaying particular elements of the tradition. Though the differences between such readings were necessarily narrow their implications could, potentially, be considerable. Minor differences in emphasis or interpretation were used to justify radically different positions.⁶¹

Alonso de Espina and the *Fortalitium fidei*

The historiographical developments of the past generation call for a new study of Alonso de Espina's *Fortalitium fidei*. Written between 1458–64, this text has long been recognized as one of the most significant works of late medieval anti-Semitism and a key text in the development of the *converso* controversy.⁶² Comprising five Books that detail the war of Christianity against its enemies – heretics, Jews, Muslims, and demons – this lengthy Latin text was a true medieval best seller.⁶³ After an *editio princeps* that appeared in Strasbourg in 1471 it went through eight further printings in one hundred and fifty years; it was translated into French and there was a partial translation into German.⁶⁴

---

⁶⁰ Miri Rubin, *Gentile Tales: The Narrative Assault on Late Medieval Jews* (New Haven: Yale University Press, 1999), p. 28.

⁶¹ See below Chapters 2 and 4.

⁶² Date and circumstances of composition: Alisa Meyuhas Ginio, *La forteresse de la foi: la vision du monde d'Alonso de Espina, moine espagnol (?–1466)* (Paris: Cerf, 1998), pp. 180–83. Authorship: B. Netanyahu, 'Alonso de Espina: Was He a New Christian?', in *Toward the Inquisition: Essays on Jewish and Converso History in Late Medieval Spain* (Ithaca: Cornell University Press, 1997), pp. 43–75, 213–31 (first publ. in *Proceedings of the American Academy for Jewish Research*, 43 (1976), 107–65). General studies on this work: Geraldine McKendrick, 'The Franciscan Order in Castile, *c.* 1440–*c.* 1560' (unpublished doctoral thesis, University of Edinburgh, 1987); Steven J. McMichael, *Was Jesus of Nazareth the Messiah? Alphonso de Espina's Argument against the Jews in the 'Fortalitium Fidei' (c. 1464)*, South Florida Studies in the History of Judaism, 96 (Atlanta: Scholars Press, 1994); Ana Echevarria, *The Fortress of Faith: The Attitude towards Muslims in Fifteenth Century Spain*, Medieval Iberian Peninsula: Texts and Studies, 12 (Leiden: Brill, 1999).

⁶³ Meyuhas Ginio, *La forteresse*, p. 213.

⁶⁴ List of editions and translations: Ludwig Hain, *Repertorium bibliographicum in quo libri omnes ab arte typographica inventa usque ad annum MD*, 4 vols

In the preface to *Fortalitium fidei*, Espina depicted himself as keeping lone watch, calling out to God from the very ends of the world.[65] If his was not quite the voice of one crying in the wilderness, it was, nevertheless the voice of a figure on the margins. From the outset of his work, Espina was seeking to clothe himself in the traditional garb of the prophet or holy man. His authority was that of the isolated outsider, fearlessly denouncing a corrupt regime and calling it to reform. There was both rhetorical display and sombre reflection in this self-fashioning.[66] Espina was a leading figure in his Order – the Observant Franciscans – and in the Castilian Church as a whole. Contemporaries depicted him as a supremely persuasive and charismatic preacher, able to inspire in his audience extremes of devotion and penitence.[67] He was likewise

(Stuttgart: Cotta, 1826–38), I: A, 94–95; *Dictionnaire de théologie catholique contenant l'exposé des doctrines de la théologie catholique leurs preuves et leur histoire*, ed. by A. Vacant, E. Mangenot and É. Amann, 14 vols (Paris: Letouzey et Ané, 1909–41), XIV, col. 2478; Klaus Reinhardt and Horacio Santiago-Otero, *Biblioteca bíblica ibérica medieval* (Madrid: CSIC, 1986), pp. 63–64.

[65] *Fortalitium*, prohemium, fol. 9ᵛ: 'Sucurre ergo, Domine, gregi tue quam precioso sanguine filii tui emisti. Sanguineos fontes lacrimarum emittit cor meum quia neminem video consolatorem gementium, et fere neminem zelatorem tue fidei catholice, specialiter in hac misera Hispania, in qua, sicut in fine mundi sita est, sic in ea congregate sunt omnes feces tuorum inimicorum.' The manuscript of *Fortalitium fidei* of 1464 held in El Burgo de Osma (Biblioteca de la Catedral, códice 154) contains a decorated initial that represents the Franciscan author writing his book in front of a tower. Rosa Vidal Doval, 'El muro en el Oeste y *La fortaleza de la Fe*: alegorías de la exclusión de minorías en la Castilla del siglo XV', in *Las metamorfosis de la alegoría: discurso y sociedad en la Península Ibérica desde la Edad Media hasta la Edad Contemporánea*, ed. by Rebeca Sanmartín Bastida and Rosa Vidal Doval (Frankfurt am Main: Vervuert; Madrid: Iberoamericana, 2005), pp. 143–68 (p. 161 with an edition of the prologue in pp. 161–64).

[66] Preachers relied on their status as outsiders, along other qualities such as asceticism, as a source of authority while often maintaining a very close relationship with the ruling elites, see Vidal Doval, 'Predicación', in *Hacia una poética del sermón*, ed. by Sanmartín Bastida, Taylor and Vidal Doval, pp. 235–38.

[67] Francisco Cantera, 'Fernando de Pulgar y los conversos', *Sefarad*, 4 (1944), 295–348 (p. 319): 'y assimismo proçedió el castigo y sancto exemplo y vida del Reuerendo padre Fray Alonso Espina, maestro en sancta Theología, fraire de los menores, que Dios tiene, que muchos años y días a sus casas los yba a buscar con muchos fieles vertiendo su sangre, lleuando ante sy la ymagen sancta del que por nos padeçió en cruz'. On penitential elements within preaching see Jeremy Lawrance, 'Homily and Harangue in Medieval Spain: The Sermon and Crowds', in *Hacia una poética del sermón*, ed. by Rebeca

active at the royal court, moving in the highest circles and enjoying the confidence of the leading men of the kingdom. Yet by the time of the completion of *Fortalitium fidei*, his star was waning and his prestige falling; it was the work of a man under whom the ground had shifted.

Despite the prominence he enjoyed during at least parts of his career, little is now known of Espina and what reliable information survives is concentrated on a period of little more than a decade in the mid-fifteenth century. His origin and background are obscure and while some evidence suggests that he was a *converso* there is no secure information concerning his date or place of birth or his family.[68] Espina first appears in the record in 1452 as the regent of Salamanca's Franciscan *studium*, having sometime earlier gained the degree of Master of Theology in the same city.[69] In 1453, Juan II

Sanmartín Bastida, Barry Taylor and Rosa Vidal Doval (= *Revista de Poética Medieval*, 24 (2010)), pp. 147–84. On violent elements within Espina's preaching and message, see Pedro M. Cátedra, 'La modificación del discurso con fines de invectiva: el sermón', *Atalaya*, 5 (1994), 101–21 (pp. 101–6). Corrie E. Norman speaks of the prevailing culture of preaching in the Late Middle Ages as one of fear where 'how well a preacher could scare his audience appears to be one of the measures of his effectiveness', 'The Social History of Preaching: Italy', in *Preachers and People in the Reformations and Early Modern Period*, ed. by Larissa Taylor, A New History of the Sermon, 2 (Leiden: Brill, 2001), pp. 125–91 (p. 176). Manuel Ambrosio Sánchez Sánchez ('Predicación y antisemitismo: el caso de San Vicente Ferrer', in *La proyección histórica de España en sus tres culturas: Castilla y León, América y el Mediterráneo*, 3 vols (Valladolid, 1993) III, 195–203 (p. 201)) warns, with regard to Vicent Ferrer, that although there are no open admonitions to violence in the texts of the sermons extant, there was a causal relationship between preaching and attacks.

[68] An anonymous letter addressed to Fernando de Pulgar in the 1480s describes Espina as a *converso*, Cantera, p. 319; but see *contra*, Netanyahu, 'Alonso de Espina'. Palencia and El Espinar (Segovia) have been suggested as possible places of birth. See, Echevarria, *The Fortress of Faith*, p. 47; and Fidel Fita, 'La judería de Segovia: documentos inéditos', *Boletín de la Real Academia de la Historia*, 9 (1886), 344–89 (p. 376).

[69] Master of Theology: Isaac Vázquez, 'Repertorio de franciscanos españoles graduados en teología durante la Edad Media', in *Repertorio de historia de las ciencias eclesiásticas en España*, 7 vols (Salamanca: Instituto de Historia de la Teología Española, 1967–79), III, 235–320, (p. 319). Regent of the Franciscan *studium*: 'In registro Generalis Angeli de Perusio invenio eum hoc tempore Regentem fuisse studii Theologici in Conventu Salamantino', Luke Wadding, *Annales Minorum seu Trium Ordinum a S. Francisco institutorum*, rev. by José Maria Ribeiro da Fonseca, 2nd edn, 25 vols (Rome: Rochi Bernabò, 1886), XII, 144 §31.

entrusted him with announcing to Álvaro de Luna his impending execution and providing the former royal favourite with spiritual counsel.[70] Such was clearly a delicate mission and demonstrated Espina to be a trusted and capable figure – contemporary sources agree that Luna approached his death in exemplary fashion and that this redounded to Espina's credit.[71]

By the mid 1450s, there is further evidence of Espina moving in court circles and operating at the heart of the kingdom. As one of the confessors of Enrique IV, he enjoyed a degree of *privanza* with the monarch and used this privilege to further the interests of his Order.[72] In 1454, he petitioned the king to transfer ownership of the Franciscan house in Segovia from the Conventual Franciscans to the Observants. Although Enrique refused, he provided an extensive endowment for the new Observant convent of San Antonio in Segovia – a significant endorsement of the reformed branch.[73] In 1456, Espina's career reached its highpoint. Enrique

---

[70] *Crónica del serenísimo rey don Juan*, p. 683; *Crónica de don Álvaro de Luna, condestable de Castilla, maestre de Santiago*, ed. by Juan de Mata Carriazo, Colección de Crónicas Españolas, 2 (Madrid: Espasa-Calpe, 1940), pp. 249–50; Alonso de Palencia, *Gesta hispaniensia ex annalibus suorum dierum collecta*, ed. and trans. by Brian Tate and Jeremy Lawrance, 2 vols (Madrid: Real Academia de la Historia, 1998–99), I, 70.

[71] Nicholas G. Round, *The Greatest Man Uncrowned: A Study of the Fall of Don Álvaro de Luna*, Colección Támesis, A111 (London: Tamesis, 1986), pp. 207–10 who explicitly rejects any interpretation of this episode through the lens of the *converso* problem. The episode, and Espina's intervention, reached such notoriety that it appeared in literary works: 'Señor, te pido perdón, | e a vos, maestro d'Espina, | honesta persona e dina, | de su parte, absolucçión', Íñigo López de Mendoza, *Doctrinal de privados fecho a la muerte del maestre de Santiago don Álvaro de Luna, donde se introduçe al autor fablando en nombre del maestre*, in *Poesía crítica y satírica del siglo XV*, ed. by Julio Rodríguez Puértolas, Clásicos Castalia, 114 (Madrid: Castalia, 1989), pp. 154–67 (p. 166).

[72] Alfonso Vázquez, Lope de Barrientos and Rodrigo de Valencia were also confessors to Enrique IV, Atanasio López, 'Confesores de la familia real de Castilla', *AIA*, 31 (1929), 5–75 (p. 67). Meyuhas Ginio suggests that Espina's role may have been to provide occasional spiritual advice and confession rather than acting as the king's sole confessor, *La forteresse*, pp. 86–87. See also Echevarria, *The Fortress of Faith*, p. 50.

[73] *Memorial de diversas hazañas: crónica de Enrique IV, ordenada por Mosén Diego de Valera*, ed. by Juan de Mata Carriazo, Colección de Crónicas Españolas, 4 (Madrid: Espasa-Caple, 1941), pp. 9–10. The two other royal foundations of the reign of Enrique IV were Hieronymite houses: Santa María del Parral in Segovia, and San Jerónimo del Paso in Madrid, William D. Phillips, *Enrique IV and the Crisis of Fifteenth-Century Castile, 1425–1480*, Speculum Anniver-

IV entrusted him with the prestigious task of preaching the bull of crusade against Granada, granted by Pope Calixtus III. As the crusade indulgences could also be granted to souls in Purgatory, the potential economic benefits from this bull were vast but so too were the dangers of the misappropriation of funds. According to the royal chronicler Diego de Valera, Espina recognised these dangers and did not hesitate to threaten the king with excommunication if any of the money raised were to be embezzled.[74] The subsequent misuse of crusade funds remained a sore point for Espina and one he would return to in *Fortalitium fidei* where he condemned preachers of the bull who accepted payments for their services.[75]

It was during the later years of the 1450s and the early 1460s that Espina began or intensified his campaigns against the enemies of the faith and, in particular, against *conversos*. As well as writing *Fortalitium fidei*, Espina was amongst those seeking the establishment of an Inquisition in Castile. In 1460, he was one of the leaders of the Observant Franciscans who lobbied Enrique IV to adopt a hard line against judaizers and religious minorities.[76] Despite the monarch's initially positive response, by the following

---

sary Monographs, 3 (Cambridge, MA: Mediaeval Academy of America, 1978), p. 90.

[74] *Memorial de diversas hazañas*, p. 41. On the negotiations to obtain the bull and the special nature of the indulgence: José Goñi Gaztambide, *Historia de la bula de la cruzada en España*, Victoriensia, 4 (Vitoria: Editorial del Seminario, 1958), pp. 355–56, 359–60; José Manuel Nieto Soria, 'Enrique IV de Castilla y el pontificado (1454–1474)', *En la España Medieval*, 19 (1996), 167–238 (pp. 174–75, 208). On Enrique's campaigns, see Ana Echevarría, 'Enrique IV de Castilla, un rey cruzado', *Espacio, Tiempo y Forma. Serie III, Historia Medieval*, 17 (2004), 143–56.

[75] 'Sicut accidit istis temporibus quoniam sic conducuntur predicatores pro pecunia quarundam bullarum colligenda. Ac si essent operarii qui ad vineas excolendas conducuntur in platea vt pro qualibet bulla quam dederunt recipiant tantum, vt ex hac auaricia dissolute sunt multe religiones in isto regno', *Fortalitium*, I, consideratio 2, fol. 13^v. On this episode see, Echevarria, *The Fortress of Faith*, p. 53.

[76] The fullest account of this episode appears in a seventeenth-century source: José Sigüenza, *Historia de la orden de San Jerónimo*, rev. by Ángel Weruaga Prieto, Libros Recuperados, 2, 2 vols (Valladolid: Junta de Castilla y León, Consejería de Educación y Cultura, 2000), I: 430–35. There is also a contemporary account in *Crónica del rey don Enrique el Cuarto*, in *Crónicas de los reyes de Castilla desde don Alfonso el Sabio hasta los Católicos don Fernando y doña Isabel*, ed. by Cayetano Rosell, 3 vols, Biblioteca de Autores Españoles, 66, 68, 70 (Madrid: M. Rivadeneyra, 1875–78), III, 3–222, (p. 130). See also Pastore, *Il vangelo*, pp. 10–12.

year there had been no action and so the Franciscans appealed for assistance from the powerful Hieronymite Order. The Franciscans wanted Enrique to enforce existing legislation about Jews and Muslims living amid Christians and to establish an Inquisition, independent from diocesan control, akin to the one operating in France.[77] Though the Hieronymites were persuaded of the need for action, under the leadership of Alonso de Oropesa they approached the king independently from the Franciscans.

Although Enrique eventually acceded to demands for an inquisition, the campaign at court was ultimately a failure for Espina and the Franciscans.[78] In a sermon intended to highlight the extent of judaizing among *conversos*, Hernando de la Plaza claimed to possess the foreskins of one hundred circumcised New Christians.[79] When Oropesa revealed the claim to be a lie, the Franciscans became associated with extreme anti-*converso* views and Espina's standing at court fell. By contrast, the Hieronymites convinced the king to place Oropesa in charge of an inquisition into *converso* heresy in Castile. Oropesa conducted proceedings personally in Toledo at the request of Archbishop Alonso Carrillo, concluding that Old and New Christians alike were guilty, the former of intolerance and the latter of faithlessness, and blaming the polluting presence of Jews

---

[77] The programme of action was spelled out in the Franciscans' letter to the Hieronymites, where Espina was one of the signatories. Sigüenza, *Historia*, I, 430–31: 'en estos nuevos tiempos y reinos vemos los infieles crecer y muchos herejes la fe de Jesucristo destruir y subvertir [...] demandar al rey nuestro señor remedio de justicia, requiriéndole de parte de Dios que provea que los infieles vivan según son obligados por los estatutos de la madre santa Iglesia y leyes imperiales, reales y que eso mismo sobre los herejes se haga inquisicion en este reino según como se hace en Francia y en otros muchos reinos y provincias de cristianos, porque los buenos sean conocidos, de entre los malos apartados y puedan vivir seguros y en paz y esta tal malicia no haya lugar de inficionar y corromper todo el bien de la nuestra santa fe católica.'

[78] Enrique petitioned Pope Pius II in December 1461 for an institution with inquisitorial powers and a strong link to the needs of royal government. In May 1462 the bull *Dum fidei catholicae* granted the papal nuncio in Castile powers to appoint inquisitors but since the tribunal proposed was eminently ecclesiastical in character it was not established. See Nieto Soria, pp. 216–19.

[79] *Crónica del rey don Enrique*, p. 130: 'en sus reynos avia grande heregía de algunos que judaizaban, guardando los ritos judaicos, y con nombre de christianos retaxaban sus hijos; suplicándole que mandase hacer inquisicion sobre ello, para que fuesen castigados. Sobre lo qual se hicieron algunos sermones; y en especial Fray Fernando de la Plaza, que predicando dixo que él tenia prepucios de hijos de Christianos conversos, que avian retaxado a sus hijos'.

living amid them.⁸⁰ Nonetheless Oropesa also censured the Franciscans' rigorist stance towards the Jews, which he argued had stoked the flames of social conflict and endangered the peace in the republic.⁸¹

This episode seems to have marked the end of Espina's career at court and he probably died soon after, perhaps around 1466.⁸² The documents of a case brought by the Inquisition against the *converso* family Arias Dávila in the late 1480s accused Diego Arias (*c.* 1400–66) of murdering Espina through the administration of poison.⁸³ According to several testimonies Arias greatly resented the friar's anti-Jewish activities and, in particular, his sponsoring of a campaign for Christians to wear a badge with the name of Jesus.⁸⁴ Ostensibly promoted as a means for Christians to differentiate themselves from Jews, it was worn 'very probably in particular by "Old Christians"' to publicly claim 'not to be of Jewish origin'.⁸⁵

---

⁸⁰ Sigüenza, *Historia*, I, 434: 'halló que de una y otra parte de cristianos viejos y nuevos había mucha culpa: unos pecaban de atrevidos, temerarios, facinerosos, otros de malicia y de inconstancia en la fe; éstos padecían no sin culpa y los otros merecían grave castigo por su insolencia y aun por su ambición. Y la culpa principal de todo era la mezcla que había entre los judíos de la sinagoga y los cristianos, ahora fuesen nuevos, ahora viejos, dejándolos vivir, tratar y conversar juntos sin distinción, porque a los unos y a los otros los prevaricaban los judíos astuta y endiabladamente, como él mismo [Oropesa] lo dice en su libro, descubriendo algunos engaños suyos y las mañas diabólicas que tenían, para hacer que los cristianos negasen la fe.'

⁸¹ Oropesa concluded that the Franciscans 'haciéndose como fiscales y mostrando mucho celo de la fe, provocaban la ira del pueblo contra los pobres judíos', Sigüenza, *Historia*, I, 433. See also Pastore, *Il vangelo*, pp. 17–19.

⁸² The remainder of Espina's career has been a matter of some speculation. For a discussion of hypotheses about Espina's career after 1464 see Echevarria, *The Fortress of Faith*, p. 55.

⁸³ *Proceso inquisitorial contra los Arias Dávila segovianos: un enfrentamiento social entre judíos y conversos*, ed. by Carlos Carrete Parrondo, FIRC, 3 (Salamanca: Universidad Pontificia de Salamanca; [Granada]: Universidad de Granada, 1986), pp. 37–38 §52. On slanders depicting Jews as poisoners see Mitre Fernández, p. 78.

⁸⁴ *Proceso*, p. 33 §42: 'Otrosí dixo que al tiempo que el frayle de la Espina, que se decía que predicaba esta santa Inquisición y decía de los sométicos, puso en tal estado esta santa Inquisición que todos los que eran christianos trayan un Jesú en el bonete, y que oyó decir este testigo a los escuderos que a la sacón bibían con Diego Arias que si llebaban el Jesú ante el dicho Diego Arias, contador, y yban por librança, que no los quería librar asta que se quitasen el Jesú del bonete, e se lo decía que no los libraría fasta que lo quitasen'.

⁸⁵ John Edwards, 'Fifteenth-Century Franciscan Reform and the Spanish *Conversos*: The Case of Fray Alonso de Espina', in *Monastic Studies: The*

Fortalitium fidei itself provides other accounts of Espina's agitation against Jews and *conversos*. He brought, unsuccessfully, an accusation of ritual murder against a Jew in Valladolid in 1454; he took part in an inquest by the Bishop of Palencia against a *converso* accused of judaizing; and he preached in Medina del Campo in 1459 after a group of judaizers was discovered in the town.[86]

Throughout his career and his writings, Espina put forward a vision of Castile as a society in crisis, besieged by religious enemies, riven by profound conflict, and in dire need of strong leadership and decisive action. He relied on a combination of legal activity and preaching, persuasion of the ruling elites and the stirring up of popular support to achieve his aims. In pursuing his goals and those of his Order, Espina was neither an agent of the Crown nor a simple conduit of popular opinions and anxieties. Instead, he used his skills as a preacher and theologian and his carefully cultivated aura of moral authority to persuade different actors in Castile of the validity of his vision.

In undertaking such activities, Espina was part of a well-established tradition of mendicant charismatic preachers. Almost always Observant Dominicans or Franciscans, these figures attempted to reform and to remake society according to a rigorist and exclusionary interpretation of Christian principles.[87] Preachers such as Vincent Ferrer (1350–1419), Bernardino of Siena (1380–1444), John Capistrano (1386–1456) and Giacomo della Marca (*c.* 1391–1476) were among the best-known and most influential religious figures in late medieval Europe.[88] In their hands, the popular sermon reached its full potential as a means of maintaining civic order, driving reform, and defining the boundaries of Christian society.[89] Alongside these public activities, most of these preachers

---

Continuity of Tradition, ed. by Judith Loades (Bangor: Headstart History, 1990), pp. 203–10 (p. 204).

[86] These episodes are discussed in Chapter 5, pp. 128–29.

[87] Cynthia L. Polecritti, *Preaching Peace in Renaissance Italy: Bernardino of Siena and his Audience* (Washington: Catholic University of America Press, 2000), p. 3, describes these figures as 'charismatic preachers who tried to reform society in one grand gesture'.

[88] On the figure of the charismatic preacher see the introduction and essays in *Charisma and Religious Authority: Jewish, Christian, and Muslim Preaching, 1200–1500*, ed. by Katherine L. Jansen and Miri Rubin, Europa Sacra, 4 (Turnhout: Brepols, 2010), and bibliography therein.

[89] On sermons and preaching in general see the essays in *The Sermon*, ed. by Bervely Mayne Kienzle, Typologie des Sources du Moyen Âge Occidental,

were also significant authors, revising their sermons for dissemination in written form and producing theological treatises and other texts.⁹⁰

Charismatic preachers formed an elite that travelled widely across Europe, attracted mass followings and had access to rulers, including popes and monarchs. These preachers saw themselves first and foremost as reformers, both of their own religious orders and of society at large.⁹¹ Their brand of reform was predicated on the identification and removal of supposedly polluting elements within society – sodomites, prostitutes, gamblers, witches, Jews, and other groups. Such was seen as the first and necessary step in the reordering of society along properly Christian lines.⁹² Their sermons often triggered dramatic change: populations would revel in a state of newly-found religious fervour that often led to the passing of legislation that sought to enforce a strictly-defined Christian morality.⁹³ Such heightened fervour was, however, often short-lived; bad habits returned and laws were repealed or contested. Yet preaching campaigns often effected significant and long-lasting change in the perception of particular social groups or religious minorities: Bernardino of Siena's preaching in Rome lead to a heightened awareness of the dangers of witchcraft and, as has been

---

81–83 (Turnhout: Brepols, 2000); *Preacher, Sermon, and Audience in the Middle Ages*, ed. by Carolyn Muessig, A New History of the Sermon, 3 (Leiden: Brill, 2002); and *Preachers and People in the Reformations and Early Modern Period*, ed. by Larissa Taylor, A New History of the Sermon, 2 (Leiden: Brill, 2001).

⁹⁰ See, for instance, Franco Mormando's account of Bernardino of Siena's written production, *The Preacher's Demons: Bernardino of Siena and the Social Underworld of Early Renaissance Italy* (Chicago: University of Chicago Press, 1999), pp. 40–45.

⁹¹ Bernardino of Siena was one of the key figures in the development of the Observant reform within the Franciscan Order. Michael Robson, *The Franciscans in the Middle Ages* (Woodbridge: Boydell Press, 2006), pp. 202–22; and John Moorman, *A History of the Franciscan Order: From its Origins to the Year 1517* (Oxford: Clarendon Press, 1968), pp. 441–56.

⁹² Christian morality as guiding principle for society in mendicant culture: Bernadette Paton, *Preaching Friars and the Civic Ethos: Siena, 1380–1480*, Westfield Publications in Medieval Studies, 7 (London: Centre for Medieval Studies, Queen Mary and Westfield College, University of London, 1992), p. 86.

⁹³ Lawrance, 'Homily', in *Hacia una poética del sermón*, ed. by Sanmartín Bastida, Taylor and Vidal Doval, p. 156: These preachers left behind a 'puritan desert […] an odious atmosphere of sanctimonious sabbatarianism.'

seen, Vincent Ferrer's visit to Castile contributed to the development of a new climate of anti-Semitism and a wave of mass conversions.[94]

Regarded by their contemporaries as extraordinary men, charismatic preachers became the paradigm of late medieval sanctity: Bernardino of Siena was canonized in 1450, while Vincent Ferrer was elevated to the altars in 1455. As such, they became role models for figures such as Espina and other friars of his generation, who consciously patterned their own behaviours and careers on such exemplars. Thus Espina promoted, and possibly even introduced into Castile, the devotion to the Name of Jesus, originally developed by Bernardino as a response to factionalism in Italian cities.[95] So closely did Espina become associated to this devotion that a sixteenth-century history of the Franciscan Order recorded an account of a miracle where the Name of Jesus had provided proof that Espina's preaching apostolate enjoyed divine sanction.[96]

---

[94] On Bernardino's career and activities see, with ample bibliography, Mormando; Paton, *Preaching Friars*; Polecritti; Nirit Ben-Aryeh Debby, *Renaissance Florence in the Rhetoric of Two Popular Preachers: Giovanni Dominici (1356–1419) and Bernardino da Siena (1380–1444)*, Late Medieval and Early Modern Studies, 4 (Turnhout: Brepols, 2001). Vincent Ferrer: Pedro M. Cátedra, *Sermón sociedad y literatura en la Edad Media: San Vicente Ferrer en Castilla (1411–1412), estudio bibliográfico, literario y edición de los textos inéditos* (Valladolid: Junta de Castilla y León, Consejería de Cultura y Turismo, 1994). New climate of anti-Semitism: Samuel K. Cohn, 'The Black Death and the Burning of the Jews', *P&P*, 196 (2007), 3–36 (p. 35).

[95] *Fortalitium*, I, consideratio iii, fol. 43ᵛ, & III, consideratio vii, fol. 125ᵛ. See also Meyuhas Ginio, *La forteresse*, p. 184 n3. On Bernardino's development of the devotion to the Name of Jesus see Polecritti, pp. 7–8. The development and use of this potent symbol by Bernardino, a tablet inscribed with the letters IHS inscribed in gold, is complex: originally it seems to have arisen as a means to fight a heretical sect from Lombardy but it soon acquired other uses and connotations, John Edwards, 'Fifteenth-century Franciscan reform', pp. 205, 207. The writing of *Fortalitium fidei*, likewise, may have been intended in part as an emulation of the activities of Bernardino, see Steven J. McMichael, 'The Sources for Alonso de Espina's Messianic Argument against the Jews in the *Fortalitium Fidei*', in *Iberia and the Mediterranean World of the Middle Ages: Studies in Honor of Robert I. Burns S.J.*, ed. by Larry J. Simon, 2 vols (Leiden: Brill, 1995–96) I, 72–95, (pp. 75–76).

[96] Espina's doubts about the efficacy of his preaching to the people of Valladolid were assuaged when a voice compelled him to draw water from a well in the cloister of his convent. Upon doing so, he found twenty-four pebbles with the name of Jesus inlaid in silver. See Francesco Gonzaga, *De origine seraphicae religionis franciscanae eiusque progressibus, de regularis*

Though Espina's recorded activities were restricted to Castile and the religious culture that he sought to change was distinctive to the Iberian Peninsula, he was thus very much representative of wider, European developments. His vision of the need to police rigorously the boundaries between the Christian majority and those elements he deemed to be outside of it would have struck a chord with numerous of his mendicant contemporaries.[97] Such a vision ran in parallel with the very ideals of Observant reform, departing, as they did, from a rigorist stance that sought to enforce a strict following of monastic rule and legislation.[98] The international dimension of the Franciscan Order, likewise, meant that individual members and congregations from different provinces were able to keep in close contact, both through writing and in person.[99]

Traditionally, *Fortalitium fidei* itself has been valued as an expression of the dominant voice in Castilian society, reflecting the majority view of *conversos* as heretics and crypto-Jews whose very presence threatened the stability of the kingdom. This vision of *Fortalitium fidei* as a statement of mainstream opinion derives most of its force from events in Castile in the decades after its publication. The establishment of the Spanish Inquisition, the expulsion of the Jews, and the conquest of the Muslim kingdom of Granada have long been seen as the enacting of the programme of reform set out in *Fortalitium fidei*. Espina's main contribution to the changes in the religious culture of fifteenth-century Spain was thus his turning of widely held opinions and prejudices into a set of guiding principles for the actions of rulers.

Despite the attractions of such a position, it is not without problems. As will be argued below, Espina's programme of action in *Fortalitium fidei* differs in significant ways from the religious policies of the Catholic Monarchs at the end of the fifteenth

---

observanciae institutione, forma administrationis ac legibus, admirabilique eius propagatione (Rome: [n. pub.], 1587), p. 863.

[97] On the actions of Dominicans in the Crown of Aragon see Robin Vose, *Dominicans, Muslims and Jews in the Medieval Crown of Aragon* (Cambridge: Cambridge University Press, 2009).

[98] Moorman, pp. 517–18; Fidel de Lejarza and Ángel Uribe, 'Introducción a los orígenes de la Observancia en España: las reformas en los siglos XIV y XV', *AIA*, 17 (1957), 17–660 (p. 60).

[99] Mormando, pp. 107–8. Marie Despina hypothesizes a meeting been Espina, John Capistrano and Bernardino of Feltre 'en algún capítulo de la Orden', 'Las acusaciones de crimen ritual en España', *El Olivo*, 9 (1979), 48–70 (p. 51).

century. He became the architect of the Spanish Inquisition only in retrospect. Moreover, determining the views of the majority concerning *conversos* presents formidable methodological problems and it is by no means certain that *Fortalitium fidei* did reflect widely held or particularly influential views. Evidence from anti-*converso* polemics cannot be used to determine whether there was a widespread animus against New Christians. By their very nature, polemical texts are persuasive rather than informative, advancing contentious points by appearing to reflect the views and prejudices of readers. Even if Espina had captured the majority opinion, this does not mean that *Fortalitium fidei* was not a work of advocacy, advancing a very particular agenda and intervening in an ongoing debate. Moreover, the outcome of that debate – and thus the fate of *conversos* in Castile – was far from inevitable. Ranged against Espina were some of the most powerful and influential figures in the kingdom, whose learning easily surpassed his own and whose views were in closer accord with long-standing Church policies. That views similar to Espina's would ultimately triumph does not mean that his victory was certain in the 1460s or that his ideas were necessarily shared by the majority of the population at the time of writing.

Determining the status of the text is made harder by the difficulties in establishing a clear context for its production, its precise aims and intentions, and even the very audience Espina sought to address. In contrast to other authors writing about the *converso* problem, Espina provided few details about the immediate circumstances of the production of *Fortalitium fidei*. The text lacks a dedicatee and Espina presents his motivation for writing solely in terms of his need to sound a warning about the dire situation facing the faith in Castile. It is possible than when Espina began writing his work in 1458 he intended to address it to Enrique IV; *Fortalitium fidei* would then be an extension of the spiritual advice the preacher offered the king when acting as his confessor.[100] At the

---

[100] There was a precedent in Espina's career for royal dedications of his work. He had addressed a now-lost *Dialogus de fortuna* to Juan II. The contents and circumstances of the production of that work are unknown but it is possible that it may have been related to Alvaro de Luna's fall, since the episode had prompted much reflection on this theme. On the *Dialogus*: *Index alphabetico digestus ordine, in quo recesentur codices manuscripti latini, qui in huius regiae bibliothecae armariis sive tabulariis per pluteos seu sectiones distributi asservantur*, in Guillermo Antolín, *Catálogo de códices latinos de la Real Biblioteca del Escorial*, 5 vols (Madrid: Imprenta Helénica, 1910–23), V, 331–487

very least, the text must have been part of the effort by Observant Franciscans to bring the issue of the supposed enemies of the faith, particularly *conversos*, to the king's attention. The failure of the Franciscans to persuade the king to adopt their views and their subsequent loss of prestige may explain why Espina could not count on royal patronage by the time he completed his work in 1464.

Fortalitium fidei itself suggests that there were certain among the Castilian episcopate who shared some of Espina's views. It recorded contacts with the bishops of Lugo, Salamanca, and Palencia who in the 1450s had reported to Espina blood libels in their diocese. It is therefore possible to speak of an 'anti-Jewish school of thought' within the Castilian ecclesiastical hierarchy and postulate that there may have been a degree of 'ideological solidarity' between Observant Franciscans and this group.[101] Espina himself may also have had ties with the bishop and chapter of El Burgo de Osma. The only manuscript of *Fortalitium fidei* extant in the Iberian Peninsula, a very early copy of the original, was produced in 1464 for Bishop Pedro Montoya.[102] The cathedral library likewise contains the only copy of a collection of sermons attributed to Espina – four texts on the devil and the afterlife.[103]

More widely, the very nature of the text affords further insight into its function and intended readership. It has long been recognized that it contains much material – particularly those parts with a more popular appeal – eminently suited to aiding preachers in the composition of sermons. Nonetheless, that *Fortalitium fidei*

(p. 336). On works after the fall of Luna, see James M. Boyden, '"Fortune has Stripped You of your Splendour": Favourites and their Fates in Fifteenth- and Sixteenth-Century Spain', in *The World of the Favourite*, ed. by J. H. Elliott and L. W. B. Brockliss (New Haven: Yale University Press, 1999), pp. 26–37 (pp. 27–28).

[101] McKendrick, pp. 133–34.

[102] [Alonso de Espina], *Fortalitium fidei*, El Burgo de Osma, Biblioteca de la Catedral, códice 154. See also Timoteo Rojo Orcajo, *Catálogo descriptivo de los códices que se conservan en la santa iglesia catedral de Burgo de Osma* (Madrid: Tipografía de Archivos, 1929), p. 244.

[103] [Alonso de Espina], 'Sermones de Reverendi Magistri de Spina de penis Inferni', El Burgo de Osma, Biblioteca de la Catedral, códice 26, fols 100ʳ–115ᵛ. Codicological description: Rojo Orcajo, pp. 739–40. Authorship and contents: *Los sermones atribuidos a Pedro Marín (B.N.M., Mss. 9433): van añadidas algunas noticias sobre la predicación castellana de san Vicente Ferrer*, ed. by Pedro M. Cátedra, Analecta Salmanticensia: Textos Recuperados, 1 (Salamanca: Universidad de Salamanca, 1990), pp. 60–61.

was written in Latin and contained primarily theological and legal material suggests a more specialized and learned audience. By writing *Fortalitium fidei*, Espina was lending intellectual authority and credibility to a message that had been understood by some contemporaries to veer very close to popular agitation. More than just attempting to elevate his message, by writing in Latin Espina was placing his work in dialogue with fellow ecclesiastics and intellectuals in Castile and beyond. Although seemingly offering the only possible programme of action to remedy the problems that faced Castile, he was, in actuality, appealing to the monarchy, to the episcopate and, even possibly, to the papacy to accept his interpretation of events and embrace his remedies.

THE CONTOURS OF THE *CONVERSO* DEBATE

The contours of the *converso* debate were shaped by a dialogue, often implicit, between authors on opposing sides. As claim met counterclaim, the terms of the debate crystallized. Discussions centred on a series of themes that addressed the place of *conversos* in society: the concept of Christian unity, the question of judaizing, and the relationship between Christianity and Judaism. If debates regarding the integration of New Christians were, in essence, narrow ones – both sides relied on the same limited number of Biblical and legal proof texts – nevertheless their implications were far-reaching. Taking place largely through apologetic tracts, such debates became the main arena for discussion of the shape of the Castilian Church and society. Though recent scholarship acknowledges the existence of this pro- and anti-*converso* dialogue there has been to date relatively little explicit study of its themes or of the impact of this dialogue itself on positions on either side.[1]

In his *Fortalitium fidei*, Espina never quoted works in defence of New Christians or even acknowledged the existence of such texts: for Espina, *Fortalitium fidei* was not a contribution to an on going debate but simply a statement of fact. The Biblical interpretations he offered, the remedies that he proposed, even his depiction of events and characters were the only possible, the only truly Christian ones. Nowhere in the *Fortalitium fidei* did Espina cite alternative interpretations, not even to condemn them; there was

---

[1] Rábade Obradó, 'Judeoconversos y monarquía', in *La monarquía*, ed. by Nieto Soria, pp. 248, 257. Recent collective studies of pro-*converso* apologetics include Bruce Rosenstock, *New Men: 'Conversos', Christian Theology, and Society in Fifteenth-Century Castile*, Papers of the Medieval Hispanic Research Seminar, 39 (London: Department of Hispanic Studies, Queen Mary, University of London, 2002); Dayle Seidenspinner-Nuñez, 'Conversion and Subversion: *Converso* Texts in Fifteenth-Century Spain', in *Christians, Muslims, and Jews in Medieval and Early Modern Spain: Interaction and Cultural Change*, ed. by Mark M. Meyerson and Edward D. English, Notre Dame Conferences in Medieval Studies, 8 (Notre Dame: University of Notre Dame Press, 2000), pp. 241–61; and Claude B. Stuczynski, 'Pro-*Converso* Apologetics and Biblical Exegesis', in *The Hebrew Bible in Fifteenth-Century Spain: Exegesis, Literature, Philosophy, and the Arts*, ed. by Jonathan Decter and Arturo Prats, Études sur le Judaïsme Médiévale, 54 (Leiden: Brill, 2012), pp. 151–76.

not a debate about *conversos* but, rather, a *converso* problem.² Yet, scrutiny of the writings of pro-*converso* authors reveals the extent to which *Fortalitium fidei* was an attempt to reply to their ideas. In this context, Espina's use of material from earlier works of anti-Jewish polemic gained new meaning. He was not simply reiterating the arguments of earlier authors within the mendicant anti-Semitic tradition but deploying them against pro-*converso* theologians to show that New Christians were part of the Jewish problem in Castile. Thus the full shape of Espina's opinions and position are revealed only when the *Fortalitium fidei* is analysed alongside the pro-*converso* texts that it was implicitly in dialogue with.

This chapter takes the writings of three authors – Alonso de Cartagena's *Defensorium unitatis christianae*, Juan de Torquemada's *Tractatus contra madianitas et ismaelitas*, and Alonso de Oropesa's *Lumen ad revelationem gentium* – as representative of the range of pro-*converso* opinions in mid-fifteenth-century Castile. Writing from the circles surrounding the Castilian crown and the papacy, these three authors addressed the discrimination and persecution of *conversos*, refuting claims of widespread judaizing, denying that Jewish ancestry influenced character negatively, and asserting the right of New Christians to partake fully in society.³ In so doing, they advanced a concept of the Christian community in Castile that Espina would radically oppose in his *Fortalitium fidei*. That the writings of Oropesa and Espina were in opposition has long been recognised but, as will be seen, *Fortalitium fidei* was also responding to the position of Cartagena and, probably, that of Torquemada.

---

² These strategies are at work elsewhere in *Fortalitium fidei*. For example, Netanyahu, *The Origins*, p. 844, has shown how Espina based his assessments of the behaviour of *conversos* on the infractions of very small numbers of individuals. Similarly, Nicholas G. Round, 'Alonso de Espina y Pero Díaz de Toledo: *odium theologicum* y *odium academicus*', in *Actas del X Congreso de la Asociación Internacional de Hispanistas, Barcelona 21–26 de agosto de 1989*, ed. by Antonio Vilanova, 4 vols (Barcelona: PPU, 1992), I, 319–30, has argued that Espina's lack of acknowledgement of his sources was not just an attempt to claim an expertise and erudition that he did not have, but also the product of his ideological opposition to a *converso* author such as Pero Díaz de Toledo.

³ Rábade Obradó, 'Judeoconversos e inquisición', in *Orígenes*, ed. by Nieto Soria, p. 249.

The Defence of the *Conversos*

If responses to the persecution of New Christians could take many forms, nevertheless it was theology that offered, potentially, the material for a comprehensive refutation of anti-*converso* arguments. It could address effectively the most socially disruptive and, for *conversos*, the most dangerous position: the denial of the equality of the faithful. In contrast, judaizing received much less attention. Its existence, albeit not its extent, was uncontested by all parties. Among the works that confronted the discrimination of *conversos* through theological arguments the most notable are those of Cartagena, Torquemada, and Oropesa. As well as revealing the false legal premises of anti-*converso* ordinances, these works defended the place of New Christians within the Church. They emphasized the value of baptism in bringing about the complete spiritual regeneration of all its recipients and in making all individuals equal within the community of the faithful.

All three pro-*converso* treatises were prompted by the Toledo revolt and the arguments of its apologists. Cartagena, Torquemada, and Oropesa sought to provide expert advice in the aftermath of the rebellion to the secular and ecclesiastical authorities: King Juan II, Pope Nicholas V, and Alfonso Carrillo, archbishop of Toledo. Just as the *converso* problem itself had rapidly transcended a local dispute to gain relevance for the whole of Castile, so these texts went beyond their primary aim of providing concrete and specific advice to rulers. They rose above their function as expositions of the legal and doctrinal basis for the integration of *conversos* and put forward a distinct political theology, emphasizing social and religious harmony and rejecting division of Christians among ethnic lines.[4] Such was possible because these texts were, in essence, theoretical explorations of a religious problem albeit ones designed to address a particular, immediate situation.

---

[4] On the political theology of pro-*converso* texts see particularly: Kaplan, *The Evolution*, pp. 58–59; Bruce Rosenstock, 'Against the Pagans: Alonso de Cartagena, Francisco de Vitoria, and *Converso* Political Theology', in *Marginal Voices: Studies in Converso Literature of Medieval and Golden Age Spain*, ed. by Amy I. Aronson-Friedman and Gregory B. Kaplan, The Medieval and Early Modern Iberian World, 46 (Leiden: Brill, 2012), pp. 117–39; Seidenspinner-Nuñez, 'Conversion', in *Christians, Muslims, and Jews*, ed. by Meyerson and English, pp. 242–47; Stuczynski, 'Pro-*Converso* Apologetics', in *The Hebrew Bible*, ed. by Decter and Prats.

For Cartagena at least, disputes about *conversos* had a personal dimension. A member of one of the most prominent Jewish families in Castile, Cartagena was baptized at the age of five in 1391 when his father, the former Shelomo ha-Levi, converted to Christianity as Pablo de Santamaría. The father's subsequent rise in the Castilian Church and the royal court was matched by Alonso's success. As Bishop of Burgos and a member of the *Consejo Real*, Cartagena acted as Castile's representative at the Council of Basle and carried out a series of diplomatic missions to the courts of Portugal, Germany, and Poland. By the time the *Defensorium* was completed in 1450, he was recognized by his contemporaries as a distinguished humanist author and translator as well as one of the leading theologians in the kingdom.[5] In writing the *Defensorium*, the first response to the Toledo rebels, Cartagena was combining his twin roles as theologian and royal counsellor.[6] As the prologue indicated, it was based on a shorter Spanish work, now lost, also addressed to the king that may have had its origin in the discussions about the Toledo rebellion in the Royal Council.[7]

The *Defensorium* was a response to the anti-*converso* party from the heart of the Castilian establishment. Cartagena wrote to condemn the discrimination of Christians of Jewish origin and to defend the privileges accrued by new men in the service of the

---

[5] The text carried the date of 1450, but Cartagena had probably written it in the summer of 1449. See Benito Ruano, *Los orígenes*, p. 49.

[6] Studies on the *Defensorium*: John Edwards, 'New Light on the *Converso* Debate? The Jewish Christianity of Alfonso de Cartagena and Juan de Torquemada', in *Cross, Crescent and Conversion: Studies on Medieval Spain and Christendom in Memory of Richard Fletcher*, ed. by Simon Barton and Peter Linehan, The Medieval Mediterranean, 73 (Leiden: Brill, 2008) pp. 311–26; Luis Fernández Gallardo, 'Alonso de Cartagena: iglesia, política y cultura en la Castilla del siglo XV', 6 vols (unpublished doctoral thesis, Universidad Complutense de Madrid, 1998), V, 1481–537; Jonin, 'De la pureté de foi', in *L'hérédité*, ed. by van der Lugt and de Miramon; Jeremy Lawrance, 'Alfonso de Cartagena y los conversos', in *Actas del Primer Congreso Anglo-Hispano*, II: *Literatura*, ed. by Alan Deyermond and Ralph Penny (Madrid: Castalia, 1993), pp. 103–20; Netanyahu, *The Origins*, pp. 528–77; Rosenstock, 'Against the Pagans', in *Marginal Voices*, ed. by Aronson-Friedman and Kaplan; idem, *New Men*, pp. 22–52; Seidenspinner-Nuñez, 'Prelude', in *Strategies of Medieval Communal Identity*, ed. by van Bekkum and Cobb; Sicroff, *Los estatutos de limpieza de sangre*, pp. 59–88; Pastore, *Una herejía*, pp. 43–47; Stuczynski, 'Pro-*Converso* Apologetics', in *The Hebrew Bible*, ed. by Decter and Prats.

[7] Fernández Gallardo, 'Alonso de Cartagena', V, 1481.

monarchy. For Cartagena, the king was the protector of the Church, obliged to uproot error and to defend Christian unity. In these tasks, the monarch was to be assisted by a cadre of legal experts, *letrados*, in whose company Cartagena clearly set himself.[8]

Structured in three parts, the *Defensorium* advocated the unity of the Church against the divisions arising in Castile. Taking a historical approach from Adam to Christ, the first part served as an introduction, putting forward a series of general considerations about Christian unity and the relationship between Mosaic Law and the Law of Christ. The second part expanded on these topics through the exploration of four theorems (*theoremata*): Israel was redeemed through Christ; the whole world received the grace of salvation in one manner and through one Saviour; baptism created a new people and erased the difference between Gentile and Israelite; and Christian neophytes had the right to recover their old nobility. The dignifying of Israel and of converts of Jewish origin that was implicit in the first part became a central theme in the second one. The third part addressed the discrimination of *conversos* in Toledo, moving away from theological discussion into juridical and political matters.

Unlike Cartagena, Torquemada's socio-religious status as Old or New Christian remains uncertain. The Toledan rebels believed his hostility to their cause to be an example of a *converso* protecting his brethren and many modern scholars regard it likely that Torquemada's mother was a New Christian, noting that marriage to *conversos* had become common among the nobility.[9] All that can be said with certainty is that Torquemada came from a noble family and quickly rose to prominence in the Castilian Church. A Dominican, he attended the Council of Basle as a member of his

---

[8] *Defensorium*, prologus, 61–63. Translation into Spanish: *Alonso de Cartagena y el 'Defensorium unitatis christianae': introducción histórica, traducción y notas*, trans. by Guillermo Verdín-Díaz (Oviedo: Universidad de Oviedo, Servicio de Publicaciones, 1992). See also Fernández Gallardo, 'Alonso de Cartagena', V, 1489. On Cartagena as *letrado*, see Seidenspinner-Nuñez, 'Conversion', in *Christians, Muslims, and Jews*, ed. by Meyerson and English, pp. 243–45.

[9] The Toledan rebels believed that Torquemada had been instrumental in persuading the Pope not to receive their envoy, sent to Rome to put forward their case against the accusations of rebellion and heresy levied by Juan II. These accusations appear in the *Memorial*, p. 109. On modern scholarship: Rosenstock, *New Men*, p. 14; Thomas M. Izbicki, 'Juan de Torquemada's Defense of the *Conversos*', *Catholic Historical Review*, 85 (1999), 195–207 (p. 197).

Order's delegation and, subsequently, entered the Curia where he would remain for the rest of his career although he retained a close interest in Castilian affairs. He was Cardinal of Saint Sixtus and Master of the Sacred Palace, providing advice to the pope on theological and juridical matters, writing over fifty works of theology, and undertaking diplomatic missions to Castile, France and the Empire. After Pius II's death in 1464, he was one of the main candidates for the papacy, although he avoided being elected.

The *Tractatus* was the product of the internationalization of the *converso* dispute, after the Toledan ecclesiastical authorities and the crown had sought the support of the papacy to defeat the rebellion.[10] Having undertaken the task of defending the rights of New Christians at the Curia, Torquemada in all likelihood advised the pope in the redaction of the bull *Humani generis inimicus* that condemned the discrimination of *conversos* as heretical.[11] Building on the theological and legal arguments already present in the bull, Torquemada put forward in the *Tractatus* a more thorough defence of *conversos* and of the unity of the Church.[12]

---

[10] Benito Ruano, *Los orígenes*, p. 66; Llamedo González, 'Juan de Torquemada', in *Tratado*, ed. by del Valle R., p. 112. Carlos del Valle R. suggests that Torquemada first turned his attention towards the defence of *conversos* at the behest of Juan II, who had commissioned a series of expert reports early in the summer of 1449. Torquemada's reply took the form of a sermon preached before the king on 28 August 1449 that would be the kernel of the future *Tractatus*, see Valle R., 'En los orígenes', in *Tratado*, ed. by del Valle R., pp. 67–68. For an alternative interpretation that attributes the sermon to Francisco de Toledo, see *Sermo in die Beati Augustini*, in *De la 'Sentencia-Estatuto' de Pero Sarmiento a la 'Instrucción' del Relator: estudio introductorio, edición crítica y notas de los textos contrarios y favorables a los judeoconversos a raíz de la rebelión de Toledo de 1449*, ed. by Tomás González Rolán and Pilar Saquero Suárez-Somonte (Madrid: Aben Ezra Ediciones, 2012), pp. 33–77 (p. 33).

[11] The tract is dated 1450. For a suggestion that it had been written prior to *Humani generis inimicus*, see Llamedo González, 'Juan de Torquemada', in *Tratado*, ed. by del Valle R., pp. 112–13. The latter date seems preferable as it allows the *Tractatus* to be a reply to the *Memorial*, see note 13 below.

[12] Studies on the *Tractatus*: Netanyahu, *The Origins*, pp. 434–85; Izbicki, 'Juan de Torquemada'; Rosenstock, *New Men*, pp. 53–68; Elvira Pérez Ferreiro, 'El tratado de Torquemada y la controversia estatutaria en la decimoquinta centuria', in *Tratado contra los madianitas e ismaelitas, de Juan de Torquemada (Contra la discriminación conversa)*, ed. by Carlos del Valle R. (Madrid: Aben Ezra Ediciones, 2002), pp. 75–85; Seidenspinner-Nuñez, 'Prelude', in *Strategies of Medieval Communal Identity*, ed. by van Bekkum and Cobb; Edwards, 'New Light on the *Converso* Debate?', in *Cross, Crescent and Conversion*, ed. by Barton and Linehan; Stuczynski, 'Pro-*Converso*

A relatively brief and hurried text, the *Tractatus* is nonetheless a comprehensive reply to the arguments of the Toledan rebels.[13] In the Preface, Torquemada stated that, having examined the documentation submitted by the Toledans to the pope in support of their case, he had found the proceedings against *conversos* and the logic that had informed them utterly erroneous.[14] Throughout sixteen chapters Torquemada disproved the legality of the persecution of *conversos* and constructed a theological case to counter their discrimination. Firstly, he rejected the accusation that converts and their descendants were suspect in their faith on account of their Jewish ancestry. Then he moved onto denying the premise of Jews as perfidious and unfaithful that underpinned the question of alleged genealogical disposition of the *conversos* towards faithlessness. Finally he refuted the Scriptural and legal proofs that supported the thesis of the rebels. In the closing chapters of the *Tractatus* Torquemada turned to a positive defence of New Christians where he highlighted the role of Jews within salvation history and firmly endorsed the equality of the Christian faithful.

As General of the Hieronymites, Alonso de Oropesa came from a very different ecclesiastical background to those of Cartagena and Torquemada.[15] The Hieronymites were essentially a contemplative

---

Apologetics', in *The Hebrew Bible*, ed. by Decter and Prats. On the unity of the Church as a central theme in Torquemada's works see Pérez Ferreiro, 'El tratado de Torquemada', in *Tratado*, ed. by del Valle R., p. 82; Izbicki, 'Juan de Torquemada'.

[13] On the hurried style of the text and its vehement tone, see: Llamedo González, 'Juan de Torquemada', in *Tratado*, ed. by del Valle R., pp. 106–7. On the *Tractatus* as a point-by-point reply to the *Memorial* of Marcos García de Mora, see Benito Ruano, *Los orígenes*, p. 66.

[14] *Tractatus*, prologus, 0.3 [sic], 127: 'falsa, impia et scandalosa ac erronea multa esse'. Torquemada's apparently detailed information about the situation in Toledo probably came from the city's archbishop, Alonso Carrillo, Llamedo González, 'Juan de Torquemada', in *Tratado*, ed. by del Valle R., pp. 103–4.

[15] My analysis of Oropesa's work will briefer than the previous two given that it has been the object of two recent studies by Pastore, *Il vangelo*, pp. 1–56; and *Una herejía*, pp. 50–71. On *Lumen*, see also Netanyahu, *The Origins*, pp. 855–96; Felipe Pereda, 'La Puerta de los Leones de la Catedral de Toledo: una interpretación en clave litúrgica y funeraria', in *Grabkunst und Sepulkralkultur in Spanien und Portugal/Arte funerario y cultura sepulcral en España y Portugal*, ed. by Barbara Borngässer, Henrik Karge and Bruno Klein, Ars Iberica et Americana, 11 (Frankfurt am Main: Vervuert; Madrid: Iberoamericana, 2006), pp. 155–91 (pp. 178–87); Albert A. Sicroff, 'Anticipaciones del erasmismo español en el *Lumen ad revelationem gentium* de Alonso de Oropesa', *Nueva Revista de Filología Hispánica*, 30 (1981), 315–

Order whose emphasis on Scriptural study, manual labour and physical isolation placed them at the vanguard of spiritual renovation in Castile while putting them at odds with the mendicant Orders. At the same time, through their acceptance of brothers of diverse socio-religious backgrounds, they became 'la Orden por excelencia de los conversos' and Oropesa himself would emerge as the leading voice in defence of New Christians in the 1460s.[16] He enjoyed the confidence of King Enrique IV: he was royal chaplain, the monarch's representative in negotiations with the nobility, and in 1461 was entrusted with conducting an inquisition in Toledo to investigate judaizing.[17]

Although Oropesa had started writing the *Lumen* shortly after the revolt of 1449 he would only complete it in 1464. He had undertaken the task at the behest of the prior of Guadalupe to address the growing dissensions between Old and New Christians in that convent and in the Hieronymite Order at large but soon abandoned it. Having been appointed inquisitor in Toledo in 1461, Oropesa returned to the *Lumen* at the request of Alonso Carrillo, archbishop of that city.[18] Thus, the *Lumen* would become a defence of *conversos* grounded on Oropesa's experiences as inquisitor.

Scholars have long regarded the *Lumen* as the culmination of pro-*converso* works in the fifteenth century, providing as it does the fullest theological exploration of those themes developed by Oropesa's predecessors.[19] The dedication to Archbishop Carrillo gives a brief account of the *Lumen*'s purpose and main themes. Oropesa wished to counter the discrimination of *conversos*, insisting on the unity of all Christians and dignifying the role of Israel as God's people.[20] However, his analysis transcended the defence of New

---

33; Stuczynski, 'Pro-*Converso* Apologetics', in *The Hebrew Bible*, ed. by Decter and Prats.

[16] Pastore, *Una herejía*, p. 62.

[17] Ibid., pp. 50–51.

[18] Luis A. Díaz y Díaz, 'Introducción', in Alonso de Oropesa, *Luz para conocimiento de los gentiles*, ed. and trans. by Luis A. Díaz y Díaz (Madrid: Universidad Pontificia de Salamanca, Fundación Universitaria Española, 1979), pp. 7–57 (p. 20). Oropesa promised a second part to his work, dealing with pastoral content, that he never undertook; there is a reconstruction of its possible contents in pp. 31–34.

[19] Pastore, *Una herejía*, pp. 50, 64.

[20] *Lumen*, dedicatoria, 77.

Christians to become a complex exploration of the whole of the Christian faith that focused on the relationship between Mosaic Law and the Law of Christ and on the meaning of a Christian life.[21]

Christian Unity

Cartagena, Torquemada and Oropesa challenged the persecution of New Christians through a defence of the unity of the Church and the equality of all the faithful.[22] In so doing they sought to efface the division between Christians of Gentile and Jewish origin that the Toledan rebels had attempted to establish and to refute the idea that ethnic origin was 'determinative of Christian identity'.[23] Despite differences in approach and emphasis among these authors, their discussions of unity and equality were restricted to confronting arguments about the inferiority of *conversos*. Overall, their defence of New Christians rested on the assertion of the efficacy of baptism in creating new individuals, cleansed of all former sins, and in acting as a gateway into the Church, engendering a new people united by ties of spiritual kinship.[24]

For Cartagena, the common destiny of mankind was to achieve salvation within the 'indivisible unity' of the Church; the building of this Church was thus an on going historical process.[25] The Church Militant was the city of Jerusalem, surrounded by the walls of the faith that had been built through the efforts of Christians of Jewish and Gentile origin.[26] This construction was still in progress:

---

[21] Pastore, *Una herejía*, pp. 50, 64; Sicroff, 'Anticipaciones', p. 319.

[22] Torquemada did not discuss the concept of unity in *Tractatus*, probably because it was structured as a response to the legal case put forward by the Toledan rebels. Nonetheless, his treatise was informed by similar notions of the nature of the Christian community as Cartagena's and Oropesa's.

[23] Rosenstock, 'Against the Pagans', in *Marginal Voices*, ed. by Aronson-Friedman and Kaplan, p. 119.

[24] On notions of Christian community as kin group see Gil Anidjar, 'Lines of Blood: *Limpieza de Sangre* As Political Theology', in *Blood in History and Blood Histories*, ed. by Mariacarla Gadebusch Bondio, Micrologus' Library, 13 (Florence: SISMEL/Edizioni del Galluzzo, 2005), pp. 119–36.

[25] *Defensorium*, II, theorema 3, iii, 137–40 (p. 137): 'indivisibilis ecclesie unitas'. On Cartagena's understanding of the history of salvation as a dialectic progression towards the unity of mankind, see Jonin, 'De la pureté de foi', in *L'hérédité*, ed. by van der Lugt and de Miramon, pp. 90–92.

[26] *Defensorium*, II, theorema 3, ii, 135: 'Semen enim est verbum dei, quod apostoli et discipuli domini et plurimi martires quia ex israel erant, seminantes sedule disperserunt. Fidelis autem gentilitas in terra bona suscipiens fructum

the walls of Jerusalem were being built and defended by theologians who scrutinized Scripture and preachers who fought against error.[27] Secular rulers assisted them bringing armed force against those who attempted to breach or bring down the walls of the faith and introduce error and infidelity, either openly or covertly.[28] All Christians, whatever their origin, were called to take part in the task; those who attempted to sow dissension, more than any other, were the ones who were failing the faithful and offending God.

Within this scheme, the entry of *conversos* into the Church was one more advance in the fulfilment of mankind's destiny. Rejecting *conversos* was to take a step back in this process, hence the tenor of Cartagena's discussion of Paul's condemnation of judaizers in the letter to Titus (1.10–14). Where the Toledan rebels had claimed that in excluding *conversos* from office they were following the Apostle's admonition, Cartagena saw their actions as sowing dissension among Christians, the most odious sin in the eyes of God.[29] In his analysis of the letter, Cartagena focused not on the

centuplum dedit, cum ex ea procedentes fideles mirabilissima dispersione fuderunt diffusumque a volucribus et vulpibus, erroribus siquidem et heresibus multis, sapiente et potentie miro mucrone accutissimo deffenderunt sanctam civitatem iherusalem, que in hac via est ecclesia militans, muris fidei cincta in unitate sua mirabiliter protegentes'.

[27] *Defensorium*, II, theorema 3, ii, 135: 'Sed fidei muros edificarunt et edificant edificatosque deffendunt, cum sancti doctores ex eis descendentes profundissima ingenii perspicuitate catholicam fidem elucidarunt. Ac continue per diversas orbis partes devotissimi cordis et elevatissimi ingenii multi sapientissimi viri verbo et scriptis elucidant, cum eius diverticula armis scripture sacre indefessa virtute tuentur.'

[28] *Defensorium*, II, theorema 3, ii, 135–36. Cartagena proposed the mystical body as an alternative image for Church and society. The Church was a mystical body structured hierarchically according to ascending degrees of theological nobility, culminating with the Pope at the top; civil society was, likewise, an organic entity structured in ascending degrees of civil nobility with the king at the head. These structures operated in parallel because both secular and ecclesiastical leaders sought the same aim: to unify mankind in the image of Christ, see Rosenstock, *New Men*, p. 27.

[29] *Memorial*, pp. 218–19: 'Por Escriptura sacra, en quanto San Pablo en la epístola que embió al Emperador Tito, vengador de la sangre de Ihesu Christo le embió a amonestar que se guardase e no consintiese elegir por prelados los convertidos del linaje de judíos, diziendo: *Oportet enim episcopum sine crimine esse, sicut Dei dispensatorem; non superbum, non vinolentum, non iracundum, etc.*, porque naturalmente son malos, vindicativos, infieles, adúlteros, soberbios, vanagloriosos e de todas malas costumbres doctados.' *Defensorium*, III, i, 271–72.

Apostle's censure of Christians practicing circumcision but on his condemnation of discord among the community in Crete. For Cartagena, Paul had been less concerned with judaizing than with those who had tried to create division among Christians, reopening old debates that had already been settled.[30]

Torquemada likewise framed his defence of *conversos* within a historical approach, presenting the persecution of New Christians as an episode of the continuing struggle between the Church and its enemies. He asserted that the anti-*converso* party was guilty of the very errors it imputed to New Christians, particularly the charge of hatred of God's people. Framing this denunciation in genealogical and ethnic terms added further force to Torquemada's argument, turning Old Christians' own discriminatory rhetoric against them. In the Prologue Torquemada identified the enemies of *conversos* with the descendants of Esau and Ishmael who, following the example of their ancestors' persecution of Jacob and Isaac, were enemies of Israel.[31] Old Christians may have believed themselves to be righteous, but their actions betrayed them as the devil's agents because they hindered God's glory and the salvation of mankind.[32] The label Edomites and Ishmaelites hinted at Torquemada's genealogical treatment of the problem: through their discrimination of *conversos* Old Christians were removing themselves from the righteous lineage of Abraham. Moreover, by identifying the anti-*converso* party explicitly as Ishmaelites, Torquemada was linking them to the Muslims further underlining the threat they posed to the kingdom.[33] As Cartagena had done, Torquemada condemned the rebels' interpretation of Paul's letter to Titus (1.7, 9–10), showing how an exegesis concluding all Christians of Jewish origin were perfidious and faithless was a deliberate distortion of Scripture. By labelling those who held such views 'pseudochristiani', he was, once more, turning the anti-

---

[30] *Defensorium*, II, theorema 1, vi, 110–11.

[31] *Tractatus*, prologus, 0.1–0.2, 125–26. Though in the title of the work Torquemada labelled the Toledan rebels, enemies of *conversos*, as Midianites and Ishmaelites, enemies of the Israel in the Old Testament, elsewhere in the *Tractatus* he preferred the identification of Edomites and Ishmaelites.

[32] *Tractatus*, prologus, 0.2, 126: 'Unde merito tales conversorum ad fidem Christi de populo Israelitico descendentium persecutores ministri diaboli in hoc et inimici Dei ostenduntur, cuius gloriam impediunt et humanae saluti praeparant impedimenta'.

[33] Netanyahu, *The Origins*, p. 414.

converso party's own logic against them.³⁴ In this designation there was an implicit equivalence between Old Christians, who accused New Christians of having converted falsely, and those Paul had reprimanded for their incomplete conversion when they clung to the practices of Mosaic Law.³⁵ Thus in the *Tractatus* Torquemada asserted that the fracture in the unity of the Church in Castile came from those who, while believing themselves to be the true Israel, removed themselves from the community of the faithful by their hatred of their brethren of Jewish origin.

Oropesa's *Lumen* transcended the censure of the Toledan rebels to become a wider theological exploration of the nature of the Church and its development within the history of salvation. Although in existence since the time of Abel as a mystical assembly of all who believed in the One God, the Church had only achieved its perfection through the Passion of Christ, when it was constituted as a perfect community of equals, united in faith and charity.³⁶ As the redemption of all mankind was achieved through the Passion so Christ's sacrifice made possible the reconciliation of Jews and Gentiles. Both peoples shared in the benefits of the Passion, both took part in the crucifixion.³⁷ Likening the Church under the Law of Christ to a body, a tree, a dove, and a seamless garment Oropesa highlighted its perfection and organic, corporate nature, where all the faithful were equal by virtue of the equal distribution of grace through the sacraments.³⁸

Oropesa's approach to the rift in Christian unity was primarily soteriological: he described his task in the *Lumen* as a defence of the rights of Christ.³⁹ Those who discriminated their brethren on the basis of the time of their arrival in the faith or their ancestral origin incurred the greatest error because they refused to share Christ's

---

[34] *Tractatus*, xi, 183–90 (7, 188).

[35] *Tractatus*, xi, 2, 184: 'Sed Paulus apostolus in hoc loco, ut glossa exponit, reprehendit Cretenses, qui erant gentiles, cum essent Graeci, et quosdam falsos apostolos, qui ex circumcisione venerant non pleni Christiani facti.'.

[36] *Lumen*, v–vi, 106–17.

[37] *Lumen*, xxxvii, 455.

[38] *Lumen*, viii, 120–24; xxxix, 484–99.

[39] *Lumen*, iv, 102: 'defender los derechos de Cristo'. On Oropesa's Christology see Díaz y Díaz, p. 38. For a critique of his position see Sicroff, 'Anticipaciones', p. 332 n48.

mercy and grace and, thus, placed limits on them.[40] Oropesa censured especially the concealed danger inherent in this ideology; those who persecuted *conversos* were destroying the Church rather than doing God's work.[41]

He also cautioned against expectations that the Church could achieve a state of further perfection, fearing such might fuel the exclusion of those deemed to be spiritually unworthy. Though within the *saeculum* the Church was a perfect entity, its members were not. The Church was like a net that contained all manner of fish, good and bad. It was the obligation of the clergy to drag the net to the shore, which was the end of time, when the sifting of the righteous and the wicked would take place.[42] Through this image, Oropesa not only defended the place of *conversos* among the faithful, but also revealed an inclusive and pragmatic notion of the Christian community.[43] His equation of unity with perfection, and his insistence on the capability of all individuals to fall into error amounted to a total rejection of divisions among Christians on the basis of genealogy and perceived spiritual and social worth.

---

[40] *Lumen*, lii, 761: 'poniendo ésos arbitrariamente un límite a la misericordia y gracia de Cristo'. In the Prologue Oropesa gave the explicit example of the brethren at Guadalupe who would claim the authority of the writings of Paul – here probably meaning the Epistle to Titus – as justification for their exclusion of *conversos*, *Lumen*, dedicatoria, 62.

[41] *Lumen*, lii, 761–62: 'oculto engaño'; dedicatoria, 64: 'como jabalí[es] salvaje[s] extermina[n] la Iglesia'.

[42] *Lumen*, xxxvi, 441–50, (pp. 447–48): 'se entiende a la Iglesia militante, que con frecuencia recibe en la sagrada Escritura el nombre de Reino de los cielos, y que sola, cual red en este mundo peligroso, mar grande e inmenso, recoge hombres, como peces, de la ciénaga profunda y juntos los lleva al puerto costero. [...] la red de la Iglesia que tenía que llenarse de toda clase de peces, es decir, de toda clase de personas: judíos y gentiles, nobles y simples, ricos y pobres, buenos y malos, como Cristo dijo; y todos los que entran en ella han de ser llevados juntos a la orilla con el mismo arrastre, cuidado, trabajo y dirección'.

[43] The Donatist author Tyconius understood the net of mixed fish from Matthew 13.47–48 as a type for the Church. Augustine, in turn, adopted this type that would become central to his thought, particularly in *The City of God*. He employed it, for instance, to censure the Donatist notion of a Church of the elect and demonstrate that in the Church Militant 'sinners can become saints and vice versa', Garry Wills, *Font of Life: Ambrose, Augustine, and the Mystery of Baptism* (Oxford: Oxford University Press, 2012), pp. 141–42.

The Problem of Judaizing and the Inheritance of Sin and Guilt

As well as putting forward their own inclusive vision of the Christian community, pro-*converso* authors addressed explicitly those ideas that informed Old Christian discriminatory ideology. They responded to accusations of judaizing and called into question the notion that Jewish descent, 'no matter how distant', made individuals liable to 'heresy and moral corruption'.[44] While these authors could not deny that there had been instances of error among *conversos* in Toledo, they rejected the existence of judaizing as a collective problem, challenged the notion that particular errors could attach exclusively to certain groups, and contested claims about the inheritability of sin and negative personal characteristics. In addressing these issues, Cartagena, Oropesa and Torquemada mounted an open attack on Old Christian ideology, concluding that persecution of *conversos* was a far greater heresy than judaizing.

Cartagena's discussion of judaizing did not go into the specifics of the situation in Toledo but remained largely at the level of general doctrinal principles and points of law. The Apostolic Church had already established that Christians should not adhere to Mosaic Law; any subsequent attempt at keeping its practices was a return to the infidelity of the Jews that should be energetically punished by the episcopal inquisition.[45] Yet Cartagena warned that the persecution of *conversos* was an even graver error. Far from regarding the accusations of judaizing as a mere pretext for discrimination he interpreted them as a means to introduce, under the guise of the defence of orthodoxy, the greater heresy of breaking the unity of the Church, which he labelled paganizing.[46] Cartagena also considered the group dynamics of the *converso* problem. He maintained that, although the existence of error among some *conversos* was undeniable, it did not extend to all. Overall, Cartagena's

---

[44] Nirenberg, 'Was There Race before Modernity?', in *The Origins of Racism*, ed. by Eliav-Feldon, Isaac and Ziegler, p. 242.

[45] *Defensorium*, III, x, 296–301.

[46] Discrimination of *conversos* as heresy: *Defensorium*, II, theorema 4, xxxiv, 266–67; paganizing: 'sic et illi qui baptismatis gurgite loti et in unum populum cum aliis effecti divisionem aliquam revivificare volunt, paganizare dicentur, cum christianam unitatem scindere', III, prologus, 270. Cartagena would also use the accusation of judaizing against Marcos García de Mora on account of his literal and erroneous interpretation of the canons of the IV Council of Toledo to justify the discrimination of *conversos*. See below, Chapter 5, p. 124 n21.

position was based on the defence of the actions of individuals to establish their virtue. Judaizing was not a collective problem, nor was error in the faith the exclusive preserve of any group. Thus, Cartagena argued that, contrary to the rebels' claim that only Christians of Jewish origin were guilty of returning to their pre-baptismal practices, Paul's epistles showed that both Christians of Jewish and Gentile origin had fallen into such error.[47]

Cartagena's focus on the individual led him to afford to every generation of Christians the status of neophytes. Thus, he argued that it was not licit to speak of New and Old Christians because all individuals were new to the faith.[48] Since the grace of baptism could not be inherited, nor could the foetus in the mother's womb be baptized, having Christian ancestors counted for nothing.[49] The acquisition of a Christian identity was an individual process, where no merit could accrue by virtue of descent.[50] Implicit in his argument was a critique of the idea, maintained by the anti-*converso* party, that an Old Christian lineage automatically conferred a degree of virtue and privilege.

Cartagena's defence of the value of an individual's actions over considerations of inheritance and collective guilt rested on two points: baptism afforded absolute forgiveness to all its recipients, and sin and culpability, with the exception of Original Sin, could not be inherited.[51] There was, however, one important qualification. Cartagena asserted that the rejection of baptism, be it in the refusal of the Jews to embrace Christianity or in the apostasy of Christians of either Gentile or Jewish origin, meant that the sins of their ancestors would fall on them.[52] This was not because such sins

---

[47] *Defensorium*, II, theorema 1, vi–vii, 109–16, quoting Titus 1.10–14, Galatians 4.8–12, and Romans 1.19–25.

[48] *Defensorium*, II, theorema 3, v, 146: 'cum nullus catholicus sit qui noviter ad fidem non venerit'.

[49] *Defensorium*, II, theorema 3, v, 147: 'provectior etate ille antiquior christianus est, si infantulus baptismum receperit.'

[50] Cartagena's argument also sought to counter the notion implicit in anti-*converso* documents that the legal status of neophytes was inheritable. See Vidal Doval, 'Nos soli sumus christiani', in *Medieval Hispanic Studies*, ed. by Beresford, Haywood and Weiss, p. 228.

[51] *Defensorium*, II, theorema 4, x, 184–87, and xi, 190.

[52] *Defensorium*, II, theorema 1, vi, 109.

were latent but rather it was the inevitable consequence of the individual's choice to reject the forgiveness offered by baptism.[53]

Yet, Cartagena did not reject fully the idea that moral qualities could be inherited. He argued for a model of latent nobility that, with baptism as its lynchpin, sought to marry the absolute value of the actions of an individual with the inheritance of virtue.[54] Baptism therefore did not entail the complete and wholesale change of a person and a total break with the past, but rather a radical transformation that brought to the fore hitherto attenuated or latent positive qualities.[55] Cartagena claimed that *conversos* could recover the civil and natural nobility of their Jewish ancestors.[56] Though the Israelites' rejection of the Gospel had led to their loss of divine grace and the forfeiture of their theological nobility, even in their captive state, the Jews had retained their natural and civil nobility that manifested itself in their understanding, moral virtues, and capacity to rule.[57] Conversion allowed these virtues to shine

---

[53] *Defensorium*, II, theorema 1, vi, 109–10: 'Quod utique commune omnibus est tam ex gentilibus quam israeliticis ad fidem catholicam venientibus ut peccata maiorum, sua quoque que iam transsierant, eis improperentur, si fidem catholicam recipere renuunt vel post receptam in errores iudaysmi seu gentilitatis recidivant, quia veritatem cognoscere vel post agnitam retroire gravissimum est et preteritorum criminum memoriam revivificare videtur. [...] Non quia ipsum originale peccatum gurgite baptismi suffocatum realiter suscitetur, sed quia penam peccantis exagerat remissio preteritorum. Nam quanto maiorem criminum sive propriorum sive parentum remissionem recepimus, presertim si in deviationem fidei aut blasfemiam tenduntur.'

[54] Nirenberg, 'Was There Race before Modernity?', in *The Origins of Racism*, ed. by Eliav-Feldon, Isaac and Ziegler, p. 259. As Nirenberg argues, Cartagena was not merely responding to the rebels but also entering into a wider debate about nobility taking place in late medieval Spain that transcended the confines of the *converso* problem, pp. 253–54. For an overview of ideas about nobility in late medieval Spain, see Isabel Beceiro Pita and Ricardo Córdoba de la Llave, *Parentesco, poder y mentalidad: la nobleza castellana, siglos XII–XV* (Madrid: CSIC, 1990).

[55] Thus Cartagena proposes a model of conversion that followed the evolution-change model where a Jewish identity matures into a Christian one. On these models of change and conversion see, Denise Kimber Buell, 'Early Christian Universalism and Modern Forms of Racism', in *The Origins of Racism in the West*, ed. by Miriam Eliav-Feldon, Benjamin Isaac and Joseph Ziegler (Cambridge: Cambridge University Press, 2009), pp. 109–31 (pp. 115–16).

[56] *Defensorium*, II, theorema 4, in particular xiv–xviii, 195–211.

[57] *Defensorium*, II, theorema 4, xviii, 210.

forth fully once again.[58] Even virtues that had remained dormant across centuries of Jewish unbelief could reappear after baptism. Such explained the military valour of certain New Christians. In the short period of time it had lapsed since their conversion it would have been impossible for them to acquire the degree of fortitude and military prowess that they displayed.[59]

The *Defensorium*, however, was more than simply a defence of *conversos*. Cartagena sought to vindicate the rapid rise of certain New Christians within Castilian society. Although the *Sentencia* had not explicitly barred *conversos* from the nobility, the possibility that it could be employed to such end was 'a legitimate concern'.[60] To counter such a threat, Cartagena devoted a significant part of the *Defensorium* to an exploration of the nature of nobility and a defence of the rights of *conversos* to access its ranks.[61] Following baptism, New Christians could maintain and augment the privileges and status they may have had as Jews. There was a clear personal element in this theory. Cartagena was defending his family's very claim to nobility on the basis of their Levite descent and of their former prominent position in the Jewish community of Burgos. In Cartagena's formulation, the unity and equality of all the faithful was not incompatible with a defence of the privileges of the elite. This was not a genealogical model free from contradictions.[62]

[58] The Jews of Spain were a particular case in point: they still maintained distinctions on the basis of civil nobility because some were descendants of the most important and noble lineages among the Israelites who had arrived in the Iberian Peninsula after the destruction of Jerusalem, *Defensorium*, II, theorema 4, xviii, 210–11.

[59] *Defensorium*, II, theorema 4, xx, 217–18: 'aliquis nobilitatis carbunculus licet non plene lucens non tamen prorsus extinctus in stomacis aliquorum ex eis qui ex vetustissima nobilitate eorum de seculo in seculum descendens aliquantulum fumigasset.'

[60] Kaplan, *The Evolution*, pp. 59–60 (quotation at p. 60).

[61] Cartagena, in line with other authors of the time, distinguishes three elements within nobility: civil, natural and theological, see *Defensorium*, II, theorema 4, xviii, 210.

[62] Writing in the context of Cartagena's treatment of judaizing Jonin notes further tensions in the argument between 'logique d'inclusion universaliste chrétienne et impératif de préservation de la singularité communautaire', 'De la pureté de foi', in *L'hérédité*, ed. by van der Lugt and de Miramon, p. 99. Furthermore, Cartagena must have known that the Bible provided more examples of the inheritance of negative characteristics than just Original Sin, see above, Chapter 1, p. 15.

Since the *Tractatus* addressed closely the arguments of the Toledan rebels, Torquemada considered the problem of judaizing among the city's *conversos* primarily from a legal point of view. Although he admitted the likelihood that some New Christians were guilty of Jewish practices, he flatly denied the existence of a judaizing heresy in Toledo.[63] He argued that the rebel faction had brought the charge against New Christians as retaliation for their refusal to take part in the revolt against Juan II.[64] After reviewing the evidence put forward in the legal proceedings brought against *conversos*, he concluded that neither there had been persistence in error, nor a large-scale, organized movement of judaizers.[65] Although the documents recorded imputations of circumcision, denial of the divinity of Christ and of the sacramental value of the Eucharist, it was only appropriate to speak of error rather than heresy. The executions of New Christians on charges of heresy had been nothing but murders.[66]

Torquemada contrasted these opportunistic and unproven accusations with the real heresy at work in Toledo: the discrimination of *conversos* by their Old Christian brethren.[67] He insisted that the sins of the parents did not fall on their children, who were not responsible for either guilt or penance. Anyone who maintained otherwise was limiting the redemptive value of Christ's passion and death and, in turn, became guilty of denying the sacramental value of baptism and penance to cleanse sin.[68] Despite

---

[63] *Tractatus*, xii, 3, 192: 'aliquos de genere Iudaeorum ad fidem conversos non bonos fuisse aut esse Christianos, sed malos et etiam in fide suspectos, servantes apud se aliquas veteris legis caerimonias'

[64] *Tractatus*, i, 2, 130: 'Plane illi, qui adversus novos fideles, pro eo quod eorum factionibus et machinationibus proprium et naturalem dominum non consenserant, rapinis et caedibus processerunt; et, ut sua maleficia aliquo fuco honestatis colorarent, processum super confictis haeresibus fiendum stabilierunt.'

[65] *Tractatus*, i, 129–38.

[66] *Tractatus*, i, 6, 136: 'Videant ergo ipsi, et maxime religiosi, qui, propterea quod ipsi dixissent quosdam captos fuisse haereticos, occasionem dederunt morti eorum, an sint homicidae et irregulares, potissime quia, cum nullus illorum convictus fuerit, aut sponte confessus, aut pertinax in aliquo errore repertus, non poterant dicere cum veritate quod essent haeretici'. See also *Tractatus*, i, 3e, 133–34.

[67] *Tractatus*, ii, 2, 139–40; 4–7, 144–48; i, 4, 134.

[68] *Tractatus*, ii, 3, 143: 'Item, non est omnino nec de virtute, nec vitio parentum aut laudandus aliquis aut culpandus, nemo inde vere aut obscurus aut clarus est'.

insisting that *conversos* should be judged exclusively by their actions as individuals, and that error was not the exclusive preserve of any given group, Torquemada recognized that there was collective dimension to the New Christian problem.[69] The deep-seated hatred felt by a group of Old Christians against *conversos* had burst forth during the revolt, triggering a persecution that he likened to the roaring and rising of the enemies of Israel in Psalm 82.3–5.[70] The *Tractatus* painted a picture of a city divided, where Old Christians, motivated by greed and envy, sought to oppress and exclude *conversos*.

In the closing sections of the *Tractatus*, Torquemada returned to the great themes of his work: the efficacy of the sacraments and the absolute value of faith and individual works. He showed how through baptism all Christians formed a new mystical body, united in spiritual kinship as children of God and partaking of the same spiritual inheritance. True membership, however, was based upon the sincere exercise of charity and love to fellow Christians.[71] Thus, claims of genealogical superiority advanced by Old Christians could not be sustained. Furthermore, it was the persecutors' membership of the Christian fellowship that should be questioned, not that of the *conversos*.[72] Converts should instead be praised and celebrated on account of their acceptance of Christianity and the debt owed by all Christians to the *conversos*' Jewish forebears should be remembered. Torquemada was not proposing a genealogical model of personal worth – he was unequivocal in his rejection of such views – but was offering recognition, in the face of slander, of the spiritual benefit that carnal Israel had bestowed upon all Christians. Rather than from the mistakes of a few *conversos* who lapsed into error out of ignorance, the gravest danger to the Church came from those Old Christians who attempted knowingly to create dissension and to manipulate events for their own gain.

The intervening years between 1449 and Oropesa's completion of the *Lumen* witnessed a deterioration of social conditions in

---

[69] *Tractatus*, xii, 3, 192–93.

[70] *Tractatus*, prologus, 0.2, 127: 'Dicuntur autem praefati persecutores fidelis populi Israelitici iuxta Glossam *insonuisse*, quia odium et malitiam quam corde adversus populum Israeliticum gestabant, et blasphemias et mali as quas occulte contra illos loquebantur, aim in publicum loqui non verentur'.

[71] *Tractatus*, xiv, 1–7, 207–11.

[72] Rosenstock, *New Men*, p. 67, speaks of Torquemada's 'counter-assault against the dignity of gentile Christians as a whole'.

Toledo and in Castile. Approaching the issue of judaizing from his perspective as inquisitor, Oropesa considered primarily its pastoral implications. Although he was clear that *conversos* who had erred should be punished, he also noted that *conversos* as a group should not be discriminated against, lest some fall in their faith.[73] New Christians were not heretics by nature, and any claims to that effect were entirely self-interested and motivated by envy. Following a path trod by Cartagena and Torquemada, Oropesa accused Old Christians of the very sins they censured in *conversos*. When Old Christians wished to exclude New Christians from office they were literally behaving like the ancient Israelites, who in accordance with the Law would allocate dignities such as the priesthood to certain lineages.[74] For Oropesa, the Old Christians, and not the *conversos*, were the judaizers. Thus, rather than representing the forces of order and orthodoxy in the city, the anti-*converso* party was a destabilizing influence, guilty of dragging the Church back to the time of the Synagogue. The actions and attitudes of the anti-*converso* party deepened the rift between Old and New Christians, without providing any means to close it. Oropesa's solution was to sweep the anti-*converso* party – the evil beasts, the thieves and highway robbers, the stinking animals – from the sheepfold of Christ.[75] Unjust persecution was to be met with just persecution.

Whereas Cartagena and Torquemada had directed their works almost exclusively at the Toledo rebels and their supporters, Oropesa also had to contend with a Castilian society in which the divisions between Old and New Christians were increasingly entrenched and those demanding radical action against *conversos* were gaining ground. Oropesa warned against such radical measures, arguing that in a Church that was a perfect body, while

---

[73] *Lumen*, iv, 102: 'No es que pretenda dejar sin castigo a cualquiera de ellos que pecase, sino tan solo establecer que no se los desprecie y que, a los que pequen, se les debe castigar según la ley de Cristo común para todos, como quedará claro en el desarrollo; y que tampoco alguno de los simples, decepcionado a causa de su ignorancia, sacudido quizás por esta peste perezca, tornando así su fe en escándalo, de forma que lo que tenía que ser causa de salvación eterna se le vuelva ocasión de perdición.'

[74] *Lumen*, dedicatoria, 63: 'De donde claramente se deducía que estos hombres destruían el evangelio queriendo defenderlo y rebajaban la Iglesia de Cristo al nivel de la sinagoga: de tal modo que, así como allí el sacerdocio, las dignidades y los oficios se asignaban por la Ley a determinadas personas de los judíos, incluso aún a determinada tribu y familia'.

[75] *Lumen*, l, 705–6.

there was no room to return to the imperfection of Mosaic Law, nor was there the possibility of achieving further perfection within historical time. Thus, he denounced as heretics both those who observed the precepts of Mosaic Law, in particular circumcision, and those who held millennarist expectations of a forthcoming Age of the Spirit.[76] Oropesa's identification of the Durango heretics as an example of the second error contained an implicit censure of the positions of Espina and the Observant Franciscans.[77] While the Franciscans equated heresy with judaizing *conversos* and argued for a papal-style inquisition led by the friars, Oropesa advocated a 'parsimonious' episcopal inquisition that would extend its investigations to Old and New Christians alike.[78] In the *Lumen*, then, Oropesa sought to discredit ideologies that were quickly gaining ground in Castile and to sound a warning of the danger inherent in pursuing purity at the expense of unity and charity.[79]

The Relationship between Christianity and Judaism

Despite their insistence that neophytes had been made new people through the grace of baptism, Cartagena, Torquemada, and Oropesa still felt compelled to address the vilification of the Jews. In so doing, they acknowledged that the discrimination of *conversos* was based largely on the assumption that anyone who possessed Jewish lineage was suspect. So strong was the association between New Christians and Jews in anti-*converso* writings that these authors were forced to neutralize the negative connotations of Jewish ancestry even if such should have been irrelevant given their assertions of the efficacy of baptism and the equality of the faithful. All three authors explored the relationship between God and Israel and between Mosaic Law and the Law of Christ to show the importance of the Jews in the foundation of the Church and thus deny the stigma attached to Jewish ancestry. These similarities did not obscure, however, divergent attitudes towards contemporary

---

[76] *Lumen*, xxi, 218–21.

[77] Pastore, *Il vangelo*, pp. 31–32. The fact that the error in Durango had started with the preaching of a Franciscan made this point all the clearer; even those who had presented themselves as the staunchest defenders of the faith and the champions of the virtuous Old Christians had heretics among their ranks.

[78] Stuczynski, 'Pro-*Converso* Apologetics', in *The Hebrew Bible*, ed. by Decter and Prats, p. 161.

[79] Pastore, *Il vangelo*, pp. 19–20. On Oropesa's insistence on charity as the leading source of interpretation of Scripture, see *Lumen*, xlvii, 583.

Jews. While Cartagena and Torquemada envisaged the relationship between Judaism and Christianity as one of covenantal continuity, Oropesa took a supersessionary view.

In the *Defensorium*, Cartagena explored the relationship between God and Israel through a history of salvation where unity was the guiding principle.[80] God had created a single man, Adam, and redeemed the whole of mankind through Christ, the second Adam.[81] In the time between creation and redemption, God had chosen the Israelites – the descendants of Isaac and Jacob who, by divine mandate, had prevailed over Ismael and Esau – as the people from whom the Saviour would come.[82] On account of this election, God had bestowed on Israel great spiritual gifts. He had given Abraham circumcision, a sign of covenant, and the Jews the Law, a sign of His favour and love that afforded them special rectitude and sanctification.[83] For the most righteous in Israel the Mosaic Law was able even to deliver the precepts of the Gospel.[84] Thus, for Cartagena, Israel and the Mosaic Law had enjoyed a privileged position: they were a people exalted by God, superior to the Gentiles in their law.

While the Jews had lost this position of pre-eminence by virtue of their rejection of Christ, Cartagena cast the relationship between Mosaic and the Law of Christ in terms of continuity and perfection. He illustrated this concept through light as allegory of the faith and understanding of Scripture and the divine.[85] Natural reason was like the light of the moon, too weak to illuminate most things; those living under it were unable to understand the divine essence.[86] In contrast, the written Mosaic Law was like fire that

[80] *Defensorium*, prologus, 64: 'in unitate principium humani generis formando possuit et ad unitatem redimendo reduxit'.
[81] *Defensorium*, I, i, 65–67, and x, 89–92.
[82] *Defensorium*, I, iii, 69–72.
[83] *Defensorium*, I, ii–iv, 68–75 (iv, 74): 'Legem igitur deus et alia et alia [*sic*] beneficia specialia illi populo exhibuit propter promissionem patribus eorum factam, illam siquidem ut ex eis christus nasceretur. Decebat enim ut populus ex quo Christus nasciturus erat, quadam pre aliis speciali sanctificatione polleret.'
[84] *Defensorium*, I, iv, 72–75, and vi, 77–80.
[85] The text never makes the point explicitly but the allegory appears to be based on the amount of light necessary for reading a book: almost impossible to do by moonlight; possible by firelight; and in ideal conditions under the sun at noon.
[86] *Defensorium*, I, viii, 82–84.

illuminated divine mysteries and foretold salvation, while the Law of Christ was like the sun, bringing spiritual illumination to the entire world. In his endorsement of covenantal continuity, Cartagena depicted the entire world congregating around Israel, under the light of Christ, and making up the Church Militant, the true Jerusalem.[87] Thus, Cartagena afforded carnal Israel a dignified place in the history of salvation.[88] He sought even to rescue the Jews from carrying exclusively the blame for the death of Christ. Since the Passion had benefitted both Jews and gentiles – with the former preaching the Gospel to the latter after their own baptism – culpability should fall on both groups.[89] The leaders of the Jews carried the greatest blame because they could see that the prophecies about the Messiah were fulfilled in Christ; the guilt of the Jewish people, although still very great, was attenuated because they had acted out of ignorance; the gentiles, having crucified Jesus, shared in the guilt too although theirs was the lesser crime because they were ignorant of the Law.[90]

Alongside this collective defence of Jews, Cartagena was also concerned with proving Mosaic Law's potential for affording righteousness to individuals. Although under a carnal understanding Mosaic Law was indeed old and senescent, under a spiritual understanding, it was always new. Meanwhile Christ's Law

---

[87] *Defensorium*, I, ix, 84–89 (p. 88): 'Quis enim dicere posset quantus numerus hominum, quanti cunei militarium virorum, diis suis reiectis, ad adorandum Christum ambulandumque sub solari lumine suo et in splendore ortus sui ad Iherosolimam, idest, ad sanctam ecclesiam venerunt. Nec enim Iherusalem ad gentes conversa est sed gentilis populus ad Iherusalem convertitur, ut ex utroque populo una vera Iherusalem, que in hac via est ecclesia militans, per quam ad supernam Iherusalem ascenditur, que est ecclesia triumphans, conderetur.'

[88] Rosenstock, *New Men*, p. 22; Edwards, 'New Light on the *Converso* Debate?', in *Cross, Crescent and Conversion*, ed. by Barton and Linehan, p. 319.

[89] *Defensorium*, II, theorema 3, iv, 143: 'ideo licet gradus culpe diversi fuerunt tamen tam israelite quam gentes in culpa illa participaverunt [...]. Ideo conveniens fuit, ut christus a iudaeis pati inciperet et postea illis tradentibus per manus gentilium eius passio finiretur, ut sic omnes in culpa participarent, sicut in merito participaturi erant.'

[90] *Defensorium*, II, theorema 3, iv, 143–44. He returns to the topic of the guilt for the death of Christ once more to highlight that the leaders of the Jews, those who were most culpable, did not wish this guilt to fall on the whole of the people: 'hinc ergo non super totum populum sed in se et in filios suos sanguinem verti illi sceleratissimi petierunt', *Defensorium*, II, theorema 4, v, 167.

alone could not confer virtue: for sinners and those who did not embrace charity, even the Law of the Gospel grew old.[91] This endorsement of covenantal continuity had positive consequences for *conversos*. For them the Law of Christ was not new but rather complemented and fulfilled the Mosaic Law, so much so that they were never true newcomers to the faith. Unlike those who came to Christianity from gentility, who were neither familiar with the precepts of the law nor knew the nature of God, through their conversion New Christians deepened their knowledge through spiritual understanding.[92]

While sharing the same basic outlook, Torquemada went further than Cartagena in defending the dignity and enduring collective role of Jews in salvation history. Israel had been and was still beloved of God, who had chosen it as the people from whom Christ would be born.[93] Torquemada tackled head on the idea of Israel as a condemned people. He examined Scriptural invective against Jews to conclude that, although there had been many among them who were impious and unfaithful, these accusations had never and could never apply to the totality of the Jews.[94] Similarly, even after its involvement in the death of Christ, God had not abandoned Israel.[95] Torquemada concluded, going against the grain of many of his contemporaries' opinions, that the proposition that the Jews were a condemned and unfaithful people was not merely false but heretical.[96]

Torquemada understood the relationship between Judaism and Christianity in terms of completion and fulfilment rather than supersession and enmity. Not content with simply highlighting the

---

[91] *Defensorium*, I, vi, 78: 'Illis tamen lex vetus est testamentum qui eam carnaliter intelligunt. Illis vetus est et senuit, quia vires suas obtinere non potest. Nobis autem qui eam spiritualiter exponimus semper nova est [...]. Peccatori autem et caritatis federa non servanti etiam evvangelia veterascunt'.

[92] *Defensorium*, I, vi, 78: 'quod non quasi ad inauditam legem et de novo recenter oblatam ex israelitico populo descendentes accedunt, sed ad implementum legis scripte eiusque plenissimam perfectionem'.

[93] *Tractatus*, vi, 1, 166: 'a Deo acceptum, carum et honoratum, [...] sive quod ab aeterno certissime apud divinam sapientiam notum erat quod multi illorum advenientem in carne Dei Filium, non modo non susciperent, sed etiam morti tradituri essent.'

[94] *Tractatus*, vii, 1–2a, 171–73; ix–x, 179–82.

[95] *Tractatus*, iii, 1, 149–55.

[96] *Tractatus*, iii, 1, 149: 'damnata tanquam mala, et infidelis, et adultera in fide'; 'sacrilegum, blasphemumque Dei ac sanctorum, et haereticum'.

importance of carnal Israel for Christianity, Torquemada also asserted that Jewish and Christian identities were not mutually exclusive. Such a position, and even more so the terms in which he expressed it, must have seemed 'startling' to many of his contemporaries, accustomed to thinking of Christians and Jews as polar opposites.[97] Torquemada insisted that Christ, the Virgin Mary, and the first generation of Christians were Israel according to the flesh. The Son had chosen to be incarnated as a Jew and was born of a Jewish woman; His flesh and blood, present in the Eucharist, were Jewish. When Christians despised the totality of the Jews as an impious, perfidious and condemned people they were insulting and rejecting the main instruments of their salvation: the Eucharist, the Virgin Mary, as well as the prophets, the apostles and many saints who interceded on behalf of Christians.[98]

Torquemada argued that first generation converts had experienced no rupture with their past because the Church had existed among the righteous of Israel since the time of Abel. The Church had not replaced Israel, but rather had sprung from it. Torquemada underlined this point through the image, taken from Romans 11.16–24, of the wild olive of Gentility grafted onto the olive tree of Israel.[99] Thus, Christians could not slander Jews without rejecting their own heritage, the founders of their Church, and the means of their salvation. As a result any attempts to disparage or besmirch the totality of the Jews, past or present, amounted to a denial of the unity and sanctity of the Church.[100]

Torquemada continued to challenge majority positions when he asserted the gap between the Jews of the Old Testament and those of the present to be minimal.[101] One of the tropes of medieval anti-Semitic discourse was that rabbinic Judaism was an illicit development, preventing Jews from fulfilling their role as witnesses to the truth of Christianity, and thus removing their right to live

---

[97] Edwards, 'New Light on the *Converso* Debate?', in *Cross, Crescent and Conversion*, ed. by Barton and Linehan, p. 321.

[98] *Tractatus*, iv, 156–59; xiv, 10, 213. Edwards, 'New Light on the *Converso* Debate?', in *Cross, Crescent and Conversion*, ed. by Barton and Linehan, pp. 321–23.

[99] *Tractatus*, xiii, 8–11, 201–4.

[100] *Tractatus*, vii, 2b, 174: 'Patet ergo quod dicere quod totum gens Iudaeorum in toto fuerit damnatum aut reprobatum est peccare in articulum fidei *unam sanctam Ecclesiam*'.

[101] Rosenstock, *New Men*, pp. 54–55.

amid Christians.[102] By contrast, Torquemada's telescoping of past and present marked out contemporary Jews as potential converts, eminently able to embrace Christianity, because they came from the same stock as those members of Israel according to the flesh, such as the apostles and the prophets, who had already achieved sanctification.[103]

With regard to the *conversos*, Torquemada spelled out the consequences of their and their ancestors' vilification. Since New Christians had already entered the Church it was pointless and absurd to castigate them for the unbelief of their forebears, all the more so since this same charge could be levelled against those of Gentile origin.[104] Any measures taken against *conversos* not only created dissension in the unity of the Church and the Christian community but also endangered their own faith, and dissuaded potential converts.[105]

Unlike the other two authors, Oropesa did not seek to dignify the Jews as a people and, as a result, Israel occupied a less prominent place within his narrative of the history of salvation. He showed how Biblical Israel had had a unique relationship with God as His chosen people and as repositories of His promises, law and prophets. Yet, even before the coming of Christ, grace and salvation had not been restricted to the Jews; these had been open to all those who had sought God.[106] Furthermore, the incarnation and ministry of Christ had meant the abolition of Mosaic Law; rather than emphasizing the continuity between Mosaic Law and the Law of Christ, Oropesa understood them primarily in opposition to one another. Christ had established the perfect Church, perfect in the faith, in the sacrifices, in the law, in the promise of salvation, and in its universality.[107] Oropesa concluded that Jews who had refused to enter this Church had severed their special relationship with God

---

[102] Cohen, *The Friars*, p. 76.

[103] *Tractatus*, xiii, 7, 200: 'quia descendentes a Iudaeis habiles sunt ad bonum et, per consequens, reparabiles ad salvationem. Et probat hoc tam ex parte apostolorum, qui ex illis processerunt, quam ex parte patriarcharum, qui fuerunt quasi radices plebis Iudaicae, qui fuerunt sancti'.

[104] *Tractatus*, xiii, 13, 205–6.

[105] *Tractatus*, 12, 214: 'cum Ecclesiae consonantiam perturbet, unitatem dirimat, dissensiones pariat, iurgia nutriat, quibus Ecclesiae unitas rumpitur et societas Christiana violatur'. See also xiv, 11–12, 213–14.

[106] *Lumen*, x–xii, 134–48.

[107] *Lumen*, xxi–xxii, 215–44.

and, as divine punishment, had lost Israel and the Temple. Their rejection of Christ and their enduring impiety meant that they were condemned to live in captivity among Christians.

According to Oropesa, Castilian Jews were the enemies of the faithful: they insulted them, encouraged some to judaize, and committed crimes against them. In order to curb their activities and influence he advocated their freedoms be restricted, particularly their contact with Christians.[108] Such demands not only reflected the traditional themes of late medieval anti-Jewish discourse but related more closely to Oropesa's own pastoral concerns. In his assessment of the situation in Toledo following his inquisition in the city, he had noted the pernicious influence that Jews had on *conversos* and had advocated their segregation to avert the danger of apostasy.[109]

Converso Theology

While these three authors sought to defend *conversos* their works display divergent opinions and differing emphases. Such is most noticeable in their attitudes towards Jews and their vision of the relationship between Judaism and Christianity. Whereas Cartagena and Torquemada presented this relationship in terms of completion and fulfilment, Oropesa asserted that the Law of Christ had superseded Mosaic Law. Cartagena and Torquemada likewise sought to dignify the Jews in the past and present, rescuing them from marginalization within salvation history and emphasizing the essential continuity between Old Testament and rabbinical Judaism. The views of Oropesa were, by contrast, closer to the traditional medieval views of Jews and Judaism. For him, there had been a fundamental rupture between the Judaism of the Old Testament and modern practices; contemporary Jews appear most often in *Lumen* as enemies of Christians and a nefarious influence on *conversos*. Ecclesiology was another area where their opinions diverged. Cartagena understood the mass conversions of Jews as a significant step in the on going and progressive construction of the Church. Persecution of *conversos* was thus an attempt to halt that progress and to impede the building of the New Jerusalem. Though Torquemada's conception of the Church was largely similar, his

---

[108] *Lumen*, xxiv, 266–82.

[109] Pereda, 'La Puerta de los Leones', in *Grabkunst*, ed. by Borngässer, Karge and Klein, pp. 185–86.

focus in the *Tractatus* was restricted chiefly to attacks on Israel and the Church. The defence of *conversos* against persecution was thus one more part of the continuing struggle of the Church against its enemies. Oropesa held a rather different view. The coming of Christ and the giving of a new Law established the Church as a perfect entity albeit one whose members would not themselves be perfected until the Last Judgement. This impossibility of perfection within historical time meant that there should be no discrimination of Christians on account of their individual merits and virtues.

Where these three authors agree is in their understanding of the nature of the *converso* problem and their suggested remedies. Through their works, Cartagena, Torquemada, and Oropesa defended *conversos* as fully Christian, rejecting any possibility of the genealogical transmission of guilt or negative personal characteristics. New Christians were entitled to all privileges and dignities available to their coreligionists of Gentile origin and were equally capable of living virtuous and pious lives. The Old Christian faction was to blame for the marginalization of *conversos* and their actions, under guise of the defence of the faith, were a far more dangerous heresy than the deeds of any judaizing New Christians. Though Cartagena, Torquemada, and Oropesa disagreed about the extent and seriousness of such judaizing, nevertheless they were united in calling for diocesan authorities to use the inquisition to remedy any errors. These and other similarities may be the result of direct textual influence – Netanyahu, for example, has suggested that Oropesa may have read Cartagena's *Defensorium* – though such relationships remain to be proven conclusively.[110] They also reflect the fundamentally reactive nature of the earliest pro-*converso* texts. Cartagena and Torquemada were responding to an agenda set by the Toledo rebels: a particular series of accusations needed to be refuted and particular interpretations of Scripture had to be challenged.

The similarities between the views of Cartagena and Torquemada have led a number of scholars – most notably Rosenstock and Edwards – to talk of a distinctive *converso* theology.[111] This amounted to a recasting of the relationship between Judaism and

---

[110] Netanyahu, *The Origins*, p. 859.

[111] Put forward initially by Rosenstock, *New Men*, and followed up by Edwards, 'New Light on the *Converso* Debate?', in *Cross, Crescent and Conversion*, ed. by Barton and Linehan; and Seidenspinner-Nuñez, 'Prelude', in *Strategies of Medieval Communal Identity*, ed. by van Bekkum and Cobb, pp. 47–74.

Christianity where, in Seidenspinner-Nuñez's words, 'the Church is the true Israel in which Jews could find their real identity and destiny' and Christianity is 'the consummation of Judaism, not its antithesis'.[112] *Converso* theology promoted a Jewish Christianity that highlighted the Jewishness of the early Church and afforded the Jews a continuing and central place in the history of salvation, culminating in their final conversion at the end of time. Such understandings derived not only from distinctive readings of Scripture – privileging particularly the literal sense – but also from an especial concentration on specific books of the Bible – for example Stuczynski has argued for the promotion of a 'Pauline' Christianity and a particular reliance on the letters of Paul.[113]

For Rosenstock, Cartagena's and, particularly, Torquemada's reading of Romans 11 is paradigmatic of *converso* theology.[114] Using the Pauline epistle as proof text, these authors provide a 'reworking of Christian theology around the centrality of the Jewish people' – 'judaizing' as Rosenstock explicitly terms it.[115] In their reformulation of salvation history, the Jews remained a positive part of the divine plan. Interpreting the Apostle's words, these authors understood the Jews' enduring unbelief as a divinely mandated service to the Gentiles, allowing for their conversion. Far from seeing it as a punishment for their rejection of Christ, Cartagena and Torquemada invested the enduring unbelief of Israel with a positive meaning and afforded the Jews an essential place within the on going process of the salvation of mankind. Thus, these theologians placed carnal Israel at the centre of the mystical body of the Church. The Jews were the 'origin and terminus' of salvation since the promises of the Old Testament would only be fulfilled once all carnal Israel converted at the end of time. Though Rosenstock acknowledged that individually all of these elements

---

[112] Seidenspinner-Nuñez, 'Prelude', in *Strategies of Medieval Communal Identity*, ed. by van Bekkum and Cobb, p. 59–60. She considers the *Instrucción del Relator* to contain some of the same tendencies, particularly the emphasis on the interconnectedness between Old and New Testament, although this work does not offer a full theological development of this position. Her study excludes Oropesa's *Lumen*.

[113] Stuczynski, 'Pro-*Converso* Apologetics', in *The Hebrew Bible*, ed. by Decter and Prats, pp. 151–55.

[114] Rosenstock, *New Men*, pp. 34–42, 55–67.

[115] *Ibid.*, p. 53.

were present in earlier Christians writings, 'their fusion into a single theological vision [...] is unprecedented'.[116]

However, Rosenstock's 'claims for novelty [...] must be rejected'.[117] These interpretations, as a whole, neither amount to a break with orthodoxy nor provide a radical re-reading of salvation history. Instead, Cartagena and Torquemada deployed an already existing set of ideas within a new context. The ideas of covenantal continuity and the enduring value of Jewish unbelief, which Rosenstock took as characteristic of *converso* theology, had long been invoked to defend the place of the Jews in medieval Christendom; Cartagena and Torquemada simply reactivated these ideas to defend *conversos* and vindicate their genealogy. Medieval theology had two parallel traditions regarding the relationship between Judaism and Christianity as repositories of the divine covenant: supersession and continuity. Although the first informed most medieval views of Judaism and in particular underpinned the Church's official position, the latter appeared in the works of a variety of authors and contexts stretching back to the Church Fathers.[118] More specifically, the notion that the existence of the Jews has an enduring purpose is based on a positive reading of Romans 11, which had started with the works of Origen and was continued by a succession of medieval theologians.[119] Cartagena and Torquemada were not self-consciously seeking to create a *converso* theology but were instead constructing a defence of New Christians out of an entirely orthodox set of existing interpretations. Favouring a particular range of interpretative possibilities does not in itself amount to the creation of a new theological paradigm.

Similarly, claims that pro-*converso* authors drew distinctively or particularly from Paul's letters need to regarded with circumspection. While it has been recognized that at least some New Christian authors grounded their own experiences and identity as converts on Saint Paul's life, both sides of the debate claimed the Apostle's words as their own.[120] The Toledan rebels had used them

---

[116] Rosenstock, *New Men*, p. 17.

[117] Jennifer Harris, 'Enduring Covenant in the Christian Middle Ages', *Journal of Ecumenical Studies*, 44 (2009), 563–86 (p. 580).

[118] Harris, p. 580.

[119] Cohen, 'The Mystery of Israel's Salvation', pp. 260–63, and 277–80.

[120] For identification with Paul, see Stuczynski, 'Pro-*Converso* Apologetics', in *The Hebrew Bible*, ed. by Decter and Prats, p. 153.

as the Scriptural basis for the discrimination of *conversos* as a whole. As will be seen, Espina would do so too. Cartagena and Torquemada, and implicitly Oropesa, invoked Paul's accounts of disputes among Christians of Jewish and of Gentile origin to challenge the positions of their opponents – positions that were buttressed by precisely the same pericopes. It is entirely possible that both sides understood themselves to take a Paulinian standpoint towards the *converso* problem. If the exegesis of the pro-*converso* side was closer to the words of the historical Paul, nevertheless these words had been read since in a variety of contexts as 'critical and condemnatory'.[121]

The very label *converso* theology remains controversial.[122] The establishment of a causal link between New Christian origin and certain intellectual positions remains problematic, while the dangers of essentialism are well known. While Rosenstock claims there was a distinctive *converso* Christianity that 'bears the strong stamp of a continuing identification with the Jewish people', the extent to which Cartagena and Torquemada identified with their former co-religionists remains unclear.[123] Indeed, in Torquemada's case New Christian descent is by no means proven. Likewise, Seidespinner-Núñez notes that the development of these theological positions can be explained primarily by their very polemical strength, rather than any pre-existing *converso* identity. To the Toledan rebels' idea of God's everlasting and utter rejection of the Jews, Cartagena and Torquemada replied with a view of carnal Israel as part of an on going plan for the salvation of mankind, to the idea of *conversos* as dangerous, foreign elements within Christianity, they responded with a Church with New Christians at its centre.[124]

---

[121] On Paul's discussion of the ongoing role of the Jews in salvation history as presented in his Epistle to the Romans and its many potential meanings, see Nirenberg, *Anti-Judaism*, pp. 60–66 (quotation p. 63).

[122] David Nirenberg, 'Review of Bruce Rosenstock, *New Men: 'Conversos', Christian Theology, and Society in Fifteenth-Century Castile*, Papers of the Medieval Hispanic Research Seminar, 39 (London: Department of Hispanic Studies, Queen Mary, University of London, 2002)', *Speculum*, 80 (2005), 315–17.

[123] Rosenstock, *New Men*, p. 16.

[124] Seidenspinner-Nuñez, 'Prelude', in *Strategies of Medieval Communal Identity*, ed. by van Bekkum and Cobb, pp. 60, 70.

The comparison of the arguments mustered by both sides of the *converso* debate reveals the extent to which both positions were indebted to existing interpretations of Scripture within Church tradition. Rather than speaking of radically new interpretations of Christianity, it is more accurate to consider the responses to the *converso* problem as being forged within a common tradition of interpretation of Scripture that was able to produce widely divergent conclusions, all of which had a place within Christian theology. One of the most remarkable features of the debate is the extent to which these authors relied on the same concepts and Scriptural passages to make entirely different points; a case in point is the readings of Paul's letters or the concept of judaizing.

Nor was this vision of an inclusive Church, able to encompass different religious sensibilities, solely the preserve of pro-*converso* authors. Just as works in defence of New Christians drew upon existing theological traditions, so their authors could look to examples of compromise within the contemporary Church. One strand of the Conciliarist movement advocated dialogue and accommodation to end religious disputes. The Council of Basle had sought to accommodate the views of the moderate Utraquists in Bohemia, permitting them to receive communion under both species, to achieve their reintegration into the Roman Church. Similarly, John of Segovia and Nicholas of Cusa departed from the norm when they advocated dialogue with Islam instead of confrontation.[125] By seeking to find a place for New Christians among the faithful and allowing for a degree of diversity within Christianity, far from marking out novel theological territory, pro-*converso* authors were amplifying voices and traditions already present in the late medieval Church.

---

[125] Thomas M. Izbicki, 'The Possibility of Dialogue with Islam in the Fifteenth Century', in *Nicholas of Cusa in Search of God and Wisdom: Essays in Honour of Morichi Watanabe by the American Cusanus Society*, ed. by Gerald Christianson and Thomas M. Izbicki, Studies in the History of Christian Thought, 45 (Leiden: Brill, 1991), pp. 175–83. Nonetheless these figures could hold seemingly contradictory positions with regard to other minority groups. For example, Nicholas of Cusa passed through Germany as papal legate in 1451–52 and, alongside his reformist agenda, he advocated the passing of restrictive legislation against the Jews copied from that in Italian cities. See, Christopher Ocker, 'Contempt for Friars and Contempt for Jews in Late Medieval Germany', in *Friars and Jews in the Middle Ages and Renaissance*, ed. Steven J. McMichael & Susan Myers, The Medieval Franciscans, 2 (Leiden, 2004), pp. 119–46 (p. 132).

*

Cartagena, Torquemada, and Oropesa all understood the *converso* problem to be fundamentally a Christian one: *conversos*, even when they erred, were a part of the Church. Whilst some among them may have been guilty of heresy or others of errors in the faith, these issues were not collective ones nor were they exclusive to New Christians. Heresy and error were not the sole preserve of any single group but could and did arise anywhere. All three authors saw the mass conversions in Spain as positive phenomena, with Cartagena and Torquemada even viewing these events as significant steps in the history of salvation, moving mankind closer to the moment when all would congregate in the faith of Christ. All, likewise, denied any relationship between genealogy, heresy, and personal character. Jews were perfectly capable of sincere and full conversions and of becoming exemplary Christians. The discrimination of *conversos* by the Toledo rebels in 1449 was problematic, even heretical, because it denied the equality of the faithful.

Despite such similarities it would be wrong to speak of a single, coherent pro-*converso* position. Cartagena and Torquemada, for example, insisted strongly on the links between Judaism and Christianity, suggesting Jews to have an advantage over Gentiles when they embraced Christianity. Oropesa, by contrast, had much less to say about Judaism and advanced an essentially supersessionary position. Nor were the methods and proof-texts employed by pro-*converso* authors distinct from those used by writers hostile to New Christians. As will be seen, both sides of the dispute invoked the same values – such as the need to defend the unity of the faith – and deployed the same scriptural passages – particularly the letters of St Paul – to justify their positions.

THE FORTRESS OF FAITH: UNITY AND ENMITY

Fortalitium fidei opens in a flurry of biblical quotations, in an invocation of the awesome power of God: He is 'a tower of strength against the face of the enemy'; 'He bringeth counsellors to a foolish end, and judges to insensibility. He looseth the belt of kings, and girdeth their loins with a cord. He leadeth away priests without glory, and overthroweth nobles'.[1] Despite this fearsome majesty, the enemies of God multiply. There are those who confess the faith with their lips but whose hearts are far from God. Others – heretics, Jews, Saracens, and demons – strive actively to overthrow the truth through word and deed. These errors and crimes go unchecked; the shepherds are avaricious, the judges venal, the preachers spinners of fables. Thus, from the ends of the earth, from wretched Spain, Espina calls out to God, begging for a consoler of the faithful and a guardian of the faith.

Mindful of this deepening crisis, Espina offered up his work – the *Fortress of the faith* – hoping God would aid him in his attempts to act as the defender of Christianity and the comforter of the faithful.[2] The fortress of the title was allegory and structuring device.[3] It was the Church, besieged by its enemies – heretics, Jews,

---

[1] *Fortalitium*, prohemium, fol. 9ʳ: '[T]urris fortitudinis a facie inimici [Psalms 61 (Vulgate 60).4]. [...] Tu adducis malos consiliarios in stultum finem et iudices in stuporem, Tu baltheum regum dissolvis et precingis fune renes eorum, Tu ducis sacerdotes eorum inglorios et optimates supplantas. [Job 12.17–19]'. For an edition and study of the Prologue see, Vidal Doval, 'El muro en el Oeste', in *Las metamorfosis*, ed. by Sanmartín Bastida and Vidal Doval. The Proloque quotes heavily and extensively from the Book of Job; such may speak of Espina's desire to present himself as the virtuous man who has fallen from favour but still retains his faith.

[2] *Fortalitium*, prohemium, fols 9ᵛ–10ʳ.

[3] Fortress as structuring device: 'hunc librum scribere quem *Fortalitium fidei* nomino'; 'sumens in tuo nomine pro fundamento nostri inexpugnabilis fortalicii verbum preassumptum: "Turris fortitudinis a facie inimici". Et premittitur figura pugne, in qua fortalicium quinque turrium cum eius ornatu', *Fortalitium*, prohemium, fol. 10ʳ. The besieged fortress contains the narrative element essential to allegory as well as a visual dimension that was reflected in the illustrations of the fortress of faith that appeared in manuscripts and printed editions. For discussion and reproductions of the images, see Vidal Doval, 'El muro en el Oeste', in *Las metamorfosis*, ed. by Sanmartín Bastida and Vidal Doval, pp. 149–50, 158–60. See also, Paulino Rodríguez Barral, *La imagen del judío en la España medieval: el conflicto entre*

Muslims, and demons – and guarded by the warriors of the faithful. So too was the fortress Espina's text itself: the five turrets of the castle were the five individual Books, recounting first the armour of the faith (Book I) and then the wars waged by each enemy (Books II to V). The work was intended both as a warning and a call to arms, underlining the seriousness and immediacy of the threat and proposing the means to counter it.

Though this monograph is concerned principally with Espina's engagement with the Jewish and *converso* problem, as the prologue to *Fortalitium fidei* makes clear his scope was wider and he perceived the apparently disparate attacks on the faith as part of a single war: the struggle of the Church Militant against its enemies. To understand how Espina builds his case against *conversos*, it is necessary to apprehend how he arranged his work overall, his broad aims and intentions, and the logic of his argument.[4] Espina employed the central image of the fortress of faith to articulate a plurality of meanings within his tract and to place his work in a number of traditions and contexts. He depicted the enemies of the faith as armies arranged against the fortress, and proposed a series of measures to combat them – in particular the promotion of a pastoral elite – that, if followed, would usher a new society in Castile.

The Fortress of the Faith

The image of the fortress and its scriptural underpinnings are key to understanding *Fortalitium fidei* and Espina's intentions for his text. The use of allegory allowed Espina to articulate a multiplicity of messages and meanings within a single unified framework.[5] Though the Church as besieged castle was a common medieval image and one likely to appeal to a Castilian society forged in warfare, Espina's choice of the fortress as his central device owed much to its considerable connotative potential.[6] Indeed, though Espina

cristianismo y judaismo en las artes góticas, Memoria artium, 8 (Bellaterra: Universitat Autònoma de Barcelona, Servei de Publicacións; Barcelona: Publicacions i Edicions de la Universitat de Barcelona, 2008), pp. 49–55.

[4] A point already made with regard to the study of the treatment of Muslims in the text by Echevarria, *The Fortress of Faith*, p. 106.

[5] David Cowling, *Building the Text: Architecture as Metaphor in Late Medieval and Early Modern France* (Oxford: Clarendon Press, 1998), pp. 5–7

[6] Fortress as common medieval image: José María Monsalvo Antón, 'Algunas consideraciones sobre el ideario antijudío contenido en el *Liber III* del *Fortali-*

writes of the fortress besieged by its enemies in the Prologue he gives no further indication of what the castle itself actually stands for; it is only through the reading of *Fortalitium fidei* as a whole that potential meanings become clear.

Espina's principal audience were conditioned to detect multiple levels of meaning within a single text or image. The system of patristic exegesis or interpretation of the four levels of meaning in Scripture – literal, tropological, allegorical, and anagogical – was central to the education of the clergy.[7] Furthermore, it was the basis of medieval hermeneutics, as Lubac observed:

> elle définit les rapports de la réalité historique et de la réalité spirituelle, de la société et de l'individu, du temps et de l'éternité; elle contient, comme on dirai aujourd'hui, toute une théologie de l'histoire, en connexion avec une théologie de l'Écriture.[8]

Examining biblical commentaries offers one means of apprehending the range of potential meanings Espina envisaged for the fortress of faith. According to Augustine's commentary on Psalm 61 (Vulgate 60) the fortress has two meanings: the Church and the soul. The castle is the Church Militant, attacked by pagans and heretics until the Last Days, but it is also the unassailable Church Triumphant, that will see its enemies vanquished at the end of

---

tium fidei de Alonso de Espina', *Aragón en la Edad Media*, 14–15 (1999), 1061–87 (p. 1061). Appeal to *Reconquista* Castilian society: Meyuhas Ginio, *La forteresse*, p. 11. Connotative potential of the fortress: 'the numerous associations that tradition linked to the edifice assured the writer who used it complex, time-honoured connotations that could materially enrich his own text's allusive power', Barbara E. Kurtz, 'Diego de San Pedro's *Cárcel de Amor* and the Tradition of the Allegorical Edifice', *Journal of Hispanic Philology*, 8 (1984), 123–38 (p. 137); and see also Ann R. Meyer, *Medieval Allegory and the Building of the New Jerusalem* (Cambridge: Brewer, 2003), and Christiania Whitehead, *Castles of the Mind: A Study of Medieval Architectural Allegory* (Cardiff: University of Wales Press, 2003). For the significance of the castle in late medieval Spanish vernacular culture, see Vidal Doval, 'El muro en el Oeste', in *Las metamorfosis*, ed. by Sanmartín Bastida and Vidal Doval, p. 152. For the use of castles and cities in polemical texts, see Cohen, *Living Letters*, pp. 170, 186, 310–11, who cites the works of Anselm of Canterbury, Odo of Cambrai, and Alain de Lille.

[7] Beryl Smalley, 'The Bible in the Medieval Schools', in *The Cambridge History of the Bible*, II: *The West from the Fathers to the Reformation*, ed. by G.W.H. Lampe (Cambridge: Cambridge University Press, 1969), pp. 197–220 (pp. 197–98).

[8] Henri de Lubac, *Exégèse médiéval: les quatre sens de l'Écriture*, 4 vols (Paris: Aubier, 1959–64), I.1, 17.

time. The castle also represents the human soul, surrounded by vices and sin that can be overcome by taking refuge in Christ. Both meanings lead to a third, for Augustine the most important: the fortress is a typological figure of Christ.⁹ On this reading, Espina's fortress is the Church, which is Christian society in Castile, under attack from its enemies. Though such attacks cannot endanger the institution, the impregnable Church of Christ, they can harm the individuals that make it up.¹⁰ Furthermore, the failure of individuals to act allows the enemies of the faith to harm society. If the clergy do not investigate heretics, if judges allow Jews and Muslims to commit crimes with impunity, then society is defenceless.¹¹ This double message of warning and reform is articulated through the image of the besieged castle that contains both social and individual dimensions.

The castle also carries connotations of purity. The tower was used widely in the Middle Ages to stand for the state of virginity and chastity, while the fortress or castle was also used to represent Mary.¹² Within *Fortalitium fidei* such connotations of purity and cleanliness would serve to underline the polluting effect of the enemies of the faith and emphasize the need to purge them from the fortress that was at once the Church, the body politic, and the individual believer. Such ideas would be strengthened if, as Round has suggested, *Fortalitium fidei* originated in a series of sermons delivered by Espina during a period of plague in Valladolid in 1457. The presence of non-believers and dissidents within Christian society was the catalyst for the plague epidemic, thus those enemies of the faith became synonymous with impurity, disease and danger.

---

⁹ Augustine of Hippo, *Enarrationes in Psalmos*, ed. by E. Dekkers and J. Fraipont, 3 vols, CCSL, 38–40 (Turnhout: Brepols, 1956), II, 125. Christ as the keep of the fortress of faith: *Fortalitium*, I, consideratio iii, fol. 14ʳ.

¹⁰ The text advertises the truth and invincibility of the central tenet of the faith already in its opening, *Fortalitium*, I, consideratio i, fol. 14ʳ: 'et iam sunt vltra mille 460 anni quod multi posuerunt omnes vires suas ad destruendam hanc altissima, turrim siue hanc veritatem, scilicet, quod Ihesus Christus est filius Dei viui, certissime firmius fundata quam celum et terra, et preciosor quam aurum in pluribus fornacibus depuratum'.

¹¹ *Fortalitium*, prohemium, fol. 9ᵛ.

¹² Christiania Whitehead, 'A Fortress and a Shield: The Representation of the Virgin in the *Château d'amour* of Robert Grosseteste', in *Writing Religious Women: Female Spiritual and Textual Practices in Late Medieval England*, ed. by Denis Renevey and Christiania Whitehead (Cardiff: University of Wales Press, 2000), pp. 109–31 (p. 110).

Fortalitium fidei was therefore a call to Castilian society to purify itself through fighting against them.[13]

The fortress also functions as a 'political metaphor' projecting a very particular image of Castile and its position in the wider world.[14] While the castle stands for Castile – Espina's multi-turreted fortress echoing the coat of arms of the kingdom – it is the belligerent Castile, in the vanguard of the fight for the faith.[15] After the disaster of the conquest of Constantinople by the Turks in 1453, the struggle against Islam in the Iberian Peninsula gained a greater significance in Western Christendom. When Pope Calixtus III sent a blessed sword and a bull of crusade for the campaign in Granada to Enrique IV in 1457, he addressed the king as the bulwark of the faith against Islam.[16] It is this vision of Castile and its monarch as the bastion of Christendom, as the fortification against the enemies of the faith, which Espina sought to invoke.

The image of the fortress also suggests something of the contexts in which Espina sought to place his work. At the most discernible level, the image placed *Fortalitium fidei* within the longer tradition of Christian polemic. Many such works employed allegories of violence and martial imagery as structuring principles and thematic devices and a number of them are among the key sources for Espina's own tract. These include *Pugio fidei* (1278) of the Dominican Raymond Martí, the *Sefer milḥamot Adonai* of Alfonso de Valladolid (presumably via the Spanish translation *Libro de las batallas del Señor*), and *Contra Iudaeos* of Jerónimo de Santa Fe.[17]

---

[13] Round, 'Alonso de Espina', p. 322.

[14] Cowling, p. 18.

[15] On Castile's coat of arms, see Faustino Menéndez Pidal de Navascués, *Heráldica medieval española* (Madrid: Hidalguía, 1982), pp. 47–49.

[16] *Memorias de don Enrique IV de Castilla: contiene la colección diplomática del mismo rey compuesta y ordenada por la Real Academia de la Historia*, 2 vols (Madrid: Real Academia de la Historia, 1835–1913), p. 156, §56: 'firmissimus murus oppositus es'.

[17] Cándida Herrero Hernández, 'Literatura latina de controversia religiosa en la Castilla del siglo XV: una aproximación a su tipología', in *Estudios de latín medieval hispánico: actas del V Congreso Internacional de Latín Medieval Hispánico, Barcelona, 7–10 de septiembre de 2009*, ed. by José Martínez Gázquez, Óscar de la Cruz Palma and Cándida Herrero Hernández (Florence: SISMEL/Edizioni del Galluzzo, 2011), pp. 425–41 (p. 438). On the sources of *Fortalitium fidei*, see McMichael, 'The Sources'; idem, *Was Jesus of Nazareth the Messiah?*, pp. 57–106; Meyuhas Ginio, *La forteresse*, pp. 203–7; Echevarria, *The Fortress of Faith*, pp. 83–96, 216–19.

The embattled fortress was likewise part of the vocabulary of late medieval mendicant reform. Among Espina's predecessors and contemporaries in Italy – notably Bernardino of Siena – it had become common to preach about the embattled city, 'under threat from alien external forces', and to stress the need for reform to vanquish the enemy without. In such preaching, the city was both the New Jerusalem and the individual soul and each and every citizen shared collective responsibility for the spiritual fight.[18]

In the immediate Castilian context, Espina's use of the fortress underlines his implicit engagement with pro-*converso* authors. Alonso de Cartagena had employed the image of the Church as a walled city, writing of 'fidei muros' constructed and defended by the faithful.[19] Espina's fortification was offered as the substitute for Cartagena's, the true fortress of the faith was that described by the Franciscan friar not that set out by the bishop of Burgos. More significantly, the scriptural quotation that opens *Fortalitium fidei* – 'Turris fortitudinis a facie inimici' – similarly opens Juan de Torquemada's *Tractatus*, as well as featuring on his coat of arms.[20] The significance of this is difficult to determine. The intention may have been disputatious – Espina's vision of the tower of strength intended to challenge and to replace Torquemada's – or conciliatory, with Espina reaching out to the expatriate Cardinal to show him the true situation in Castile and to correct his errors. Certainly, Archbishop Alonso Carrillo seems to have provided Torquemada with detailed information about the situation in Toledo prior to his writing of the *Tractatus* and Espina's intervention might be understood in similar terms.[21] Whether Espina's choice of scriptural quotation means that, lacking favour at court, he was addressing his work particularly to Cardinal Torquemada, seeking his patronage or a sympathetic ear in the Curia remains unclear.[22]

---

[18] Paton, *Preaching Friars*, pp. 91, 130–32 (quotation p. 130). See also eadem, '"Una Città Fatticosa": Dominican Preaching and the Defence of the Republic in Late Medieval Siena', in *City and Countryside in Late Medieval and Renaissance Italy: Essays Presented to Philip Jones*, ed. by Trevor Dean and Chris Wickham (London: Hambledon Press, 1990) pp. 109–23.

[19] *Defensorium*, II, theorema 3, ii, 135.

[20] *Tractatus*, prologus, 0.1, 125. For the coat of arms, see *ibid.* p. 243 n3. The tower of strength was a pun on the Latin form of the surname, Turrecremata.

[21] See above, Chapter 2, pp. 39 n14.

[22] In a personal communication, María de Pilar Rábade Obradó has suggested to me that *Fortalitium fidei* may be interpreted as an attempt by Espina to

The Besieged Fortress and the Knights of Christ

In the prologue to *Fortalitium fidei*, Espina outlines the attacks the enemies of the faith make. Heretics, the enemies within, undermine the fortress; the Jews, blindfolded and chained, commit hidden and unheard of crimes; Saracens engage in earthly warfare against Christian armies; devils contend with angels.[23] Books II to V give a detailed account of the war waged by each individual group and the threats that they pose to contemporary Castile.[24] Each Book begins with an account of the origins of the enemy detailed therein. Espina then outlines the theological attacks that they make on Christianity, showing how they are refuted and defeated. Next he details the physical attacks that these enemies make and lays out the mechanisms that exist to overcome them.[25] The presentation of information is effectively chronological, moving from the earliest attacks to the more recent with the focus narrowing in on Castile. Thus the longest part of the discussion of contemporary heresies in Book II is allocated to those found in Castile, while the extensive accounts of the wars between Muslims and Christians in Book IV focuses on battles fought on Iberian soil.[26] Espina closes each Book with a description of the part the enemy will play at the end of time.[27] Across Books II to V as a whole, there is also a sense of

garner support at the papal court for the Observant Franciscan agenda through engagement with Cardinal Torquemada.

[23] *Fortalitium*, prohemium, fol. 10ʳ. The end of the twelfth century saw the appearance of a 'new genre of polemical treatise, which debated systematically and in turn against heretics, Saracens, and Jews' that had its first manifestation in Alain de Lille's *De fide catholica contra haereticos*, Cohen, *Living Letters*, p. 157.

[24] *Fortalitium fidei* is a *summa* about the enemies of the Church, compiling materials from a variety of sources and traditions. See, Echevarria, *The Fortress of Faith*, p. 101. Monsalvo Antón, 'Algunas consideraciones', pp. 1062–63 explains, with reference to Book III, that it 'debería encuadrarse en el característico discurso anfibiológico de los teólogos medievales y verse más bien como una suma de argumentos heterogéneos, como una obra de aluvión, un compendio sistemático de argumentos antijudíos de muy diversa procedencia', but I would reject his notion that it is fruitless to seek an ideological coherence in the text.

[25] Meyuhas Ginio, *La forteresse*, pp. 11–12.

[26] *Fortalitium*, II, consideratio vi, fols 50ᵛ–66ʳ; IV, consideratio ix, fols 186ᵛ–221ʳ.

[27] *Fortalitium*, III, consideratio xii, fols 154ᵛ–156ᵛ; IV, consideratio xii, fols 223ʳ–224ᵛ; V, consideratio xii, fol. 240ʳ. Cf. Revelation 20.7–8 about the forces of Antichrist attacking the castle of the saints.

chronological development: Book II is concerned with the earliest form of attack, namely dissent from within or heresy; Book III deals with the Jews but principally with Judaism after the Incarnation rather than Old Testament Judaism; Book IV with Muslims; Book V ends the narrative, laying out the activities of demons and detailing in particular their final battle at the end of time.[28] Each of the Books makes clear the ultimate victory of Christianity: the Church is unassailable and the enemies of the faith will be defeated and damned in eschatological time. Within historical time, however, individuals and communities are vulnerable and anyone outside the fortress of the faith – heretic, Jew, Muslim – cannot achieve salvation.

The structural similarities across the four Books underline that for Espina the enemies of the faith are all fundamentally the same.[29] Despite the varied nature of their attacks and the varied nature of their errors, their effects – the imperilling of the Christian faithful – and their ultimate fate – damnation – are the same. Likewise, all the enemies are part of the same narrative arc, the same story of the struggles of the Church Militant. By extension, regardless of the complexities of Espina's refutations of error and the copious detail in which he outlines the different attacks on Christianity, the overall message is the same. Despite the certainty of ultimate victory, the enemies of the faith pose a serious danger at the quotidian level and what is required is constant vigilance and combat, extreme intolerance and the excision of all religious difference.[30]

---

[28] The first group of heretics mentioned is the Nicolaites, mentioned in Revelation 2.6–15, *Fortalitium*, II, consideratio iv, fol. 49ʳ.

[29] This notion was well established already by the twelfth century when authors began attributing similar characteristics and, hence, a similar hostility towards Christendom to Jews, Muslims, and heretics, Cohen, *Living Letters*, p. 158. On Bernardino of Siena's notion of the fundamental unity of danger to the faith embodied on the image of the bark of Saint Peter shaken on all sides, see Mormando, p. 81. Espina's treatment of each of the enemy groups, however, is sufficiently detailed and thorough to stand on its own. Thus, for instance, the German translation of *Fortalitium fidei* is a summary of the third expulsion of the Jews (*Fortalitium*, III, consideratio ix) in Stuttgart, Württembergische Landesbibliothek, HB I 26, fol. 247, lines. 23–45. See Reinhardt and Santiago-Otero, p. 64.

[30] There is a tension in Espina's account because, although measures can be taken against the enemies of the faithful, their attacks are part of the divine plan and will not cease until the end of time. See, for example, the discussion of the providential role of Islam when he observes that 'prouidit Deus electo

Though all Books set out measures against the enemies of the faith, Book I underlines the importance of individual action and collective responsibility, under the leadership of a pastoral elite. Employing the well-worn allegory of the Christian soldier of Ephesians 6.11–17, Espina emphasizes that all the faithful of whatever rank and status have at their disposal the means to protect themselves against the temptations of the devil.[31] It is their duty to furnish themselves with the armour of truth, justice and hope, to mortify their flesh and to show contempt for the world. Just as Castile was surrounded by enemies, so each Castilian Christian was beset by temptation and danger. Fighting for the faith was not an extraordinary action but one more part of the obligations placed upon every Christian.

If such combat was a universal duty, nevertheless certain groups had greater obligations. For Espina, in the vanguard of the fight for the faith were the preachers, the true champions of the Church, wielders of the sword that was the word of God.[32] True preachers carried out spiritual warfare through their rooting out of error and their rebuking of crimes, preaching sermons that were sober in style and that sought to warn and to exhort, to teach and to edify.[33] They discerned the perils facing society and guided those who governed and administered justice. Poverty was the first requirement of the preacher; he must be an outsider, distant from the secular world and yet deeply engaged with it. He should also be fearless in his task, putting the defence of the faith above all other considerations and having no thought for his own welfare.[34] Such

---

suo populo Christianorum de flagello correctionis scilicet populum Sarraccnorum', *Fortalitium*, IV, consideratio v, fol. 167ʳ. See also Echevarria, *The Fortress of Faith*, p. 114.

[31] *Fortalitium*, I, consideratio i, fols 10ʳ–11ʳ.

[32] *Fortalitium*, I, consideratio i, fol. 11ʳ: 'Et quia veri predicatores in bello spirituali singularissimum bellum gerunt et nimium vtile in ecclesia Dei'. On this section, including a transcription and translation into Spanish, see now Constanza Cavallero, 'Miles Christi: la construcción del ethos en el *Fortalitium fidei* de Alonso de Espina (Castilla, siglo XV)', *Estudios de Historia de España*, 13 (2011), 149–98.

[33] *Fortalitium*, I, consideratio ii, fols 11ʳ–14ʳ. Espina based this section largely on Alain de Lille's *Summa de arte praedicatoria*, in *PL*, 210, cols 109–97.

[34] Poverty and contempt for the world: 'Ad primum quod praedicator verbi divini debet esse in habitu exteriori camelus, id est, debet indui vestibus pauperrimis et despectis in quo reluceat mundi contemptus'; rejection of the world: 'nec semper sit inter turbas sed aliquando recedat ab eis et vadat in

true preachers would be rewarded with eternal life, ranking in heaven above virgins and martyrs.[35]

As throughout the rest of the text, the inferences that the audience is meant to draw from this depiction of the true preacher are left unstated. Instead, Espina's logic is juxtapositional: the Prologue condemned preachers as storytellers and the clergy as avaricious, Book I outlined the qualities of those who should lead the fight against the enemies of the faith. By implication, for Espina, the majority of his contemporary churchmen fell short in the fulfilment of their duties. The secular Church in Castile, particularly its bishops, had not moved against heretics nor warned sufficiently of the dangers of social contact with Jews and Muslims. Although he never mentioned his rivals by name, such criticisms clearly encompassed the actions of pro-*converso* clergymen such as the bishops of Cuenca, Segovia, and Zamora and authors such as Cartagena and Oropesa.[36] Thus, the fight against the enemies of the faith could not be left to those who had so far failed to act. What was needed was a body of true of preachers devoted entirely to the defence of Christianity. Though Espina is never explicit, the cumulative weight of his words makes clear his meaning: the Observant Franciscans had the required spiritual qualities and were ready to take on the necessary tasks. They were the most active champions of orthodoxy in Castile, equipped and capable of acting as inquisitors, promoting crusade, staging disputations with Jews and Muslims, and preaching to Christian and non-Christian alike. The ideals of the Franciscans matched the qualities of the true preacher – poverty, humility, and evangelical zeal – and from the outset their Order had sought the conversion of infidels through disputation, mission and the practice of exemplary piety, and had been papally commissioned to preach to the Jews.[37] In this sense,

---

desertum locum exemplo Christi'; engagement with the world: 'debet esse predicator ewangelicus in praedicatione. Dico quod debet esse Marta et ignis: Marta in solicitudine […] ignis in feruore'; fearlessness: 'debet esse animo leo quia non debet aduersitate terreri', *Fortalitium*, I, consideratio ii, fols 12ᵛ–13ʳ.

[35] *Fortalitium*, I, consideratio ii, fol. 14ʳ, where Espina also notes that prelates who have failed to preach will not achieve this reward.

[36] On pro-*converso* bishops, see McKendrick, pp. 133–34.

[37] Cohen, *The Friars*, pp. 39–40. On the Franciscan ideal of mission, with an emphasis on the element of aggressive attempts to convert the Jews, see also Bert Roest, 'Medieval Franciscan Mission: History and Concept', *Strategies of Medieval Communal Identity: Judaism, Christianity and Islam*, ed. by Wout J. van Bekkum and Paul M. Cobb, Mediaevalia Groningana New Series, 5

Fortalitium fidei can be seen as very much typical of the mainstream of European mendicant thought, where friars perceived themselves as 'not only heavenly mediators, prayer-mongers, and representatives of Mother Church, but as the active formulators of civic ethics and the moral voice of the public'.[38]

If Espina sought to place his own Order at the forefront of the fight for orthodoxy, nonetheless his text served also to reinforce his own authority and exemplarity. As has been seen, by the time Espina wrote *Fortalitium fidei* he had established a reputation as a preacher of note, styling himself on such figures as Bernardino of Siena and Vincent Ferrer. Throughout his career, he had cultivated an image of himself as an outsider, willing to castigate the errors of the ruling elite. Again, Espina's logic in *Fortalitium fidei* is implicit: he never speaks of himself directly but 'la imagen que el fraile pretende mostrar de sí mismo mediante *el modo de su enunciación* se ajusta o pretende ajustarse al *contenido del mensaje,* esto es a las cualidades del "verdadero predicador", del "soldado de Cristo".'[39] The portrayal of the ideal preacher in *Fortalitium fidei* was thus an open advertisement of Espina's own qualities and a demonstration of his veracity: true preachers, he states, were the organ of truth.[40]

Fortalitium fidei was an embodiment of the very principles that Espina was setting out: writing was a form of preaching.[41] Moreover, Espina's tract followed many of the precepts of the composition of the ideal sermon and sought both to provide a moral lesson and also to move the faithful to action. The Prologue, for example, opens with the *thema* 'Turris fortitudinis a facie inimici', there then follows a prayer or *prothema*, invoking God and seeking help to complete the task. Next the *divisio* outlines how the material is arranged, enumerating the enemies of the faith, and then the *prosecutio* or amplification of each of the sections sets out

---

(Paris: Peeters, 2004), pp. 137–61. On Pope Nicholas III's commission to preach to the Jews in 1278 in the bull *Vineam Soreth*, see Cohen, *The Friars*, pp. 82–83.

[38] Paton, *Preaching Friars*, p. 35, and see also p. 52.
[39] Cavallero, p. 154, author's emphasis.
[40] *Fortalitium*, I, consideratio ii, fol. 12^v: 'praedicatores enim sunt organum veritatis'.
[41] *Fortalitium*, I, consideratio ii, fol. 12^r: 'Sunt predicacionis tres species: vna que est verbo [...], alia scripto [...], alia est in facto.'

the attacks of these enemies. The prologue ends with a *peroratio* explaining how *Fortalitium fidei* is arranged into five books.⁴²

The authority that Espina established in Book I continued to be reinforced throughout the rest of the text. A key way in which this was achieved was through the use of personal information and first hand accounts; all Books contain material taken from Espina's own life and activities as a preacher and churchman.⁴³ These accounts, told in the first person, paint a vivid picture of a life spent fighting the enemies of Christianity. Among other examples, Espina tells his readers of his unease at the mischief making of a demon; his denunciation to the bishop of Palencia of Alonso de Béjar's antimendicant sermon; his uncovering of ritual murder in Zamora and subsequent – and unsuccessful – attempts to bring the culprits to justice.⁴⁴ Though these stories add colour and interest to the text, their purpose goes beyond this.⁴⁵ They serve to reinforce the credibility of the claims Espina made about the nature of the attacks on Christianity while teaching how the faithful should respond to them.⁴⁶ By talking about events in contemporary

---

⁴² For an extended discussion of the Prologue as sermon, see Vidal Doval, 'El muro en el Oeste', in *Las metamorfosis*, ed. by Sanmartín Bastida and Vidal Doval, pp. 145–48. On the structure of sermons, see Thomas Worcester, 'Catholic Sermons', in *Preachers and People in the Reformations and Early Modern Period*, ed. by Larissa Taylor, A New History of the Sermon, 2 (Leiden: Brill, 2001) pp. 3–33 (p. 4). On the Prologue as prayer, see Steven J. McMichael, 'Friar Alonso de Espina, Prayer, and Medieval Jewish, Muslim and Christian Polemical Literature', in *Franciscans at Prayer*, ed. by Timothy J. Johnson, The Medieval Franciscans, 4 (Leiden: Brill, 2007), pp. 271–304.

⁴³ Such accounts, seen as the most original material in *Fortalitium fidei*, have been regarded as Espina's main contribution to late medieval religious discourse. See, for instance, Netanyahu, *The Origins*, pp. 814–47.

⁴⁴ Domestic evil spirit ('duen [*sic*] de casa'): *Fortalitium*, V, consideration x, fol. 234ᵛ. Denunciation of Alonso de Béjar: II, consideratio vi, haeresis 5, fol. 58ᵛ. Ritual murder in Zamora: III, consideratio vii, punctus 3, crudelitas 11, fols 125ᵛ–126ʳ.

⁴⁵ These accounts have been traditionally interpreted as means to adapt Espina's message to the taste and interests of a wider public – aside from the clerical elite. See, for example, José María Monsalvo Antón, 'Mentalidad antijudía en la Castilla medieval: cultura clerical y cultura popular en la gestación y difusión de un ideario medieval', in *Xudeos e conversos na historia: actas do congreso internacional, Ribadavia 14–17 de outubro de 1991*, ed. by Carlos Barros, 2 vols (Santiago de Compostela: Editorial de la Historia, 1994), I, 21–84 (p. 41).

⁴⁶ Rubin, *Gentile Tales*, p. 144 notes, in the context of host desecration accounts, that *exempla* fulfil a double function. They indicate what kind of

Castile, Espina was also able to underline the gravity of the current dangers to the faith and present himself as someone actively engaged in the struggles to protect Christianity. Espina was thus a figure who knew through personal experience both the nature of the threats and the best remedies to counter them.

To the many problems facing Castile, Espina proposed a single unifying solution: an active, engaged and fearless pastoral elite who would guide the faithful and remind the rulers of their Christian duty. This last area was crucial for Espina. Though all the faithful had the obligation to defend Christianity and success could only come when all did so, Espina afforded particular importance to the ruling classes whose actions affected the whole of society.[47] As history demonstrated, the weaknesses and sins of rulers brought harm to their kingdoms. Thus in Book V, Espina reminded his readers of how King Rodrigo's sexual incontinence had been the cause of the conquest of Spain by the Muslims, with the king's lust resulting in the betrayal of his kingdom and the captivity of his people.[48] Moreover, good governance required not just personal probity but policing the faith, fighting against its enemies, and following the counsels of the wise. In Book III, Espina recounted how the king of England had finally freed his kingdom from war, plague and civil strife by following the advice of his counsellors first to force the conversion of the Jews and then to punish those who were insincere in their new faith.[49] Even in the present day, the exercise of power was fraught with difficulty; the dangers of sin were greatest for the rulers as the combat between good and evil was fiercest around them.[50]

> behaviour could be expected from Jews and the appropriate response of Christians and they lent credibility to the stories by placing them in 'named communities'.

[47] Bernardino of Siena expressed a similar understanding of the role of rulers in a sermon delivered in Florence in 1425: 'if the official or ruler is good, then the citizens and subordinates are good; but if he is bad, they are bad, since he is for them a sign and a light', quoted in Debby, p. 66.

[48] For Espina's account of the legend of the Fall of Spain, see *Fortalitium*, V, consideratio ix, bella 11–12, fols 188^r–189^r.

[49] *Fortalitium*, III, consideratio ix, expulsio 3, fol. 144^v. This story seems to originate with Espina, see Meyuhas Ginio, *La forteresse*, p. 70.

[50] *Fortalitium*, V, consideratio v, fol. 229^v. For a discussion of demons in *Fortalitium fidei*, see Alisa Meyuhas Ginio, 'The *Conversos* and the Magic Arts in Alonso de Espina's *Fortalitium Fidei*', *Mediterranean Historical Review*, 5 (1990), 169–82 (p. 170).

The City of God and the Reform of Castile

Fortalitium fidei offered not just a warning or simply a sharp critique of Castile's ruling classes but a concrete programme of action for the reform and renewal of Castilian society. At its heart, such a programme rested on the exclusion of those elements of society deemed non-desirable by Espina – heretics, dissenters, non-believers, witches and all other enemies of the faith. An inquisition, organized along lines similar to the Papal Inquisition, should be established to identify and to root out error, particularly among judaizing *conversos* and to supplement the all too few episcopal inquests.[51] The various ordinances and laws, civil and canon, regarding Jews and Muslims living amid Christians should be applied, in particular the *Leyes de Ayllón* of 1412, that severely restricted the autonomy of Jewish and Muslim communities, should be reinstated. Ultimately, the Jews should be reduced to a state of extreme servitude and destitution and the conquest of Muslim Granada completed.[52]

What would be the result of this programme of action? As so often, Espina did not answer this question directly but rather guided readers towards the inferences they should draw. *Fortalitium fidei* closes with an extended depiction of the fortress of faith as the City of God.[53] If the faithful followed his lead and heeded his advice, Espina offered up no less than the embodiment of the City of God on Earth. His formulation of the ideal society followed closely that of his fellow mendicant reformers; although firmly rooted in Castile's particular and distinctive religious landscape, *Fortalitium fidei* reveals itself to be part of wider and well-established European traditions. Mendicant culture saw Christian morality as the guiding principle for society and the friars' 'aim was to change reality to conform to the moral and doctrinal prescriptions of the *auctores*, the ultimate purpose of their didactic literature was to delineate the model of the Christian community they sought'.[54]

---

[51] See below pp. 140–44.

[52] *Leyes de Ayllón*: *Fortalitium*, III, consideratio xi, fols 147^r–152^v; conquest of Granada: IV, consideratio x, fol. 222^v. For a discussion of the treatment of the Jews, see below pp. 114–17.

[53] *Fortalitium*, V, consideratio ix, fols 232^r–234^r. See also Meyuhas Ginio, *La forteresse*, p. 175.

[54] Paton, *Preaching Friars*, p. 86.

The account of the fortress of faith as City of God is included in a section detailing the war waged by demons in the period between the Incarnation of Christ and the Last Judgment. The city was a paragon of order, harmony, virtue, and good governance all under the salvific influence of Christ who had freed it from the captivity of the Devil. It was a place of abundance, health, and beauty, well situated and appointed, and enclosed by circular walls. These walls were surrounded by a series of advanced defences, manned by the vanguard of its citizens: the first was the ditch of charity, manned by prelates, bishops, and clerics; the second, the ditch of justice, whose defence was allotted to princes and secular rulers; the last and most advanced was the ditch of humility, defended by those who preach.[55] It was, in essence, a depiction of the idealised late-medieval city, in sharp contrast to the stifling, over-populated, and violent urban communities of fifteenth-century Spain.[56]

This ideal city was not just held up as a model for emulation, its depiction and description played a vital part in Espina's construction of a logic of exclusion. This City of God was not imagined or solely anagogical, it was not simply indicative of something that was to come after the end of time. Instead, Espina made clear that such a state of affairs had existed during the age of the Apostles; his City of God was also the Primitive Church.[57] Espina's reform thus took on the traditional medieval guise of a return to the original purity of the early Jerusalem community.[58] Such a strategy was necessary because Espina was in actuality seeking to effect a radical change in the way the kingdom organised itself religiously, socially, and politically. Despite the tensions and deteriorating religious climate, Castile was not, and never had been, the City of God that Espina longed for. It was not a bastion of an exclusionary Christianity, pitted in permanent war against unbelievers and dissenters, but a society that still operated under rules of coexistence. The lives and activities of Jews and Muslims were tightly regulated and many of their freedoms curtailed but some among them were able to thrive and to prosper. Crusade against Granada remained impor-

---

[55] *Fortalitium*, V, consideratio ix, fol. 232ᵛ.

[56] Meyuhas Ginio, *La forteresse*, p. 176.

[57] *Fortalitium*, V, consideratio ix, fol. 232ᵛ: 'Talis fuit hec ciuitas in primitiua ecclesia quando ipsis fidelibus erat cor vnum et anima vna'.

[58] As revealed, for example, in the work of Glenn W. Olsen. See his 'Reform after the Pattern of the Primitive Church in the Thought of Salvian of Marseille', *Catholic Historical Review*, 68 (1982), 1–12 for further references.

tant but armed conflict was not the sole mode of interaction between the two kingdoms.[59] The defence of orthodoxy, in particular with regard to the alleged apostasy of New Christians, had become a vexatious issue but so far had been addressed by the traditional means of episcopal inquisitions. Espina's appeal to the purity of the primitive Church was a means of concealing the radical nature of the reforms he proposed. His reform was not remaking but return, not the introduction of novelty and innovation but the stripping away of accumulated errors.

Other meanings were also in play. Espina exploited to the full the range of possible meanings the City of God could have and the potential for ambiguity.[60] As well as the Primitive Church, for Espina the City of God was the good Christian: the physical beauty of the city stood for moral integrity, its good governance for the place of reason above desire. The City of God was also the New Jerusalem that awaited the saved after the Last Judgment and, potentially, Castile if it followed Espina's programme of reform.[61] By juxtaposing and conflating these different identities, Espina was able to open up the possibility of perfecting the Christian community in the present, of removing impure and corrupting elements permanently. Espina acknowledged Augustine as the source for the idea of the City of God but his own use of it was very different.[62] For Augustine, in historical time, and 'till the final

---

[59] The frontier provides a good example of alternative forms of interaction. See Angus MacKay, 'Religion, Culture, and Ideology on the Late Medieval Castilian-Granadan Frontier', in *Medieval Frontier Societies*, ed. by Robert Bartlett and Angus MacKay (Oxford: Clarendon Press, 1989), pp. 217–43; and Miguel Ángel Ladero Quesada, *Las guerras de Granada en el siglo XV* (Barcelona: Ariel, 2002).

[60] Heikki Kotila, quoted in Meyer, p. 55, speaks of the Augustinian concept of the Church underpinning medieval allegories of the New Jerusalem as 'simultaneously historical and eschatological, institutional and spiritual, visible and invisible'.

[61] *Fortalitium*, V, consideratio ix, fol. 232^v: 'Ista est illa ciuitas Iherusalem descendens de celo ornata a Christo sicut sponsa pulchra et excellens'. Cf. Italian friars describing the city as New Jerusalem in Paton, *Preaching Friars*, p. 91.

[62] Espina conceived the City of God and the city of the Devil as two distinct places in historical time. Unable to exercise dominion over the City of God, the Devil had set up his own city, as the base for the attacks of his infernal host against the City of God. See *Fortalitium*, V, consideratio ix, fol. 233^{r-v} and cf. V, consideratio vi, fol. 230^r. This seems to contrast with Augustine's vision of the citizens of the heavenly city captive in the earthly city in this life.

judgement, wheat and weeds grow together, often mistaken for each other.'[63] That is, the wicked and the just are mingled in society and difficult to discern; it is ultimately impossible to separate them fully until the Last Judgment.[64] This vision of a Christian community that necessarily contained both the saved and the damned, the elect and the reprobate, was one championed by pro-*converso* authors, particularly Alonso de Oropesa. Through his image of the net of mixed fish, Oropesa put forward a specifically Augustinian model for the Church in Castile – perfection was not possible until the Last Days and *conversos*, whatever their individual errors and imperfections might be, were part of the Christian community. By contrast, through his seeming conflation of historical and eschatological time, Espina suggested that the separation of wheat from weeds was both possible and desirable in contemporary society. The City of God had been realised in historical time and could, therefore, be realised again. If the final separation of the saved from the damned could not occur until the Last Judgment, nevertheless Espina held out the possibility of approaching perfection.

Espina's programme of reform, although based around the personal responsibility of the individual faithful as outlined in Book I, was thus at its heart exclusionary. It promoted the identification of certain groups and people as polluting elements, to be excised from Christian society. The danger such groups posed was not solely religious or, rather, for Espina the political community and the Christian community were or should be coterminous. The mere presence of heretics, Jews, and Muslims in Castile was sufficient to trigger a cycle of decline and decay in the kingdom.[65]

See *De civitate Dei*, ed. by B. Dombart and A. Kalb, 2 vols, CCSL, 47–48 (Turnhout: Brepols, 1955), XIX. xvii.

[63] Garry Wills, *Saint Augustine* (London: Weidenfeld & Nicolson, 1999), p. 118. For a detailed exposition and analysis of these ideas see Robert Markus, *Saeculum: History and Society in the Theology of St Augustine* (Cambridge: University Press, 1970), pp. 45–121.

[64] Augustine of Hippo, *De Genesi ad litteram*, ed. by J. Zycha, Corpus Scriptorum Ecclesiasticorum Latinorum, 28.1 (Vienna: Tempsky, 1894), XI. xv.

[65] This is expressed most succinctly in relation to judaizing *conversos* in *Fortalitium*, II, consideratio vi, haeresis 1, fol. 54ᵛ: 'Sicut eciam faciendum est in republica que pro vnum malum hominem, latronem, homicidam, adulterum, crimine pessimo maculatum et cetera, huiusmodi corrumpitur; unde tales circumcidenti sunt per iusticiam et mortem, sicut ouis morbida ne

Such was a powerful message in a Castile caught in a succession of economic crises and urban uprisings, pervaded by a sense of inexorable social decay, and sliding towards civil war as Enrique IV lost his grip on power.[66] For Espina, such problems were not the result of the systematic malfunctioning of the late medieval political system in Castile but were the consequences of the failure of those in power to combat the enemies of the faith.[67] Once these dangerous polluting elements were eliminated, prosperity and harmony could follow.

The attempts to refashion Castilian society according to a rigorist interpretation of doctrine that left no room for compromise or accommodation have an unmistakeably mendicant flavour. Espina's aims were in essence identical to those of Bernardino of Siena, the creation of 'a total Christian theocracy, [a] morally and socially homogeneous society in which Christian doctrine had the first and final word [via] the elimination or at least the drastic isolation of those subversive "foreign" elements within the "Body of Christ".'[68] The longing to recreate the heavenly Jerusalem on Earth also had similarities with the ideals of apocalyptic reform movements. While Espina was clearly no millenarian – he refused

---

pereat grex.' The Toledo rebels of 1449 had employed a similar rhetoric, blaming *conversos* for the ruin of the city in the *Sentencia*, pp. 26–27. For a discussion of this motif in the *Sentencia*, see Vidal Doval, 'Nos soli sumus christiani', in *Medieval Hispanic Studies*, ed. by Beresford, Haywood and Weiss, pp. 230–31. On the link between pollution and political decline more widely, see Geraldine Coates, *Treacherous Foundations: Betrayal and Collective Identity in Early Medieval Spanish Epic, Chronicle, and Drama*, Colección Támesis, A281 (Woodbridge: Tamesis, 2009), p. 92.

[66] MacKay, 'The Hispanic-*Converso* Predicament', p. 159: 'When faced with rampant inflation, arbitrary reductions of bullion coins, rising taxation, bad harvests, famine, and plague, the urban populace tended to turn onto the Jews and *conversos*.' Political and economic situation: Teófilo F. Ruiz, *Spain's Centuries of Crisis, 1300–1474* (Oxford: Blackwell, 2007), pp. 86–109, 139–63. Contemporary perceptions of crisis: Jeremy Lawrance, 'Representations of Violence in 15th-Century Spanish Literature', in *Late Medieval Spanish Studies in Honour of Dorothy Sherman Severin*, ed. by Joseph T. Snow and Roger Wright (= *BHS*, 68 (2009)), pp. 95–103.

[67] On the social and political conservatism of mendicant models of reform, see Mormando, p. 36.

[68] Mormando, pp. 47–48. Similarly Rubin, p. 192, observes that mendicant prescription for reform relied on 'antagonistic populism which advocated self-improvement thorough the creation and expulsion of bearers of pollution' and that, 'having excised them, deems the work done, the cleansing and purification achieved'.

to be drawn into speculations about the timing of the Second Coming – his remark that it was possible Antichrist had already been born suggests he may have shared some of the apocalyptic expectations of his contemporaries.[69] The mass conversions of Jews in Castile, the advance of the Turks and the conquest of Constantinople were deemed by many to be portentous, as signs of the nearness of the End of Days.[70] Whatever Espina's eschatological expectations, *Fortalitium fidei* would serve as a reminder of the dangers ahead, as a statement of what was needed from individuals and society to combat the enemy, and, finally, as assurance that ultimate victory awaited Christianity and the true faithful:

> Hec erit pax de qua dicit Apostolus. Cum fuerit tranquilitas magna et securitas tunc veniet repentinus introitus a quo liberari mereamur feliciter per Ihesum Christum Dominum nostrum, qui est turris fortitudinis a facie inimici cui sit honor et gloria sine fine. Amen.[71]

*

Through the central image of the fortress of faith, Espina articulated his entire vision for Castilian society. As pro-*converso* authors had done, he asserted strongly the need for Christian unity, yet Espina's was a belligerent and uncompromising unity that functioned through repression and exclusion. If defending this fortress of Christianity was the duty of all the faithful nevertheless the secular and ecclesiastical powers had particular responsibility. Espina censured strongly those who had so far failed to act, calling on the elites to heed his warnings and implement his reforms. At the heart of this programme of reform was his own Order – the Observant Franciscans – serving as shock troops in the fight for the faith. It was their task to identify and to uproot error and to spur others to act. *Fortalitium fidei* was nothing less than the advertisement of the exemplarity of Espina and his Order.

The fortress allowed Espina to place his work in dialogue with other texts and traditions. Through it he positioned himself in a

---

[69] *Fortalitium fidei*, III, consideratio xii, punctus 7, fols 155ᵛ–156ᵛ. See also Echevarria, *The Fortress of Faith*, pp. 205–8.

[70] On the apocalyptic expectations of authors in the *converso* controversy, see Rosenstock, *New Men*, pp. 70–71. More widely, see Alain Milhou, *Colón y su mentalidad mesiánica en el ambiente franciscanista español*, Cuadernos Colombinos, 11 (Valladolid: Casa-Museo de Colón, Seminario Americanista de la Universidad de Valladolid, 1983); and José Guadalajara Medina, *Las profecías del anticristo en la Edad Media* (Madrid: Gredos, 1996).

[71] *Fortalitium*, V, consideratio xii, fol. 224ᵛ.

long line of authors employing martial and military imagery to warn of the dangers of infidels and heretics, while counterposing his own fortification with those of pro-*converso* authors. The fortress also stood for Christian Castile, under attack and threatened by a series of enemies – Jews, heretics, Muslims, and demons. If the Christian faith was ultimately impregnable, nevertheless its enemies could inflict grave damage on the kingdom and its people. Through spiritual combat, legislation, expulsion, and war these foes had to be neutralized – only then could Castile be the true embodiment of the fortress of faith. Such a vision was not utopian but a promise of how the kingdom would be if Espina's ideas were only implemented. Where authors such as Oropesa were doubtful of the possibility of perfection in this world, Espina, in line with other mendicants, held out the possibility of achieving the City of God on Earth.

JEWS AND JUDAISM:
CARNALITY AND CRIMINALITY

Of the enemies of the faith discussed by Espina in *Fortalitium fidei*, it is the Jews who are the focus of most attention. Book III – 'On the War of the Jews' – is the longest of the five and there is also extensive discussion of Judaism in the final sections of Book I. Any attempt to understand Espina's position regarding *conversos* must begin with a consideration of his treatment of Jews and Judaism: for Espina, *conversos* were, in essence, Jews.[1] Though *conversos* were, strictly speaking, Christian heretics – and Espina discussed them as such in Book II – their heresy was judaizing and all the characteristics and errors that Espina attributed to the Jews could also apply to New Christians. Such a position was well-established in anti-*converso* literature by the time Espina wrote and, as has been seen, even pro-*converso* authors felt compelled to discuss Judaism in their works.[2] In addition, exploring Espina's treatment of Jews and Judaism offers one means of understanding his ideas on a number of concepts that are central to the *converso* problem – chief among these genealogy and inheritance.

The division of the material between Books I and III is effectively chronological; Book I deals principally with the Old Testament, while Book III explores Jews and Judaism after the Incarnation, with a particular focus on late medieval Castile.[3] This division is not absolute – Book I, for example, makes reference to the Talmud

---

[1] In a section about the status of Jews in his contemporary Castile Espina stated that many Christians were secret Jews: 'cum multi christiani facti sunt iudei, uel melius dicam erant occulti iudei et facti sunt publici', *Fortalitium*, III, consideratio xii, articulus 8, fol. 151ᵛ. See also Meyuhas Ginio, *La forteresse*, p. 112.

[2] Seidenspinner-Nuñez, 'Prelude', in *Strategies of Medieval Communal Identity*, ed. by van Bekkum and Cobb, pp. 54–55, has noted that the texts of the Toledo rebellion essentialized *conversos* as Jews. Cf. *Memorial*, p. 203 that refers to them as 'judíos baptizados'.

[3] Espina's division of Jewish history has similarities with Thomas Aquinas' organization into two eras 'the time under the Law and the time after the Law – with a crucial hinge in between: the period A. D. 30–70', John Y. B. Hood, *Aquinas and the Jews* (Philadelphia: University of Pennsylvania Press, 1995), p. 38.

– but is sufficiently marked to suggest a deliberate choice on Espina's part.[4] There are also differences in purpose between the two Books. Book I explores Judaism and Mosaic Law to demonstrate both the truth and the superiority of Christianity. Christ was the Messiah promised by God and Christianity the true fulfilment of the Abrahamic covenant and the only vehicle for salvation. Thus consideration iii, an exposition in six articles, argues Jesus Christ to be the Son of God and Christianity to be older, more stable, more noble, perfect and more useful than the Mosaic Law, whose validity had ceased with the coming of Christ.[5] Book III, by contrast, focuses on the attacks, intellectual and physical, made by the Jews on Christianity. The Book opens with a discussion of how the Jews are unable to perceive Christ to be the Messiah prophesized in their own Scripture, then explores the putative origins of the Jews before setting out their dissensions and religious disagreements.[6] Considerations iv–vi then spell out the intellectual assaults against the truth of Christianity, showing how the Jews attempt to employ arguments from Mosaic Law, from the Gospels, and from nature.[7] The ultimate failure of these intellectual assaults leads to the physical attacks and crimes outlined in considerations vii and viii, while considerations ix–xi set out the various means by which the Jewish problem can be addressed – expulsion, conversion, and legislation.[8] The Book ends with a discussion of the eschatological role of Jews.[9]

---

[4] See, for example, *Fortalitium*, I, consideratio iii, articulus 6, fols 28^v–29^r.

[5] Jesus Christ as living Son of God: *Fortalitium*, I, consideratio iii, articulus 1, fols 14^r–16^v; Law of Christ is older: articulus 2, fol. 17^r; is more stable: articulus 3, fol. 17^v; is more noble and perfect: articulus 4, fols 18^r–19^r; is more useful: articulus 5, fols 19^r–20^v; the Law of Moses is no longer valid: articulus 6, fols 20^v–47^r.

[6] About the blindness of the Jews: *Fortalitium*, III, consideratio i, fols 71^r–72^v; the origins of the Jews: consideratio ii, fols 72^v–73^r; religious dissensions: consideratio iii, fol. 73^{r-v}.

[7] Attacks against Christianity with arguments from Mosaic Law: *Fortalitium*, III, consideratio iv, fols 73^v–95^v; from the Gospels: consideratio v, fols 95^v–108^v; from the laws of nature: consideratio vi, fols 108^v–122^r.

[8] Acts of cruelty committed by the Jews: *Fortalitium*, III, consideratio vii, fols 122^v–129^v; stupidity of Jews: consideratio viii, fols 129^v–140^r; expulsions: consideratio ix, fols 140^r–145^r; obstinacy and iniquity of Jews: consideratio x, fols 145^r–147^r; legislation about Jews living amid Christians: consideratio xi, fols 147^r–152^v.

[9] *Fortalitium*, III, consideratio xii, fols 152^v–156^v.

In essence, Espina's treatment of Jews and Judaism sought to emphasize two key points. Firstly, that there was 'no theological reason' for their continuing existence since 'they had no positive role in the divine plan for salvation except for their conversion *en masse* at the onset of final redemption'.[10] Secondly, that the presence of Jews in Castile was actively damaging to the Christian faith and to the stability of the kingdom. In Book I, Espina demonstrated that Judaism was, effectively, a spent force and that the status of the Jews as a people chosen by God had ceased with their rejection of Christ. Book III laid out the charges against Espina's contemporary Jews, in particular those in Castile, and made the case for a kingdom free from their corrupting influence. Espina's ideas, both about the status of Jews and the need for their neutralization, were by no means novel – friars had long made similar arguments about the pernicious presence of Jews in Christian societies – but his was a distinctive voice in Castile at the time and his intervention occurred at a pivotal moment in the history of Jewish-Christian relations in the Iberian Peninsula.

Mosaic Law and the Law of Christ

Espina's discussions of Jews and Judaism in Book I occur as part of a demonstration of the truth and superiority of Christianity and an assertion that Christ was the Messiah and Son of God. His presentation of such subjects as the Mosaic Law or the Abrahamic Covenant were thus subsumed within these overall aims; Book I was not intended to provide a detailed or systematic analysis of Judaism in its own right but to confirm the triumph of Christianity.[11] If Book I does not contain a sustained study of the Jews and Judaism, nevertheless something of Espina's conception of the nature of Biblical Judaism can be grasped. Overall, Espina's discussion in Book I consideration iii, attempted to marginalize the Jews within salvation history and to dilute the strength and exclusivity of their bond with God. At the same time, he sought to demonstrate Christianity to be the older faith, effectively recasting

---

[10] McMichael, *Was Jesus of Nazareth the Messiah?*, p. 54.

[11] Book I, consideration iii, which contains this discussion, is among the least studied sections of *Fortalitium fidei*. See Steven J. McMichael, 'Alonso de Espina on the Mosaic Law', in *Friars and Jews in the Middle Ages and Renaissance*, ed. by Steven J. McMichael and Susan Myers, The Medieval Franciscans, 2 (Leiden: Brill, 2004), pp. 199–223 (pp. 200–12); and idem, *Was Jesus of Nazareth the Messiah?*, pp. 110–43.

the chronological relationship between Judaism and Christianity. This exploration was wide-ranging but concentrated on two areas: the nature and purpose of the Mosaic Law and the meaning of the Abrahamic Covenant. To a time bound, fleshly and now-expired Mosaic Law, Espina contrasted the eternal, spiritual, and salvific Law of Christ. To Jewish claims that they were the exclusive heirs to the Abrahamic Covenant, Espina countered with a vision of the Covenant's universal realization in Christianity.[12]

For Espina, the Mosaic Law was preparatory and foreshadowing in function and limited and imperfect in scope. At the most basic level, the Mosaic Law had been intended to check abuses and wrongdoing. Before the Law, men had been ignorant of their weaknesses and failings – Espina does not explore these transgressions in detail but elsewhere suggests that the Jews' greatest failing was idolatry.[13] Though the Law made men aware of their sins, its precepts were limited in terms of morality and offered only imperfect understanding of God – for instance, Mosaic Law provided no knowledge of the Trinity.[14] Equally, Mosaic Law offered no possibility of healing since it could not bestow grace but could only promise imperfect and worldly things.[15] Its sacraments were limited and were concerned only with external acts, purifying but not removing sin, and their efficacy depended upon the virtues of their performer.[16] Such moral precepts as the Law offered were taught principally through fear and were obeyed through fear; the Law often spared the guilty and punished the innocent.[17]

Though the Law had a value in itself and may have curbed some of the worst excesses of the Jews, its chief purpose was to prepare

---

[12] On the notion of Judaism as the polar opposition of Christianity in Christian hermeneutics see Rosemary Radford Ruether, *Faith and Fratricide: The Theological Roots of Anti-Semitism* (New York: Seabury Press, 1974), p. 181; and now also Nirenberg, *Anti-Judaism*, pp. 55–56.

[13] Purpose of the giving of the Law: *Fortalitium*, I, consideratio iii, articulus 4, fol. 18^r; Israel's idolatry: articulus 4, fol. 28^r.

[14] Moral limitations of the Law: *Fortalitium*, I, consideratio iii, articulus 6, fol. 38^r; lack of knowledge of the Trinity: articulus 6, fol. 37^v.

[15] Imperfection of the Law's promises: *Fortalitium*, I, consideratio iii, articulus 6, fol. 42^r.

[16] The Law cannot bestow grace: *Fortalitium*, I, consideratio iii, articulus 4, fol. 19^r, and articulus 6, fol. 39^{r-v}; efficacy of its sacraments dependant on the performer: articulus 6, fol. 36^v.

[17] Fear and injustice and the Law: *Fortalitium*, I, consideratio iii, articulus 6, fol. 38^v.

the way for the Coming of Christ. Through their observance of the Law the Jews were made aware of their sinfulness so that they would understand the need for a Saviour and be ready to receive the promise that was Christ.[18] Obeying the Law was an obligation for the Jews because the Messiah would come from their seed and it was for this reason that God had chosen them and worked miracles through them.[19] Like all of the Old Testament, the Law was also a figure, a sign of things that were to come, most importantly Christ and His Law. The time of the Law of Moses was a time of shadow, prefiguring the Law of the Gospel.[20] Such was most discernable through the ceremonies and rituals of Mosaic Law; dietary regulations prefigured the spiritual purity of the New Law given by Christ, while the Passover feast and other sacrifices prefigured Christ's Passion. Likewise, Moses, David, and Solomon had ordered ceremonies and offerings to show the mystery of grace pertaining to the Messiah.[21]

Because Mosaic Law both prepared for and foreshadowed the Incarnation and was fulfilled in the Law of Christ, the Jews no longer had a Law. Before the coming of the Messiah, the Mosaic Law had been an obligation; once the promise had been fulfilled the Law was empty. Though Jews claimed to be obliged to follow the Law of Moses, with the Passion this Law had ceased to be divine and thus served no purpose in establishing and maintaining a relationship between man and God.[22] By following Mosaic Law after the Coming of Christ the Jews were attending only to its literal and fleshly sense and thus ignoring its true spiritual meaning and in so doing were incurring the wrath of God. The Mosaic Law was particular because it was limited to a single people, the Jews, to a single place, the Promised Land, and to a single time, the period

---

[18] Law promises Christ: *Fortalitium*, I, consideratio iii, articulus 4, fol. 18^r.

[19] Obligation of the Jews to follow the Law: *Fortalitium*, I, consideratio iii, articulus 6, fol. 20^v.

[20] Law of Moses as time of shadow: *Fortalitium*, I, consideratio iii, articulus 6, fol. 23^r.

[21] Diet prefigures spiritual purity: *Fortalitium*, I, consideratio iii, articulus 6, fol. 41^r; Passover and sacrifices prefigure the Passion: articulus 6, fol. 22^r; ceremonies and offerings of Moses, David, and Solomon: articulus 6, fol. 20^v.

[22] Law of Moses was no longer valid: *Fortalitium*, I, consideratio iii, articulus 6, fols 20^v–22^v; Jews attend only to the literal sense of the Law and incur the wrath of God: consideratio iii, articulus 6, fol. 23^{r-v}.

from the Moses to the Incarnation. The Law of Christ, by contrast, was universal, incumbent upon all peoples for all of time.[23]

As well as stressing the temporally and geographically bound nature of Mosaic Law, Espina asserted that it was not the only route to faith. While the Jews had been obliged to follow the Law of Moses because the Messiah would come from their seed, many others were saved by following natural law.[24] Though this idea was not unique to Espina – Thomas Aquinas had allowed that the precepts of natural law might be apprehended solely by reason – his formulation maximised the potential for salvation amongst Gentiles before the Coming of Christ.[25] In doing so, Espina seems to downplay the centrality of Mosaic Law to facilitating understanding of the most complex moral precepts. Aquinas had, for example, argued that natural law consisted of three levels, ranging from the simplest and most general principles to the most complex and obscure. Whilst the first tier was understood almost universally to be true, understanding of the third and highest level was open only to the wisest. In apprehending this third level, the Jews had an advantage in that such moral precepts formed a part of the Mosaic Law.[26] It was this advantage, this potential for greater insight, that Espina seems to undermine.

Alongside the ending of Mosaic Law, the Passion of Christ had also meant the end of the obligation of circumcision.[27] For Espina, circumcision had been given by God to Abraham as a sign of faith in the coming of the Messiah. The giving of this sign was the origin of the distinction between Jews and Gentiles: though Abraham was the father of both peoples, circumcision and Mosaic Law were instruments of obligation only between God and the Jews and through fulfilling them the Jews were made worthy of receiving His

---

[23] Law of Moses is particular and Law of Christ universal: *Fortalitium*, I, consideratio iii, articulus 6, fol. 37ʳ.

[24] *Fortalitium*, I, consideratio iii, articulus 6, fol. 20ᵛ. Espina does not explain what he means by the term *salvi* in this context.

[25] Hood, p. 45.

[26] Hood, p. 47

[27] On the debate about the exact point in time when Mosaic Law had been abrogated see, Nancy L. Turner, 'Jewish Witness, Forced Conversion, and Island Living', in *Christian Attitudes toward the Jews in the Middle Ages: A Casebook*, ed. by Michael Frasetto (New York: Routledge, 2007), pp. 183–209 (p. 189).

grace.[28] Circumcision, though an obligation for the Jews, was not from Mosaic Law; Espina insisted on their essential separation.[29] Like the Law, however, circumcision was also preparatory, imperfect, and time bound. It prepared for Christ and prefigured the sacrament of baptism, imperfectly, for though it lifted Original Sin it could not confer grace, and its practice should have ceased with the coming of the Messiah.[30] The obligation of circumcision had ended because the time of promises was over: God had fulfilled His greatest promise to the Jews in Christ and those who rejected Him were acting as if God had not fulfilled His promise.[31]

While Mosaic Law and circumcision, at least carnally understood, had ended with the Passion of Christ, Espina was clear that the Abrahamic Covenant was enduring and extended to all peoples. Drawing on Paul's Letter to the Galatians, Espina argued the Law of Christ to be older than the Law of Moses, noting that Abraham had been justified by his faith and that the Covenant God made with him and his descent was on account of this faith alone.[32] Likewise, as Espina noted, the Letter to the Hebrews stated that Abel, Enoch, Jacob, Joseph and Moses had all been justified before the Law. The promises that God had made to Abraham – many descendants, the Promised Land, the multiplication of his seed, and the blessing of all peoples – though all literally fulfilled ought more correctly and more properly to be understood as fulfilled spiritually in Christianity. Thus the Promised Land of Canaan stood spiritually for the entire congregation of the Christian faithful, Jews and Gentiles. Many descendants and the multiplication of Abraham's seed spiritually understood meant Christ and the blessed, true Christians.[33]

---

[28] Giving of circumcision to Abraham: *Fortalitium*, I, consideratio iii, articulus 6, fol. 20ᵛ.

[29] *Fortalitium*, I, consideratio iii, articulus 5, fol. 19ʳ, and cf. articulus iii, 17ᵛ.

[30] Imperfection of circumcision: *Fortalitium*, I, consideratio iii, articulus 6, fols 39ʳ, 40ᵛ.

[31] Implications of the rejection of Christ: *Fortalitium*, I, consideratio iii, articulus 6, fol. 22ᵛ.

[32] Abrahamic covenant: *Fortalitium*, I, consideratio iii, articulus 2, fol. 17ʳ. Cf. Galatians 3.6–19.

[33] *Fortalitium*, I, consideratio iii, articulus 2, fol. 17ʳ. Cf. Hebrews 11. See also McMichael, 'Alonso de Espina on the Mosaic Law', in *Friars and Jews*, ed. by McMichael and Myers, p. 200.

Christians were, through their kinship with Christ, the spiritual descendants of Abraham and, as adherents of the faith through which he was justified, heirs to the Covenant between him and God.[34] For Espina, this spiritual descent was through the line of Isaac and Jacob and Christians were like the stars in heaven, whereas the descendants of Ishmael, Seth, and Esau were wicked and sterile like the sands of the sea.[35] Though such phrasing looked back to the words of the angel to Abraham, it also underlined that the descendants of Ishmael, Seth, and Esau were to be identified with some at least of the Jews, those whose descendants would reject Christ and Christianity. The phrase '[h]arena maris' is used in Revelation 20.7 to refer to the multitude of people gathered together by Satan at the End of Days. Espina understood this passage from Revelations to refer to Antichrist gathering the sons of Israel, imprisoned since the time of Alexander the Great in the Caspian Mountains, as well as the rest of the Jews scattered throughout the world, before descending on Jerusalem.[36]

Espina's vision of twin lines of descent from Abraham – one perfidious and sinful, one pious and faithful – was a means by which he implied, though never stated fully, the existence of two peoples within the Old Testament, the reprobate Jews and those 'heroes and prophets, whose lineage is fulfilled in the future

---

[34] Christians as coheirs with Christ: *Fortalitium*, I, consideratio iii, articulus 5, fol. 17^v. On Ambrosiaster's notion that the inheritance of Abraham was by faith and not by law, see *Ancient Christian Commentary on Scripture, New Testament* VIII: *Galatians, Ephesians, Philippians*, ed. by Mark J. Edwards (Downers Grove: InterVarsity Press, 1999), p. 43.

[35] *Fortalitium*, I, consideratio iii, articulus 2, fol. 17^r: 'Boni qui ex ipso descendunt per Ysaac et Iacob sunt sicut stelle celi. Sed precipue vere Christiani qui sunt eius semen spirituale et semen Dei repromissum in quantum eius fidem imitantur. Sed mali qui ex eo descendunt per Hismahelem et filios Sethure et per Esau fuerunt sicci et steriles velud harena maris.'

[36] *Fortalitium*, III, consideratio xii, punctus 6, fols 154^v–155^r. See also McMichael, 'The End of the World', p. 254. On ideas about the role of Antichrist and the Jews at the end of time, see Roberto Rusconi, 'Antichrist and Antichrists', in *The Encyclopedia of Apocalypticism*, ed. by Bernard McGinn and John J. Colli, 3 vols (New York: Continuum, 1999), II, 287–325; Andrew C. Gow, *The Red Jews: Antisemitism in an Apocalyptic Age 1200–1600* (Leiden: Brill, 1995), especially pp. 37–63; and Robert E. Lerner, *The Feast of Saint Abraham: Medieval Millenarians and the Jews* (Philadelphia: University of Pennsylvania Press, 2001), especially pp. 2–31. Medieval tradition believed these Jews to be the ten lost tribes of Israel.

Church.'[37] In hinting at such a division, Espina appears to be operating within a tradition that saw the Patriarchs as obeying the natural law from their hearts and thus being members of a universal race rather than Jews.[38] The purpose was to efface the position of the Jews as the true heirs of Abraham and to replace them with Christians; Abraham, Isaac, and Jacob, as well as other righteous Old Testament figures, were effectively Christians *avant la lettre*.[39]

In his discussion in Book I of the relationship between Christianity and Judaism, Espina put forward a model of extreme supersessionism: the Coming of Christ had altogether abrogated Mosaic Law, replacing it with the Law of Christ and ending any special relationship between God and the Jews. Mosaic Law had been an essential stepping-stone in the history of salvation but was a measure that had applied only to the Jews, from whom the Messiah would arise, and only during a particular historical period. With the Incarnation, death, and resurrection of Christ the special role of Jews in salvation history had effectively finished. However, even during the period of the Law, when the Jews had been especially chosen by God, their relationship with the divine was not exclusive or unique – natural law offered a means to salvation.

In making such points, Espina was operating within well-established traditions and drawing on ideas and concepts that had

---

[37] Rosemary Radford Ruether, 'The *Adversus Judaeos* Tradition in the Church Fathers: The Exegesis of Christian Anti-Judaism', in *Aspects of Jewish Culture in the Middle Ages: Papers of the Eighth Annual Conference of the Center for Medieval and Early Renaissance Studies, State University of New York at Binghamton, 3–5 May, 1974*, ed. by Paul E. Szarmach (Albany: State University of New York Press, 1979), pp. 27–50 (p. 35). Augustine put forward a similar model of parallel ancestries in the Old Testament but to a much more positive purpose, see Fredricksen, *Augustine*, pp. 194, 245.

[38] Ruether, 'The *Adversus Judaeos* Tradition', in *Aspects of Jewish Culture*, ed. by Szarmach, p. 42.

[39] Elsewhere in Book I (consideratio iii, articulus 6, fol. 28ʳ) Espina would hold up Noah, Abraham, Lot, Jacob, Joseph, Moses, Judith, and others as examples of particular virtues to be emulated by contemporary Christians, describing them as the saints of the Old Testament. Racial concepts also existed among the Jews in late medieval Castile. The possibility of conversion to Judaism allowed escaping the polluted blood of Essau, who stands for Rome and Christianity, and to partake of the blood of Jacob, that stands for Israel. See David Biale, *Blood and Belief: The Circulation of a Symbol between Jews and Christians* (Berkeley: University of California Press, 2007), p. 107. On concerns about genealogy in the Christian and Jewish cultures of the Iberian Peninsula, see Nirenberg, 'Mass Conversion', pp. 3–9.

long histories. Nonetheless, a comparison of Espina's stance with those adopted by pro-*converso* authors demonstrates the extent to which the medieval tradition, although narrow, was flexible and could be reshaped and recast to serve particular contemporary needs. Where Espina had stressed spiritual descent from Isaac and Jacob, presenting them as the fathers or forerunners of Christians, Alonso de Cartagena focused on fleshly descent; Isaac and Jacob were the fathers of the Jews. Similarly, where Espina had hinted that the Jews were the descendants of Ishmael and Esau, for Juan de Torquemada the Ishmaelites and Edomites were the Old Christian persecutors of *conversos*. Like Espina, Torquemada had acknowledged the presence of numerous reprobate and faithless Jews amongst the Israelites of the Old Testament and that the Church had existed among the righteous before the giving of Mosaic Law. Yet Torquemada, unlike Espina, stressed the essential identity of the Patriarchs and the Jews; faithful and faithless were part of the same people, the tree onto which Gentile Christians had been grafted.

Differences also existed in attitudes towards Mosaic Law. Cartagena viewed the Law in fundamentally positive terms, a gift from God to the Jewish people, while Espina emphasized the punitive aspects of it and its limitations. Moreover, for Cartagena those of the Jews who were closest and dearest to God seemed to observe the Law of the Gospels in their actions and were truly more disciples of the Gospel than of the Law. To a privileged few who understood it spiritually, Mosaic Law could deliver the Gospel. Alonso de Cartagena had likewise compared the pale illumination of natural reason to the fire-like light of Mosaic Law, the former teaching nothing of the true nature of God, the latter communicating something of the divine mysteries. Espina, by contrast, though allowing for the existence of righteous Jews under the Law, insisted also on the ability of natural law to deliver salvation. Alonso de Oropesa adopted a similar, though subtly more positive, position. He acknowledged that Jews under the Law had had a unique relationship with God but nevertheless stressed that Mosaic Law had not even then been the only vehicle for salvation.

Where Cartagena and Torquemada viewed the relationship between Judaism and Christianity in terms of continuity, completion and perfection, Espina insisted on ending and replacement. Oropesa, too, saw Mosaic Law and the Law of Christ in opposition, arguing, as Espina had done, that the Jews no longer had a relationship with God. Though Oropesa had opposed publicly many of Espina's views and his *Lumen* might be termed a pro-*converso* work, it is clear that he and Espina shared an essentially similar outlook on the nature of the relationship between Judaism and Christianity. Cartagena and Torquemada, by contrast, built their defence of *conversos* around a fundamentally more positive vision of Jews and Mosaic Law.

Reading and Blindness

At the end of Book I, Espina spelled out the punishments the Jews had suffered on account of their culpability for the death of Christ: the loss of their status as God's people, the destruction of Jerusalem and the Temple, and their own desolation. Their future punishment was damnation.[40] Having established that Biblical Judaism had been superseded with the Coming of Christ, in Book III Espina moved on to consider medieval Judaism.[41] Alongside the grave threat Jews posed to Christian society, they were a people apart from the main fold of mankind and constituted a parenthesis in the history of salvation. While the Jews of the Old Testament had prepared the way for the coming of the Messiah and those in apocalyptic times would convert to Christianity ushering the End of Days, Espina allowed medieval Jews a very limited role within providential history.[42]

In consideration xi, he addressed the question of why, despite their many crimes, the Jews were still allowed to live amid Christians rather than being killed or expelled. He offered five reasons for their continued toleration: so that Christians might exercise charity; to confirm the truth of the Christian faith, since the enduring servitude of the Jews was eloquent testimony to their divine punishment for deicide; in remembrance of Christ's suffering; and to allow them to fulfil their apocalyptic role.[43] Though Espina cast this discussion in terms of the long-established

---

[40] *Fortalitium*, I, consideratio xii, articulus 6, fols 46^v–47^r.

[41] On Book III of *Fortalitium fidei* see particularly, Alisa Meyuhas Ginio, *De bello iudaeorum: Fray Alonso de Espina y su 'Fortalitium fidei'*, FIRC, 8 (Salamanca: Universidad Pontificia de Salamanca, 1998); and eadem, *La forteresse*, pp. 132–49.

[42] Jews's role at the End of Days: *Fortalitium*, III, consideratio xii, puncti 6–8, fols 154^v–156^v.

[43] *Fortalitium*, III, consideratio xi, articulus 1, fol. 147^{r-v}, quotation fol. 147^r: 'Pocius enim videtur quod deberent omnis occidi et expelli de mundo'.

Augustinian tradition, his rationale for toleration was almost exclusively a negative one. Where Augustine and others had allowed some continuing value to Judaism, for Espina contemporary Jews had no positive theological role, their presence was largely a reminder of their culpability for the most heinous crime of deicide.[44] Though he could not have proposed, or even envisaged, a world without Jews, throughout Book III Espina holds up the possibility of a Castile without them.

For Espina, the defining characteristic of medieval Jews was spiritual blindness. Such prevented them from discerning the self-evident truth of Christianity and made them cling tenaciously, but entirely mistakenly, to the literal observance of Mosaic Law. The blindness was, in effect, a hermeneutical disposition: the Jews refused or were incapable of reading their own Scriptures correctly and were thus unable to interpret properly – that is spiritually – the prophecies they contained.[45] Instead, contemporary Jews persisted in the fleshly, literal readings of their ancestors.

This blindness of the Jews was the result of sin.[46] The Jews sinned and so turned away from God, this led to the withdrawal of God's grace, leaving them blind and further mired in sin.[47] Failure to recognize Jesus as the Messiah prophesized by Scripture was the supreme act of blindness that separated all Jews from God. The severing of this relationship resulted in enduring blindness: the Jews ceased to receive divine illumination and so continued to reject the truth of Scripture.[48] The enduring blindness of the Jews

---

[44] On the notion of the enduring value of Judaism, see Fredricksen, *Augustine*, pp. 328, 351.

[45] *Fortalitium*, III, consideratio i, fol. 71ʳ–72ʳ. On this section, see McMichael, *Was Jesus of Nazareth the Messiah?*, pp. 47–48; and Meyuhas Ginio, *De bello*, pp. 15–17.

[46] *Fortalitium*, III, consideratio i, fol. 71ʳ: 'causa cecitatis Iudeorum est quia Domino peccauerunt [...] quodam singulari modo Domino peccauerunt Ihesum Christum filium dei iniuste crucis supplicio interimendo propter quod spirituali modo facti sunt ceci inter omnes gentes, ut non solum paciantur cecitatem ignoracie super omnes, propter quam ignoranciam scripturam proprie legis minime intelligunt [...] populus igitur iudaicus merito dicitur cecus qui vetus testamentum recipit et que in eo scripta est recte intelligere nescit'.

[47] McMichael, *Was Jesus of Nazareth the Messiah?*, p. 48.

[48] *Fortalitium*, III, consideratio i, fol. 71ᵛ: 'Homo enim auertens se a Deo meretur ut iuste Deus retrahet graciam suam ab eo, cuius effectus est illuminare intellectum et mollificare affectum, et ideo ipsa substracta homo excecatur et obduratur ex sua malicia. Et hoc fuit impletum quando ad

was, however, theologically problematic. Paul himself had grappled with it but his overwhelming sense of the nearness of the eschaton had allowed him to resolve the problem by suggesting it to be a short-term state, providentially ordained to allow for the conversion of the gentiles.[49] As the centuries passed and the Second Coming receded into a distant and unreckonable future, theologians were forced to gloss Paul's words and to provide answers that adjusted to the new reality. Already in Augustine's thought, the tenor of the blindness – or the hardening of the heart of the Jews – changed from strategic and temporary to punitive and enduring, a result of the secret sins of the Jews.[50]

The notions of Jewish unbelief and enduring blindness were problematic to theologians because at their core were questions about the interaction of divine providence and justice, and human free will.[51] Espina devoted little time to working through the theological implications of these ideas but asserted Jewish unbelief to be the result not of direct divine intervention but defective free will.[52] The rejection of Christ was a conscious decision by the Jews that, in turn, invited their enduring blindness by way of divine punishment. Espina even went as far as stating that the culpability of contemporary Jews was far greater than that of the generation that crucified Christ; those living in the fifteenth century had had fourteen hundred and sixty years of accumulated proof that Jesus was the Messiah and yet still refused to believe.[53]

---

predicacionem Christi Iudei per magna parte fuerunt obdurati [...]. In qua excecacione ac eciam duricia usque in presens tempus perduret generacio ista'. This very blindness would cause the Jews to accept Antichrist as the true Messiah. *Fortalitium*, III, consideratio xii, punctus 6, fol. 154ᵛ. See also Gow, pp. 123–25.

[49] Romans 11:25–26: 'For I would not have you ignorant, brethren, of this mystery (lest you should be wise in your own conceits) that blindness in part has happened in Israel, until the fullness of the Gentiles should come in. And so all Israel should be saved'.

[50] Fredricksen, *Augustine*, p. 284.

[51] *Ibid.* p. 364.

[52] *Fortalitium*, III, consideratio i, fol. 71ᵛ: 'Hic notat Nicolaus de Lyra quod talis excecacio et obduracio non est a deo directe sed a liberi arbitrii defectibilitate.'

[53] *Fortalitium*, III, consideratio i, fols 71ᵛ–72ʳ: 'Et hinc est quod idem dubium quid habebant antequam veniret tenent nunc postquam transierunt mille quadringentisexaginta anni a sua nativitate, et nolunt attenti videre quomodo prophetie iam sunt implete permanentes in maledictione dicte scripture: liga testimonium, signa legem, et iterum [...]. Hec est magna cecitas et azinina

Espina's discussion of Jewish blindness is followed by an exploration of genealogy as an example of the consequences of the Jews' literal disposition.[54] In one of the most frequently cited passages of the entire *Fortalitium fidei*, Espina writes of the double ancestry of the Jews: alongside illustrious ancestors such as Abraham, Isaac, and Jacob, were monstrous progenitors. Espina outlines the Talmud's account of the ignominious descent of the Jews, observing how their brethren are monsters, the product of intercourse between Adam and the animals, and noting their stepmothers to be the ass and the sow. On account of Adam's intercourse with Lilith before the creation of Eve, the Jews were also kinsmen of demons and their offspring shared in the malice and cunning of the serpent.[55] Though this section has been read most often as the quintessential manifestation of Espina's deep and irrational anti-Semitism, it also provides crucial insight into his understanding of genealogy and the inheritance of moral characteristics.[56] Espina explained that such stories were necessarily false since they were impossible. Nevertheless the Jews truly partook of that ignominious, demonic, and monstrous heritage because they were the only people who maintained such ideas.[57] Whilst Adam was the father of all mankind, there was division according to belief: only those who believed in its existence shared in the inferior and shameful heritage promoted by the Talmud. In essence, the very acceptance of false texts caused the ignominy of

    bestialitas quia si primi excecati non cognouerunt bonum plus sunt culpandi isti vltimi qui vident tamen tempus transisse et legunt Sanctas Scripturas et non intendunt in eis sigillum amotum manentes in sua perfidia sicut patres eorum'.

[54] *Fortalitium*, III, consideratio ii, fols 72ᵛ–73ʳ. Meyuhas Ginio, *De bello*, pp. 15–17.

[55] *Fortalitium*, III, consideratio ii, fols 73ʳ: 'Sunt eciam eorum nouerce asina et porca et omnes alie femelle bestiales, sunt fratres non minus demonum, et filii dyaboli necnon habentes pro vitrico serpentem eiusdem mores imitantes.' On the long-standing association in medieval thought of the Devil and the Jews, see Joshua Trachtenberg, *The Devil and the Jews: The Medieval Conception of the Jew and its Relation to Modern Anti-Semitism*, introd. by Mark Saperstein, 2nd edn (Philadelphia: Jewish Publication Society, 2002).

[56] Nirenberg, 'Was There Race before Modernity?', in *The Origins of Racism*, ed. by Eliav-Feldon, Isaac and Ziegler, p. 257, observes that stories of the monstrous kinship of the Jews 'doubtless seemed as fantastic to many medieval readers as they do to us'.

[57] *Fortalitium*, III, consideratio ii, fol. 72ᵛ: 'quod soli Iudei affirmant supradicta turpissima et non alii homines'.

the Jews. As with the fleshly interpretation of Scripture, what were at issue were the consequences of literal, and therefore faulty readings.[58] Just as their literal reading of Scripture was both cause and consequence of their moral defectiveness, so the Jews' rejection of Scriptural accounts of man's origin in favour of those of the Talmud was the cause of their tainted inheritance.[59]

Espina offered a model of Jewish error in which genealogy and hermeneutics were thoroughly intertwined but it was a model that remained only partially developed. He offered no explicit indication of whether or when the erroneous reading of Scripture or other texts turned from a learned cultural practice into an inherited characteristic.[60] Espina certainly did not adhere to a fully deterministic genealogical framework for the perfidy of Jews. Instead, fleshly, literal reading of Scripture engendered a negative moral disposition based on carnality rather than spirituality that, in turn, produced further carnality. As each generation of Jews rejected Jesus as the Messiah and compounded its guilt, so each generation of Jews consciously enacted and re-enacted its carnality. Implied in this scheme, was the possibility, however remote, that at any given point an individual or group might embrace the spiritual reading of Scripture and therefore leave behind their tainted inheritance. Yet, crucially, the boundary was permeable in both

---

[58] The paradox in Espina's critique of Jewish literalism was that, following the well-trodden path of medieval anti-Jewish polemics, he read these Talmudic passages literally and, therefore, fundamentally misinterpreted them. On this literalism, see Meyuhas Ginio, *De bello*, pp. 16–17 and Dahan, p. 458.

[59] Cf. with Peter the Venerable's argument (quoted in Cohen, *Living Letters*, p. 262) that 'the Talmud's contrived stories contrast sharply with the truly divine miracles recorded in Scripture; these talmudic tales have degraded the contemporary Jew, holding his heart in their grip, incapacitating the exercise of his reason, and rendering him subhuman.' See also his statement, quoted in Gavin I. Langmuir, 'Peter the Venerable: Defense against Doubts', in *Toward a Definition of Antisemitism* (Berkeley: University of California Press, 1990), pp. 197–208, 382–84 (p. 207): 'because I recognize that reason, that which distinguishes humans from [...] beasts, is extinct in you or in any case buried [...] Truly why are you not called brute animals? [...]. The ass hears but does not understand; the Jew hears but does not understand'. The notion that literal, fleshly reading made one akin to beasts or slaves was well established in the Christian tradition. See, for example, Nirenberg, 'Figures of Thought', pp. 409, 422.

[60] On models of inheritance of personal behaviour and cultural characteristics in late medieval Castile, see Nirenberg, 'Was There Race before Modernity?', in *The Origins of Racism*, ed. by Eliav-Feldon, Isaac and Ziegler, pp. 247–60.

directions. As will be seen, for Espina, *conversos* had willingly travelled in the opposite direction. By abandoning Christian hermeneutics in favour of literal Jewish readings of Scripture, they again partook fully in the tainted descent of the Jews. Espina did not and could not deny the salvific value of baptism or its ability to make men new but instead put forward a model of latent inheritance, activated by personal and deliberate choice.[61]

Alongside this latent inheritance of negative characteristics was the possibility of the inheritance of guilt and culpability.[62] Espina had already referred in Book I to the division of Abraham's descent into two branches: one that began with Isaac and Jacob and encompassed all of the faithful and another that began with Ishmael, Seth, and Esau and included some at least of the Jews. As heirs of this second branch, medieval Jews were from their very beginnings a people apart, distinguished by a series of negative characteristics – faithlessness, perfidy, rejection and persecution of the prophets – that would eventually lead to the severing of their relationship with God after their deicide.[63] For Espina, so great was their desire for the death of Jesus that they were willing to take upon themselves and their descendants the guilt and penalty for this deicide.[64] This guilt, and the penalty that it carried, extended throughout all generations into the present and would last until the end of time.

Espina countered head on attempts by Spanish Jews to deflect this culpability. He noted that they claimed to have arrived in the Iberian Peninsula before the death of Christ and therefore did not share in the guilt for deicide. Espina asked, however, whether they had departed willingly or under compulsion. If willingly, then they were apostates since they could not have observed the Law, if

---

[61] Cartagena also invoked a notion of latent inheritance to explain certain positive personal characteristics, such as valour, among *conversos*. See Chapter 2, p. 48.

[62] For a discussion of early Christian ideas concerning the culpability of the Jews for the murder of Christ, see Paula Fredricksen, *From Jesus to Christ: The Origins of the New Testament Images of Jesus*, 2nd edn (New Haven: Yale Nota Bene, 2000); eadem, *Augustine*, p. 82–83.

[63] *Fortalitium*, III, consideratio vii, punctus 2, fol. 122ᵛ. Ruether, 'The *Adversus Judaeos* Tradition', in *Aspects of Jewish Culture*, ed. by Szarmach, p. 30: 'The rejection and murder of Christ is the foreordained conclusion of the evil history of a perfidious people'. On this so-called trail of blood motif, see also Fredricksen, *Augustine*, p. 92.

[64] *Fortalitium*, III, consideratio vii, punctus 2, fol. 122ᵛ, citing Matthew 27.25.

unwillingly then they should have returned to Israel when permitted by King Darius and their failure to do so was a betrayal of their faith.⁶⁵ The Jews of Spain had further ancestral impediments. According to Espina, the majority of the Jews of Spain, of Castile, and particularly of the city of Burgos were Sadducees and therefore heretics.⁶⁶ It is hard not to see this passage as a thinly veiled attack against Alonso de Cartagena and the Santamaría family, given their claims to nobility on account of their Levite ancestry and descent from the Virgin Mary, as well their powerbase in the city of Burgos.⁶⁷

The Crimes of the Jews

In persisting in their erroneous hermeneutical stance, medieval Jews maintained the same attitude that had lead their forebears to murder Christ. Their refusal to read signs correctly extended not just to the Gospels or their own Scriptures but also to the book of nature. It amounted to an open and conscious rejection of the universally witnessed truth of Christianity. If this rejection was problematic in and of itself, nevertheless its consequences for Christian society were far more severe. Throughout Book III Espina sought to demonstrate the hatred contemporary Jews felt for Christianity and the constant attacks they made upon the faith and upon the faithful. He characterized these attacks in collective terms; they were not simply the work of a few isolated and hateful individuals but were intrinsic to the practice of medieval Judaism and to the nature of medieval Jews.

Espina dealt first with the theological attacks made by the Jews, focusing on three aspects: whether the obligation to observe Mosaic

---

⁶⁵ *Fortalitium*, III, consideratio ix, expulsio 1, fol. 142ʳ⁻ᵛ. On other legends that attempted to exculpate Spanish Jews for the death of Christ, see Rica Amran, 'Calumnias y falsificación histórica: dos casos de correspondencia apócrifa relacionadas con judios hispanos durante el medioevo', *Cahiers de linguistique hispanique médiévale*, 29 (2006), 317–26 (pp. 321–23).

⁶⁶ *Fortalitium*, III, consideratio iii, fol. 73ᵛ.

⁶⁷ Fernández Gallardo notes how the Santamaría family 'se atribuía nobleza pluscuamperfecta, descendencia del linaje de la Virgen María', 'Alonso de Cartagena', p. 115. For more general discussion on fictive genealogical stategies, see Isabel Beceiro Pita, 'La conciencia de los antepasados y la gloria del linaje en la Castilla bajomedieval', in *Relaciones de poder, de producción y parentesco en la Edad Media y Moderna: aproximación a su estudio*, ed. by Reyna Pastor, Biblioteca de la Historia, 1 (Madrid: CSIC, 1990), pp. 329–49.

Law still stood; whether Jesus Christ was the Son of God; and whether He was the Messiah prophesized in Scripture. Espina structured his discussion in the format of a disputation, setting down supposed Jewish objections to Christian doctrines based on their interpretation of the Old and New Testaments as well as natural philosophy before refuting them at length.[68] In challenging these theological attacks, Espina drew on a varied array of materials and sources. Key amongst these was the record of actual Jewish-Christian disputations, most notably that held at Tortosa in 1414.[69] He also relied extensively on Raymond Martí's *Pugio fidei* in these sections, using it particularly to substantiate his claims that even Talmudic literature contained proof that Jesus was the Messiah.[70] Espina's discussion displays neither great theological refinement nor depth and, despite attempts to appear an expert in Hebrew sources, is largely a simplification and abridgement of earlier Latin works.[71]

If for Espina attempts to undermine the truth of Christianity were inevitably doomed to failure, nevertheless the Jews' hatred of the faith provoked them into physical attacks against Christians and Christian society, attacks that could have grave consequences for the kingdom and its people. Espina's account of the seventeen acts of cruelty carried out by the Jews against Christians is without doubt the most-studied section of *Fortalitium fidei* and is viewed as his most significant contribution to anti-Jewish and anti-*converso* polemic.[72] Although Espina claimed to have relied on written accounts and testimonies 'of faithful men', a significant portion of his material, especially that relating to contemporary episodes, is not otherwise attested outside of *Fortalitium fidei*.[73]

---

[68] On this section see, Meyuhas Ginio, *De bello*, pp. 18–59; and McMichael, *Was Jesus of Nazareth the Messiah?*, pp. 143–71, where he discusses Espina's method of reasoning.

[69] Ginio, *De bello*, p. 58; and McMichael, *Was Jesus of Nazareth the Messiah?*, pp. 222–23.

[70] Ginio, *De bello*, p. 13.

[71] Netanyahu, 'Alonso de Espina', pp. 53–70; McMichael, *Was Jesus of Nazareth the Messiah?*, pp. 272–74.

[72] On this section see particularly Netanyahu, *The Origins*, pp. 821–39; Meyuhas Ginio, *De bello*, pp. 59–75; eadem, *La forteresse*, pp. 132–49; and McKendrick, 'The Franciscan Order', pp. 130–55.

[73] *Fortalitium*, III, consideratio vii, punctus 3, fol. 123^r: 'ut colligere potui ex diuersis scripturis et relatione virorum fidelium vsque in presens tempus'.

Though Espina's list of crimes contains many of the typical accusations made against Jews and other marginalized groups in the Middle Ages – infanticide, sorcery, poisonings – there was clearly an underlying logic to his selection.[74] The material was intended to show the link between past and present Jewish criminality and to offer up previous remedies against such activities as exemplars for contemporary rulers.[75] The specific crimes Espina selected for inclusion seem to have been designed to emphasize particularly the threat the continued presence of Jews posed to the body politic of Christian Castile: collaboration with political enemies, attacks against the public peace, prayers against Christians, and usury. The crimes also underlined the Jews continuing re-enactment of their persecution of Christ: ritual murder, host desecration, and blasphemy amongst others.[76] Just as contemporary Jews persisted in the same faulty hermeneutics that had condemned their ancestors, so they persisted in perpetrating acts of the same kind of violence.

Espina also insisted on the group dimensions of these crimes. They were representative, even typical, of Jewish activities and were the inevitable consequence of Jews living alongside Christians. Ritual murder was an essential part of their Passover celebrations and could thus be expected anywhere Jews might be living.[77] On

---

[74] For a brief discussion of these accusations see, for instance, Moore, pp. 27–44, 60–65.

[75] Meyuhas Ginio, *De bello*, pp. 60–61: '[Espina] no escogió los actos de crueldad aleatoriamente. Por el contrario, desea trazar una analogía entre los diversos actos de crueldad cometidos en diversas épocas y lugares con lo succdido en su época y lugar.'

[76] On the truth of these accusations Meyuhas Ginio, *De bello*, p. 61, observes: 'Vale la pena examinar los actos de crueldad mencionados por el autor y tratar de entender la lección que quería dar a los autores. La importancia de esta lección es mayor que la importancia de la verdad histórica'. Anthony Bale, *Feeling Persecuted: Christians, Jews and Images of Violence in the Middle Ages* (London: Reaktion, 2010), pp. 26–27, notes that, in reality, it was Christians who persecuted Jews, but these accounts of crimes and cruelties allowed the former 'to make an aesthetic and rhetorical feeling of persecution concordant with the religious ideal of gentle victimhood'. The fantasy of being persecuted could, at times, lead to instances of real persecution. On notions of these crimes as re-enactments of the Passion, see Jeremy Cohen, *Christ Killers: The Jews and the Passion from the Bible to the Big Screen* (New York: Oxford University Press, 2007), pp. 93–112.

[77] The account of the ritual murder in France of Saint Richard indicates that every year the Jews commit one such murder on the eve of Passover, *Fortalitium*, III, consideratio vii, punctus 3, crudelitas 2, fol. 123^{r-v}.

account of their deicide, Jews were subject to great sufferings that would cease only when they admitted the blood crime committed against Christ. This suffering could only be palliated by the blood of Christians and each year Jewish communities decided by lot who would murder a Christian to obtain the required blood.[78] Other crimes demonstrated that Jews saw social interactions with Christians only as a means to harm them and the faith. They encouraged their Christian servants to judaize and to misuse sacred vessels; they enacted violent revenges on their neighbours; they practiced medicine to harm and kill their patients; and they oppressed rich and poor alike through usury.[79] Such stories denied Jews any useful function in society and portrayed their actions as motivated only by cruelty, self-interest, and criminality. Exemplary punishment for Jewish crimes was expected from good rulers and Espina mentions approvingly a number of penalties visited on entire communities after crimes perpetrated by only some of their members.[80]

Espina's examples also underlined that all Christians were threatened by Jewish attacks. Not only did the Jews target Christ and the faith itself, but also no individual Christian could be safe from their hatred. Though Jews actively plotted and schemed, their crimes could also be opportunistic and their victims chosen at random. In the village of Távara in 1457 two Jews had tried unsuccessfully to murder two children who happened to be playing alone in an isolated area.[81] In the same village, a Jew who wished to

---

[78] *Fortalitium*, III, consideratio vii, punctus 3, crudelitas 5, fols 124^v. Meyuhas Ginio, *De bello*, pp. 65–66. On the symbolic nature of blood as definer of the Christian community and object of veneration, see Caroline Walker Bynum, *Wonderful Blood: Theology and Practice in Late Medieval Northern Germany and Beyond* (Philadelphia: University of Pennsylvania Press, 2007).

[79] Encouragement of Christian servants to judaize and misuse sacred vessels: *Fortalitium*, III, consideratio vii, punctus 3, crudelitas 2, fol. 123^{r-v}; enactment of violent revenge on neighbours: crudelitas 10, fol. 125^v; practice of medicine for murderous purposes: crudelitas 13, fols 126^v–127^r; usury: crudelitas 17, fol. 129^{r-v}.

[80] For instance by the King of France in cruelties 2–4 (expulsions, mass executions); the margrave of Baden in cruelty 5 (mass executions) and the German emperors in cruelties 6–7 (mass executions); and the lord of Távara in cruelty 10 (executions), *Fortalitium*, III, consideratio vii, punctus 3, crudelitates 2–7, fols 123^r–124^v; crudelitas 10, fol. 125^v.

[81] *Fortalitium*, III, consideratio vii, punctus 3, crudelitas 12, fol. 126^{r-v}. See also Meyuhas Ginio, *De bello*, p. 70.

take revenge for the execution of his criminal son, attacked all his Christian neighbours, spreading caltrops on the street, locking the doors of houses and setting fire to them so that those who were not burned alive injured themselves while trying to escape.[82] The poisoning of wells and springs were likewise indiscriminate and whole cities could suffer at the hands of Jews.[83] Espina invoked the well-known episode of the Jews betraying the city of Toledo to Muslim invaders during the time of King Rodrigo. The Jews treacherously allowed the enemy into the city, whereby it was conquered without fight and all Christian inhabitants were murdered.[84] The meaning of such accounts was clear: no one could be safe as long as Jews lived with impunity amid Christians.

If all were threatened by the continued presence of Jews, nevertheless Espina insisted that the danger was particularly acute for rulers, whose interactions with Jews could threaten the safety of the whole kingdom.[85] He invoked two examples from Castilian history to demonstrate that when monarchs associated with Jews they placed their entire kingdom in danger. Thus, under the influence of two Jewish advisors, Pedro I had ruled tyrannically and in consequence was murdered by his brother Enrique in Montiel. Similarly, Alfonso VIII came under the influence of a Jewish concubine and so isolated himself from his subjects. His misrule came to an end only when the concubine was murdered by a group of noblemen.[86] Though complaints about Jewish influence on

---

[82] *Fortalitium*, III, consideratio vii, punctus 3, crudelitas 10, fol. 125ᵛ. See also Meyuhas Ginio, *De bello*, pp. 68–69. On anti-Semitic legends in Távara: Rafael Ramos, '"Que si a Távara passáis vós serés apedreado por hebreo": una nota a la poesía del Comendador Román', *Hispanic Research Journal*, 10 (2009), 193–205.

[83] *Fortalitium*, III, consideratio vii, punctus 3, crudelitas 6, fol. 124ᵛ.

[84] *Fortalitium*, III, consideratio vii, punctus 3, crudelitas 1, fol. 123ʳ. Cf. the use of this accusation by the Toledan rebels of 1449, see Vidal Doval, 'Nos soli sumus christiani', in *Medieval Hispanic Studies*, ed. by Beresford, Haywood and Weiss, p. 229.

[85] *Fortalitium*, III, consideratio vii, punctus 3, crudelitas 14, fol. 127ʳ⁻ᵛ: 'O quam periculosa est conuersacio Iudeorum Christianis omnibus specialiter magnatibus et regibus. [...] Non ergo possum approbare conuersacionem Christianorum cum Iudeis specialiter magnatum, prelatorum et regum cum tot mala exempla et pericula non solum corpum sed etiam animarum et rei publice legamus et experiamur.'

[86] *Fortalitium*, III, consideratio vii, punctus 3, crudelitas 14, fol. 127ᵛ. On the accusations that Peter favoured the Jews: Clara Estow, *Pedro the Cruel of Castile, 1350–1369* (Leiden: Brill, 1995), pp. 154–79. On Alfonso's

monarchs were a common means of expressing discontent about a ruler's actions or justifying rebellion, Espina reversed the causality: the presence of Jews near the person of the monarch was the cause of tyranny and misrule.[87]

Christian Responses

The implications of the material assembled by Espina in considerations i–viii of Book III were easily comprehensible but far-reaching in their effects. The current religious status quo in Castile had failed. The Jews were and always had been a people apart, entirely alien to Castile and pitted against the Christian majority. The Augustinian-inspired ideals of toleration, permitting the Jews to live alongside Christians albeit 'subject to a special and oppressively restricted legal status', were no longer working.[88] Jews refused to accept their inferior place in society and plotted constantly to harm and overthrow Christian order.

In considerations ix–xi Espina set out the attempts that had been made to deal with the Jewish problem in the past: expulsion, conversion, and legislation. Though he drew on examples from across Christendom, Espina devoted particular attention to the Visigothic past as a model for contemporary monarchy and society.[89] Such allowed him to demonstrate that there were precedents within Castilian history for the policies and actions he was advocating.[90] As he had done elsewhere in *Fortalitium fidei*,

concubine and political uses of accusations of philosemitism: David Nirenberg, 'Deviant Politics and Jewish Love: Alfonso VIII and the Jewess of Toledo', *Jewish History*, 21 (2007), 15–41.

[87] On accusations of undue Jewish influence on monarchs as justifications for rebellion, see Nirenberg, 'Figures of Thought', pp. 421–22. On the application of such rhetoric to *conversos* by the Toledan rebels of 1449, see Vidal Doval, 'Nos soli sumus christiani', in *Medieval Hispanic Studies*, ed. by Beresford, Haywood and Weiss, pp. 222–23.

[88] Mark R. Cohen, 'Anti-Jewish Violence and the Place of the Jews in Christendom and in Islam: A Paradigm', in *Religious Violence between Christians and Jews: Medieval Roots, Modern Perspectives*, ed. by Anna Sapir Abulafia (Basingstoke: Palgrave, 2002), pp. 107–37 (pp. 113–14).

[89] On the treatment of Jews under the Visigothic monarchy, see Rachel L. Stocking, 'Early Medieval Christian Identity and Anti-Judaism: The Case of the Visigothic Kingdom', *Religion Compass*, 2 (2008), 642–58 <DOI: 10.1111/j.1749-8171.2008.00087.x>, and bibliography therein.

[90] See Echevarria, *The Fortress of Faith*, pp. 119–21 for a discussion of the role of history in *Fortalitium fidei*.

Espina presented his radical programme of reforms in terms of restoration and return. Moreover, the Gothic past had long been invoked as one of the sources of national identity in Castile and in the fifteenth century, through works such as Alonso de Cartagena's *Anacephaleosis*, it had become one of the central ideological pillars of the Castilian monarchy.[91] Likewise, the significance and meaning of Visigothic legislation concerning Jews had been much debated in the context of the Toledo revolt of 1449.[92]

Espina's discussion of historical expulsions of Jews explored four examples: the Roman destruction of Jerusalem and the Second Temple; the expelling of the Jews from France at the time of Philip IV; their expulsion from England; and their expulsion from Spain during the reign of King Sisebuto. If Espina did not openly advocate the expulsion of Jews from Castile, the arrangement of his material and the information that was included suggest that he was advancing this as a solution worth contemplating, particularly for insincere converts.[93] Though the crimes that had lead Philip to expel the Jews from France were the same offences Espina claimed contemporary Jews in Spain were perpetrating, it was in his discussion of the expulsion of English Jews that Espina made the comparison with Castile explicit.[94] Espina gave two reasons for this expulsion – actually extermination in his account. The first was the ritual murder of a child in Lincoln – presumably 'Little' St Hugh though Espina gives his name as 'Alfonsus'. The second related to a mass conversion of Jews. On the advice of his counsellors, an unnamed king of England had forced all Jews to be baptized in order to avert the disasters that God was inflicting upon the

---

[91] Fernández Gallardo, *Alonso de Cartagena (1385–1456)*, pp. 303–19. On *letrado* uses of the Visigothic past in the fifteenth century, see Seidenspinner-Nuñez, 'Conversion', in *Christians, Muslims, and Jews*, ed. by Meyerson and English, pp. 242–47.

[92] Vidal Doval, 'La matriz medieval', in *Disidencia religiosa*, ed. by García Pinilla. See also Francisco Francisco Márquez Villanueva, 'Sobre el concepto de judaizante', in *De la España judeoconversa: doce estudios*, Serie General Universitaria, 57 (Barcelona: Edicions Bellaterra, 2006), pp. 95–114 (at p. 96) [first pub. in *'Encuentros' and 'Desencuentros': Spanish Jewish Cultural Interaction through History*, ed. by Carlos Carrete Parrondo and others (Tel Aviv: University Publishing Projects, 2000), pp. 519–42].

[93] For a stronger statement of Espina's attitude towards expulsion from Castile, see Meyuhas Ginio, *De bello*, p. 61.

[94] *Fortalitium*, III, consideratio ix, expulsiones 2–3, fols 142ᵛ–144ᵛ. See also Meyuhas Ginio, *De bello*, pp. 80–81.

kingdom in punishment for all their crimes and unbelief. When the wars, hunger, and plague did not cease, the king was advised to test the sincerity of the Jews' conversion. His advisers claimed that after baptism the former Jews were committing worse crimes than before and had risen so far in their fortunes that the Christians were almost their captives. The monarch ordered two tents be put up by the shore; in one they placed a Torah, in the other a cross and he offered the converts a free choice between them. They all rushed rejoicing towards the tent with the Torah and as they entered it they were killed and their bodies then thrown in the sea. Thus England was purged of their influence and the calamities that afflicted the kingdom ceased. Espina concluded the account by observing that the Spanish should see whether there was not a similar, ever-growing plague in Spain.[95]

This story seems to have originated with Espina himself and was surely intended as a thinly disguised allegory of the current situation in Castile – a kingdom sliding towards civil war and anarchy with an ever-growing *converso* problem. Crucially in this account, the advisers that had interpreted the sign and proposed the remedies were religious men ('seruos dei'), the very position that Espina claimed for himself and his order. The converts themselves were depicted in terms reminiscent of anti-*converso* writings, being accused of religious insincerity and using their rapid social advancement to oppress Christians.[96] The implication that expulsion was an appropriate solution to the Jewish problem in Castile, particularly the issue of *conversos*, was reinforced by the final account of the expelling of Jews, that during the Visigothic period. Espina recounted how King Sisebuto had compelled the Jews to convert to Christianity and, seeming to conflate his reign with that of Chintila, subsequently expelled them from Spain only for them to be permitted to return by a later monarch. Espina noted the rewards Sisebuto had gained from his actions and contrasted these with the ill luck suffered by his successor.[97] The logic was implicit but clear. England had regained its prosperity

---

[95] *Fortalitium*, III, consideratio ix, expulsio 3, fol. 144ᵛ: 'videant hispani si similis plaga viget et continuo inter eos crescat.'

[96] In the *Sentencia* (pp. 24–27) of 1449 the Toledo rebels had accused *conversos* of the very same crimes: keeping the Mosaic Law and using public office and any other means available to them to oppress Christians.

[97] *Fortalitium*, III, consideratio ix, expulsio 4, fol. 144ᵛ–145ʳ. See also Meyuhas Ginio, *De bello*, p. 81.

after getting rid of its converted Jews and the Visigothic past both confirmed this causality and provided a clear Spanish precedent.

These examples also demonstrated clearly the problems presented by conversion. Was it possible for Jews to convert sincerely? Could they be brought to embrace the truth of Christianity? When discussing the faulty hermeneutics of the Jews, Espina allowed for the small, remote possibility that Jews might be healed of the blindness that prevented them from reading Scripture spiritually. He listed prayer, preaching, and mild persecution as possible means to bring about this change in attitude.[98] Yet such relied on their acceptance of a spiritual cure akin to that they had already rejected during the time of Christ and the Apostles. When Espina returned to the subject of conversion in considerations x and xii his material reinforced the same message. Though some individual Jews might eventually be brought to the faith, genuine mass conversions were highly unlikely, if not altogether impossible.

The account of eleven miracles that comprises consideration x underlines the obduracy and iniquity of Jews, painting a bleak picture of their prospects for conversion.[99] There were, to be sure, individuals capable of sincerely embracing Christianity – the Jew of Constantinople who converted after the sacred image that he stabbed began to bleed or the Jewess in Segovia unjustly punished for adultery and subsequently saved from death by the Virgin Mary – but the great majority refused to believe even after witnessing these and other miracles, preferring instead to cling to their erroneous expectation of a messiah.[100] Likewise, the Jews did not hesitate to punish cruelly anyone who showed an inclination towards Christianity, such as the father who threw his son into an oven after the boy had received communion.[101] Even when they did seek baptism, Jews did not exhibit a sincere desire for conversion. Espina's list of

---

[98] *Fortalitium*, III, consideratio i, fol. 72^{r-v}.

[99] *Fortalitium*, III, consideratio x, fols 145^r–147^r. Note that there is a mistake in the layout of the *editio princeps*: miracles 11 and 2 are missing from the main body of the text and have been inserted after the table of contents at fol. 8^{r-v}.

[100] *Fortalitium*, III, consideratio x, miracula 6 (Jew of Constantinople), 8 (Jewess of Segovia), fol. 146^r.

[101] *Fortalitium*, III, consideratio x, miraculum 3, fol. 145^r. Espina seems to follow Bernardino of Siena's line with regard to conversion. Bernardino was skeptical of the capability of Jews to convert and never sought to bring them to Christianity, seeking instead to isolate them and render them invisible. Furthermore, he regarded converts from Judaism, which he labelled 'baptized Jews', as fundamentally unstrustworthy. See Mormando, pp. 196, 200, 216.

miracles opens with water disappearing from a font when approached by a Jew seeking baptism, thus revealing his perfidy.[102]

In consideration xii 'How God will Redeem the Jews', Espina returned again to the issue of Jewish unbelief, outlining four reasons why they continued to refuse to convert to Christianity. Alongside their failure to read properly both the Talmud and Scripture, Espina argued that familial ties among the Jews were so strong as to deter conversion among the few who sought it. Not only would embracing Christianity mean abandoning their families – Espina gives the example of a wise Jew who, despite recognizing the truth of Christianity, feared that if he converted his father would die of a broken heart – but those very relatives would seek to hinder conversion and to drag them back to Judaism. The avaricious nature of the Jews also inhibited conversion for becoming Christian meant abandoning usury and the supposedly easy wealth it promised. Mired in sin, bound by family ties, and impeded by their very nature, the prospect for the sincere conversion of Jews was minimal.[103]

Minimal, but not impossible and Christians were obliged, however doubtful they may be about the sincerity of the act, to receive converted Jews into the faith. Though Espina claimed many Jews accepted baptism as a means of obtaining material benefits, nevertheless through practising Christianity and through the grace of God they or, more likely, their descendants might eventually come to embrace the truth of Christianity and be saved.[104] Nonetheless, Espina asserts that the problem of dishonesty ought to be addressed during the catechumenate. This period should be long enough to deter the insincere catechumen, who would wish to rush through the preparation, but not so long as to allow the sincere to be tempted to relapse. Espina suggests eight months to be the ideal

---

[102] *Fortalitium*, III, consideratio x, miraculum 1, fol. 145^r: 'perfidiam demonstrauit'.

[103] *Fortalitium*, III, consideratio xii, punctus 2, fols 152^v–153^v. See also McMichael, 'The End of the World', pp. 245–47.

[104] *Fortalitium*, III, consideratio xii, punctus 2, fol. 153^v: 'propter lucrum temporale tales baptizati sunt'. For general discussion of the insincerity of neophytes of Jewish origin, see Jonathan M. Elukin, 'From Jew to Christian? Conversion and Immutability in Medieval Europe', in *Varieties of Religious Conversion in the Middle Ages*, ed. by James Muldoon (Gainesville: University Press of Florida, 1997), pp. 171–89; Rubin, pp. 85–87. For a more general discussion of ulterior motives for conversion, see John Van Engen, 'Christening the Romans', *Traditio*, 52 (1997), 1–45 (p. 38).

period. Even after the completion of the catechumenate, the baptizand should be accepted at the font only with 'great caution'.[105] The point for Espina was that although baptism as a sacrament could confer God's grace on the recipient, 'since true faith is born of good will, everything is therefore centred on the will of the Jew'.[106] As Thomas Aquinas had established, for baptism to offer justification to the recipient, he or she would have to embrace baptism and its effect – insincerity blocked its grace and virtue.[107]

Espina also grappled with the question of the lawfulness of the baptism of Jewish children without their parents consent. Though he notes that Aquinas and other authorities had rejected such a practice, Espina followed John Duns Scotus in asserting that it was not only licit but also desirable. Just as a monarch might demand children be separated from their parents to serve in the army, so a ruler could compel the baptism of infants if that might bring them to salvation. Again, following Scotus, Espina argued that even the forced baptism of adults could be permissible: it was better for Jews to be compelled towards good behaviour than to commit evil with impunity as they were accustomed to do. Against claims that the Church should not actively seek the conversion of the Jews because a remnant of them would be converted at the End of Time, Espina invoked Scotus' notion that all that was required for this to happen was that a small number of Jews survived on 'some island' (*aliqua insula*) somewhere.[108] Again, though it is not spelled out, the implication of such a statement is clear: there was no theological reason for the presence of Jews in Castile. Even if there remained no Jews in Europe, enough would survive in the world to fulfil the Biblical prophecy. As Espina demonstrated at the end of Book III,

---

[105] McMichael, 'The End of the World', p. 248. Cf. *Fortalitium*, III, consideratio xii, punctus 3, fol. 153ᵛ.

[106] McMichael, 'The End of the World', p. 247. Cf. *Fortalitium fidei*, III, consideratio xii, punctus 2, fol. 153ᵛ.

[107] Thomas Aquinas quoted Augustine who distinguished four types of insincerity: lack of belief, scorn for the sacrament itself, being baptized under an unapproved rite, and through lack of devotion, Thomas Aquinas, *Summa Theologiae*, in *Corpus Thomisticum*, <http://www.corpusthomisticum.org/sth4066.html> [accessed 6 September 2012], 3a 69. 9.

[108] *Fortalitium fidei*, III, consideratio xii, punctus 4, fols 153ᵛ–154ʳ. See also McMichael, 'The End of the World', pp. 248–49. On Scotus' position, see Turner, 'Jewish Witness', in *Christian Attitudes*, ed. by Frasetto, pp. 196–200. Note that Espina did not follow Scotus' more positive assessment of Mosaic Law.

the sons of Israel were imprisoned in the Caspian Mountains and would return to Jerusalem at the End of Days.[109]

Alongside expulsion and conversion, Espina set out the role legislation could play in the amelioration of the Jewish problem.[110] Throughout eight considerations, Espina explored in detail the conditions for Jews living amid Christians set out in canon and civil codes. He produced a comprehensive review that touched upon most aspects of Jewish life: the practice of their religion and their relationship with the Christian cult; social and economic interactions with Christians; the marking of their inferior status, be it through distinctive clothing or through certain prohibitions that would deny them any authority over Christians. Castilian royal ordinances were discussed in some detail, particularly the *Leyes de Ayllón* passed in 1414 during the minority of Juan II at the instigation of Vincent Ferrer.[111] Although largely a compilation of earlier laws, the *Leyes de Ayllón* were a significant step in the oppression of Jewish and Muslim communities in Castile, redefining their relationship with the Christian majority and dismantling the principle of coexistence. So restrictive was this legislation, both socially and economically, that the viability of many Jewish communities was severely compromised and significant number of Jews sought baptism. The excessively oppressive nature of this legislation was quickly recognised; it soon ceased to be enforced and was revoked by the *Consejo Real* in 1418.[112] In effect, Espina was holding up the precedent of the most restrictive legislation that had been enacted in Castile and was demanding its reinstatement.

In discussing existing legislation, Espina concentrated particularly on the sanctions for false conversion and the measures that could be put in place to prevent new converts from lapsing. Among items prohibiting social contacts between Christians and Jews were two admonitions concerning *conversos*. Espina labels them 'Jews

---

[109] *Fortalitium*, III, consideratio xii, punctus 6, fol. 154^v.

[110] *Fortalitium*, III, consideratio xi, fols 147^r–152^v.

[111] On Espina's discussion of the *Leyes de Ayllón*, see *Fortalitium*, III, consideratio xi, articulus 7, fols 149^r–151^v.

[112] On the *Leyes de Ayllón*, see Ana Echevarría, 'Catalina of Lancaster, the Castilian Monarchy and Coexistence', in *Medieval Spain: Culture, Conflict and Coexistence, Studies in Honour of Angus MacKay*, ed. by Roger Collins and Anthony Goodman (Basingstoke: Palgrave Macmillan, 2002), pp. 79–122 (pp. 98–102).

converted to the faith' ('Iudei conversi ad fidem') and notes particularly that they were forbidden from any contact with 'the other Jews' ('aliis Iudeis') for fear that they may be corrupted. Similarly, children of Jews or of converts ('conuersi') ought to be separated from their parents to avoid being corrupted and should instead be raised in a monastery or adopted by good Christians.[113] Even those who had converted with sincere intent were at risk from social and cultural contacts with Jews and even after conversion parents could still put at risk their children's faith.[114] Elsewhere in Book III, Espina discussed the punishments meted out to Jews 'who returned to their vomit', holding up the Visigothic *Fuero Juzgo* as the model.[115] This code had decreed confiscation of property and death as the appropriate punishment for converted Jews who returned to Judaism or for any Christian who undertook Jewish rituals.

Nor, according to Espina, was it just royal legislation that decreed such punishments: the Jews themselves had agreed to these measures. Espina gives the example of the Jewish community of Toledo who had entered into a legal agreement to convert to Christianity with the seventh-century king, Sisenando.[116] As part of this contract they pledged to observe Christianity faithfully and to sever all ties with other Jews and with Judaism. If they failed to uphold these pledges, they agreed to the penalty of death or, if the

---

[113] *Fortalitium*, III, consideratio xi, articulus 4, fol. 148^(r–v).

[114] Contact between neophytes and their former correligionists was a long-standing concern. Bernard Gui, in his *Practica inquisitionis heretice pravitatis*, quoted in Cohen, *The Friars*, pp. 90–91, speaks of the need to prevent interaction with Jews to prevent converts relapsing into Judaism. Vincent Ferrer had insisted greatly on the need for all Christians to avoid any contact with Jews. As he put it: 'Car nunqua será bon christià, lo qui és vehí de juheu', quoted in David Nirenberg, 'Une société face à l'alterité: juifs et chrétiens dans la Péninsule Ibérique 1391–1449', *Annales. Histoire, Sciences Sociales*, 62 (2007), 755–90 (p. 769 n42).

[115] *Fortalitium*, III, consideratio xii, punctus 5, fol. 154^r: 'iudei conuersi redeuntes ad vomitum iudaysmi'. On this section, see Alisa Meyuhas Ginio, 'El concepto de "perfidia judaica" de la época visigoda en la perspectiva castellana del siglo XV', *Helmántica*, 46 (1995), 299–311.

[116] *Fortalitium*, III, consideratio xii, punctus 5, fol. 154^(r–v). See also Meyuhas Ginio, *De bello*, pp. 96–97. Note this is probably Chintila, see Bernard S. Bachrach, *Early Medieval Jewish Policy in Western Europe* (Minneapolis: University of Minnesota Press, 1977), p. 13. Cartagena seems to refer to the same document although he attributed it to Recesindo, *Defensorium*, II, theorema 4, xxxii, 261.

monarch was inclined to clemency, penal servitude and confiscation of property. Though a local agreement, Espina argued it to be binding on all Jews in Spain who underwent conversion, for Toledo was the imperial city. Thus judaizers broke both the laws of the kingdom and their own contract. Espina concludes this passage with the observation that were an inquisition to be carried out now, innumerable fires would smoke with the bodies of those apprehended in their judaizing.[117]

It was in his discussions of legislation that Espina provided the most detail concerning the situation in contemporary Castile and was most explicit about his vision of the extent of the *converso* problem. In the final sections of consideration xi, Espina lamented that many Christians had converted to Judaism or, rather, many Christians who secretly had been Jews now carried out the commandments of Mosaic Law openly, some were even circumcised. Other supposed Christians embraced Islam, becoming Saracens. At the same time, the Jews were stripping the kingdom of its wealth and damaging the body politic and yet were still protected by certain nobles and courtiers. Invoking once again the Arab conquest of Spain and the fate that had befallen King Rodrigo, Espina warned of the dangers to the rulers and to the kingdom if this situation were allowed to go on unchecked. The state of affairs in Castile was singularly dire – none in France or England, Espina noted, suffered at the hands of the Jews in the same way Castilians did. Even the Saracens took the crimes of Jews more seriously and punished them more harshly than rulers in Spain.

At the close of consideration xi, in the closest he came to programmatic statement of action, Espina called on popes, kings, and princes to enforce the legislation and to return the Jews to their proper state of servitude. What Espina meant by servitude was underlined by a succession of Biblical quotations. Citing Deuteronomy 23 (*recte* 28), the Jews were to 'serve thy enemy, whom the Lord will send upon thee, in hunger, and thirst, and nakedness, and in want of all things: and he shall put an iron yoke upon thy neck, till he consume thee' (28.48). For each and every Jew

---

[117] *Fortalitium*, III, consideratio xii, punctus 5, fol. 154ᵛ: 'Credo quod si vera fieret inquisicio presertim isto tempore quod innumerabiles ignibus traderentur de hiis qui iudaizare realiter inuenirentur'.

life shall be as it were hanging before thee. Thou shalt fear night and day, neither shalt thou trust thy life. In the morning thou shalt say: Who will grant me evening? and at evening: Who will grant me morning? for the fearfulness of thy heart, wherewith thou shalt be terrified, and for those things which thou shalt see with thy eyes.' (28.66-67)

It was not intended that Jews should live freely and without restraint and allowing them do so, Espina asserted, led them to rebel and was the cause of the disasters that had descended upon the kingdom.[118]

*

Across Books I and III, Espina sought to marginalize the role of Jews in salvation history and to dilute the exclusivity of the bond they had enjoyed with God before the Incarnation. Mosaic Law had been limited and preparatory and was entirely superseded after the Passion; even before the Coming of Christ it had not been the exclusive path to salvation. When Mosaic Law had been an obligation upon them, the Jews' observance of it had been imperfect and dilatory, once the obligation had ceased they clung to it blindly. Within the Old Testament Espina could detect two separate lineages: one line was the righteous of Israel, its prophets and saints, the heirs of Isaac and the forebears of Christians, the other line was the sinful and faithless, the heirs of Ishmael and the forebears of the Jews.

From such ancestry sprung contemporary Jews, oblivious to the spiritual truth of their own scriptures and caught in an ever-tightening spiral of blindness and carnality. Hating Christianity and despising Christians, Jews were guilty of terrible crimes and threatened the stability of the whole kingdom. It was, however, the false or relapsed converts who presented the most serious danger and it was for these whom Espina reserved the harshest punishments. Though he explored four historical expulsions of Jews, it was the English expulsion – that of insincere converts – that Espina held up for emulation. Likewise, when Espina wrote of the flames of numerous pyres, they were burning the bodies of judaizers. After the worst elements had been excised, the rest of the Jews might be permitted to remain in Christian society. Though Espina had allowed for the possibility of a Castile free from Jews, in the last resort it was their return to a state of servitude and penury that he

---

[118] *Fortalitium*, III, consideratio xi, articulus 8, fols 151^v–152^v. See also Meyuhas Ginio, *De bello*, pp. 92–93

espoused not their expulsion or execution. Powerless, destitute, and living in fear, the Jews would no longer threaten Christian society.

FROM CONVERTS TO JUDAIZERS

Given the importance afforded to *Fortalitium fidei* by modern scholars of the *converso* problem, Espina says surprisingly little about New Christians in his work. Of the five Books that make up the work, *conversos* feature prominently only in Books II and III. As has been seen, he reserves for them the harshest and most draconian punishments outlined in Book III but the most systematic treatment of *conversos* occurs in Book II under the heading of heresy.[1] Even here, Espina adds relatively little new material to that which was already circulating. What is significant in Espina's account of New Christians was the size and scope of the problems he saw and thus the sense of urgency that he lent to the situation. Whereas authors such as Torquemada had written of isolated cases and individual error, Espina insisted on the collective and organized nature of *converso* judaizing – it was a dangerous and widespread heresy.

All parties in the *converso* debate accepted the existence of behaviours that they labelled judaizing. What was contested was the meaning of the term – what, exactly, was judaizing, how did a Christian behave like or resemble a Jew – and the extent and significance of the problem. In Book II, Espina sought to provide as broad a definition as possible, encompassing a wide range of behaviours and beliefs, a number of which would seem to have only a tangential connection with the practice of Judaism. The significance of such behaviours was clear – they amounted to the conscious rejection of Christ. As Espina had established in Book I, Mosaic Law and, indeed, the Jews as a people had existed to prepare the way for the Messiah; adherence to Mosaic Law or other Jewish practices after the Passion was thus a denial of Christ. Throughout *Fortalitium fidei*, Espina sought to present the religious situation of Castile in simple, polarized terms. With *conversos*, he rendered a complex social and religious reality in stark and unambiguous terms: those who engaged in judaizing of any kind were consciously and fully rejecting the Law of Christ.

---

[1] For a general study of Book II, see Meyuhas Ginio, *La forteresse*, pp. 112–32

The Problem of Judaizing

The accusation of judaizing was at the root of anti-*converso* polemic. It was invoked by the enemies of New Christians as both cause and proof of *converso* criminality and the charge of judaizing was employed to construct an enduring Jewish status for neophytes and their descendants and to justify their exclusion and discrimination. The anti-*converso* texts produced by the Toledan rebels used the term to describe the religious practices of New Christians, seeking to create an identity between the sociological category of *converso* and the religious one of heretical judaizer.[2] The *Sentencia-Estatuto* claimed *conversos* to be 'sospechosos en la fe de nuestro Señor e Salvador Ihesu Christo, en la qual frecuentemente vomitan de ligero judaizando, [...] guardando los ritos e çeremonias de la ley vieja'.[3] The *Memorial*, similarly, insisted *conversos* to be guilty of 'judaizar e guardar todas las çeremonias judaicas e ayunando los días de ayunos introductos por la ley mosaica y guardando los sábados'.[4] Excluding these *conversos* from office was justified, according to the *Memorial*, by the stance taken by the Apostle Paul in his letter to the Emperor [*sic*] Titus. The rebels read this letter as excluding from office converts from the lineage of Jews on account of their inherent bad character: 'porque naturalmente son malos, vindicativos, infieles, adúlteros, soberbios, vanagloriosos e de todas malas costumbres doctados.'[5]

The accusations made in these texts covered a wide array of beliefs and behaviours, ranging from the fulfilment of essential precepts of Judaism, such as circumcision and keeping the Sabbath, to broader cultural practices, such as taking the belts of pregnant women to the synagogue to aid in their childbirth. Accompanying these activities was the explicit rejection of Christianity, a lack of piety and frequent blasphemy, and hostility towards Old Christians. *Conversos* were accused of denying the divinity of Christ and Mary, of impugning the truth of Christian doctrine, and of seizing any opportunity to harm Christians or insult the faith.[6] For the Toledan rebels, judaizing meant heresy and the rejection of

---

[2] Márquez Villanueva, 'Sobre el concepto de judaizante', p. 98.

[3] *Sentencia*, pp. 23–24.

[4] *Memorial*, p. 214.

[5] *Memorial*, pp. 218–219.

[6] *Sentencia*, pp. 24–25, and, for a longer version of the list of *converso* errors, see *Memorial*, p. 214.

Christian doctrine and practice in favour of Jewish ones; *conversos* were nothing but 'judíos bautiçados'.[7]

By labelling behaviour or individuals as 'judaizing', the Toledan rebels were privileging one particular interpretation of phenomena that could have a range of causes, meanings, and motivations. Gavin Langmuir drew a distinction between religion and religiosity. The former was 'what people are commanded to believe by those exercising social authority', the latter was 'what individuals do in fact believe about themselves and their universe — which can vary greatly and may or may not be in harmony with what they have been told to believe'.[8] If certain *conversos* erred in their religious observances that need not imply they thought themselves to be anything other than good Christians.[9] Furthermore, cultural practices — such as the changing of clothes and house linen on Saturdays or certain dietary habits — could be ascribed a religious significance that they were in truth lacking.[10] This would all be

[7] *Memorial* p. 203.

[8] Gavin I. Langmuir, 'The Transformation of Anti-Judaism', in *Toward a Definition of Antisemitism* (Berkeley: University of California Press, 1990), pp. 63–99, 362–65, (p. 65).

[9] Rosenstock, *New Men*, pp. 74–75. For the suggestion that some *conversos* may have judged judaizing as congruent with Christianity, see p. 81.

[10] Márquez Villanueva, 'Sobre el concepto de judaizante', pp. 104–5. From the earliest days of the Church there had been an acknowledgement of the complexities of conversion, involving as it did a change in a person's belief system and a process of acculturation that encompassed aspects such as diet, dress or behaviour. See Robert Markus, *The End of Ancient Christianity* (Cambridge: Cambridge University Press, 1990), p. 5. Such was, at times, recognised in fifteenth-century Spain, see the case of Hernando de Talavera discussed with regard to Muslims by Roger Highfield, 'Christians, Jews and Muslims in the Same Society: The Fall of *Convivencia* in Medieval Spain', in *Religious Motivation: Biographical and Sociological Problems for the Church Historian*, ed. by Derek Baker, Studies in Church History, 15 (Oxford: Published for the Ecclesiastical History Society by Basil Blackwell, 1978), pp. 121–46, (pp. 139–40), and with regard to *conversos* by Felipe Pereda, *Las imágenes de la discordia: política y poética de la imagen sagrada en la España del cuatrocientos* (Madrid: Marcial Pons, 2007), pp. 42–43. See also the comments about how anxieties about representations of the deity suggest a response towards the religious sensibility of *conversos*, Tom Nickson, 'The First Murder: Picturing Polemic c. 1391', in *The Hebrew Bible in Fifteenth-Century Spain: Exegesis, Literature, Philosophy, and the Arts*, ed. by Jonathan Decter and Arturo Prats, Études sur le Judaïsme Médiéval, 54 (Leiden: Brill, 2012), pp. 41–59, 279–81; and idem, 'Reframing the Bible: Genesis and Exodus on Toledo Cathedral's Fourteenth-Century Choir Screen', *Gesta*, 50 (2011), 71–89.

compounded by extremely low standards of religious instruction amongst both clergy and laity. Erroneous beliefs, defective religious observances, and superstitions were extremely common and careful scrutiny of any community of the faithful would inevitably expose heterodoxy.[11]

Against this complexity, the rebels insisted that these phenomena amounted to heresy and simply and unambiguously signalled Jewishness and Judaism, allowing the full force of medieval anti-Semitic discourse to be brought to bear on *conversos*. Such accusations were activated in individuals through genealogy: 'judaizers were to be identified by their behavior, but that behavior only gained meaning in light of their flesh's ideology'.[12] Errors only became proof of judaizing, only acquired their full heretical interpretation, when they were associated with Jewish descent. At its fullest extent, in this form of anti-*converso* discrimination an individual's genealogy was sufficient to attach a marker of heresy to his or her behaviour.[13]

Pro-*converso* authors employed the accusation of judaizing to make very different points. Though they accepted there had been instances of religious error among *conversos* in Toledo, they disagreed as to whether these amounted to heresy. Cartagena acknowledged the possibility that some *conversos* returned to Judaism after their baptism, proposing inquisition as the means to root out any such judaizing.[14] Oropesa, drawing on his own experience as an inquisitor in Toledo, wrote of certain *conversos* returning to Judaism, strongly implying such to be heresy.[15] Torquemada, by contrast, rejected all accusations of heresy. Though some *conversos* may have continued to practice certain Jewish rites, such was individual error and not heresy.[16] Both Cartagena and Torquemada

[11] Márquez Villanueva, 'Sobre el concepto de judaizante', pp. 107–8.

[12] Nirenberg, 'Was there race before modernity?', p. 259. On perceptions of individuals as *conversos* on the basis of their genealogy, see also Jean Pierre Dedieu, '¿Pecado original o pecado social? Reflexiones en torno a la constitución y a la definición del grupo judeo-converso en Castilla', *Manuscrits*, 10 (1992), 61–76 (particularly pp. 63–70).

[13] For a wider discussion of this exclusionary logic, see Vidal Doval, 'Nos soli sumus christiani', in *Medieval Hispanic Studies*, ed. by Beresford, Haywood and Weiss, pp. 225–32.

[14] *Defensorium*, III, ix, 294.

[15] *Lumen*, xxiv, 274.

[16] *Tractatus*, xii, 3, 192. See also Chapter 2, pp. 42–44.

also contested the rebels' reading of Paul's letter to Titus. For Cartagena, the letter showed Paul to be more concerned with those who would sow dissension and disunity amongst the Christian population of Crete than with those who practiced circumcision. Torquemada condemned what he saw as the faulty reading of Paul's words: to claim all Christians of Jewish descent to be of bad character was itself sinful and marked out a person as a pseudo-Christian.[17]

Pro-*converso* authors turned accusations of judaizing against the Toledan rebels, privileging a metaphorical interpretation of the term over a literal one.[18] For Cartagena and Oropesa, a judaizer was less someone who clung to Mosaic Law and the practice of circumcision after baptism and more a Christian who sought to break the unity of the faithful. Thus Oropesa accused Old Christians of lowering the Church to the level of the synagogue; by seeking to exclude *conversos* from office because of their Jewish descent, Old Christians were behaving like the ancient Israelites who sought to restrict certain offices to certain lineages.[19] Cartagena charged Marcos García de Mora, the ideologue of the Toledan rebels and the author of the *Memorial*, with reading like a Jew, of spiritual judaizing in his interpretation of texts.[20] Mora had defended the exclusion of *conversos* from office on the basis of what Cartagena termed a literal reading of Visigothic conciliar legislation. Where Mora had understood the legislation to refer to anyone of Jewish descent, for Cartagena it was a reference to

---

[17] *Defensorium*, III, i, 271–72; *Tractatus*, xi, 183–90. See also Chapter 2, pp. XX.

[18] On the use of the term 'judaizing' as 'basic negative charge' to censor behaviour irrespective of its relationship with real Jews or Judaism, see Nirenberg, *Anti-Judaism*, p. 94, and see also pp. 59–60. For an extended study of the use of the images of Jews as vehicles to map negative characteristics onto Christian attitudes and behaviours, see Sara Lipton, *Images of Intolerance: The Representation of Jews and Judaism in the Bible moralisée* (Berkeley: University of California Press, 1999), particularly pp. 28–45. The Toledan rebels had used the term, as well as in its literal sense, in the metaphorical one when they had accused King Juan II of interpreting the law literally as he protected his favourite Álvaro de Luna and *conversos* and persecuted the Old Christians of Toledo. See, Nirenberg, 'Figures of Thought', pp. 421–23; Vidal Doval, 'La matriz medieval', in *Disidencia religiosa*, ed. by García Pinilla. Cf. *Memorial*, 200.

[19] *Lumen*, dedicatoria, 63.

[20] *Defensorium*, II, theorema 4, xxvi, 238.

behaviour, excluding from office those Christians, whatever their origin, who practiced circumcision and returned to Mosaic Law – literal judaizers.[21]

Judaizing and Heresy in *Fortalitium fidei*

By the 1460s, then, there existed significant debate about how widespread judaizing was – in the sense of the keeping of Jewish practices and the precepts of Mosaic Law – whether such judaizing as there was amounted to heresy, and what, if anything, this said about the character of *conversos*. Though Espina used the word judaizing only infrequently in *Fortalitium fidei*, it is clear his vision of the problem was closer to that of the ideologues of the Toledan rebellion, though he would introduce fundamentally important innovations in his discussions. It is possible that there existed ties between the rebels and the Observant Franciscans, although conclusive proof is now lacking. In contrast to the clergy, the Franciscans chose to remain in Toledo during the rebellion, suggesting that they may have been amenable to the agenda of the rebels even if they did not actively support it.[22] Likewise, when Oropesa conducted his inquisition in the city in the 1460s he found that Franciscans were stoking anti-*converso* factionalism among the Old Christian community.[23] Links between the rebels and the Franciscans would go some way to explaining Espina's choice of material in *Fortalitium fidei* – he relied extensively on evidence gathered in Toledo when outlining the crimes and heresies of New Christians, making considerable use of a *pesquisa* that may be identical with that conducted during the first months of the rebellion.[24]

---

[21] In the *Memorial*, p. 220, Marcos García de Mora had justified the exclusion of *conversos* from office on the basis of the decree of the IV Council of Toledo of 633 that stipulated that 'Iudei aut qui ex Iudeis sunt' were forbidden from holding public office. For the text of the conciliar decree, see *Concilios visigóticos e hispano-romanos*, ed. by José Vives (Barcelona: CSIC, Instituto Enrique Flórez, 1963), p. 213. In Visigothic times, the restriction seems to have been applied to those Christians who had been forcibly converted from Judaism, P. D. King, *Law and Society in the Visigothic Kingdom* (Cambridge: University Press, 1972), p. 136. For Cartagena's interpretation, see *Defensorium*, II, theorema 4, xxiv, 227–31, and xxvi, 235–39.

[22] Round, 'La rebelión toledana', p. 435.

[23] See Sigüenza, *Historia*, I, 433; and Chapter 1, p. 25.

[24] On the similarities between the *Sentencia*, the *Memorial*, and Espina's account of the heresy of *conversos*, see McKendrick, pp. 158–61.

In his discussion of *conversos* in Book II, Espina sought to establish a series of ideas. Firstly, that *converso* heresy was widespread throughout Castile; the situation in Toledo was far from an isolated exception. Secondly, that the great majority of *conversos* were heretics, guilty of judaizing and other crimes and were intrinsically opposed to Christianity. Espina stated explicitly and without qualification that Christians of Jewish origin who returned to the practices of Judaism should be treated as heretics.[25] Thirdly, that these crimes and heresies were indicative of fundamental character flaws amongst *conversos*. Espina's logic in addressing these issues was two-fold. In the first instance, he expanded the possible range of *converso* heresies. Such served not only to sully further the reputation of *conversos* but also to contaminate with the taint of Judaism – as Espina would have seen it – a whole range of other behaviours and practices, seemingly unrelated to Mosaic Law. Secondly, particularly through his discussion of circumcision, Espina argued that judaizing was, in and of itself, an explicit denial of Christ. Where the Toledo rebels had connected judaizing and the rejection of Christ, with the same individual guilty of both, for Espina the former necessarily and absolutely implied the latter.

The treatment of heresy in Book II follows the same overall schema as the other Books in *Fortalitium fidei*. There is a discussion of the nature of heresy (considerations i–v), followed by a catalogue of contemporary heresies (consideration vi), and the measures that should be adopted to deal with heretics (considerations vii–xii).[26] For Espina, in historical time heresy was an inevitable phenomenon and the Church Militant, though ultimately invincible, would always be subject to its attacks. He likened this relentless fight against heresy with the deeds of ancient heroes: no sooner had they slain one monster than another would rise to take its place.[27] Although an evil, heresy did serve a purpose. Not only was the defence of the faith by pious Christians a meritorious act in and of

---

[25] *Fortalitium*, II, consideratio xii, questio 2, fol. 69^r.

[26] *Fortalitium*, II, considerationes i–v, fols 47^v–50^v; consideratio vi, fols 50^v–66^r; considerationes vii–xii, fols 66^r–70^r.

[27] *Fortalitium*, II, fol. 47^v. A common motif of heresiology contrasts 'the alleged unity and consistency of orthodoxy with the multiplicity and divisiveness of heterodoxy', John B. Henderson, 'The Multiplicity, Duality, and Unity of Heresies', *Strategies of Medieval Communal Identity: Judaism, Christianity and Islam*, ed. by Wout J. van Bekkum and Paul M. Cobb, Mediaevalia Groningana New Series, 5 (Paris: Peeters, 2004), pp. 11–27 (p. 11).

itself but combatting heresy, in particular, compelled the faithful to reflect and meditate on the truth of Christian doctrine.[28]

Drawing particularly on the work of Francis of Mayrone, Espina discussed at length the definition and meaning of heresy. Distinguished from error and schism, heresy always arose from the same circumstances: the exercise of free, personal choice in the interpretation of the Christian faith and the persistence in that erroneous choice in the face of correction.[29] Heresy was thus to be distinguished from lesser problems, like error and doubt, and was similarly distinct from infidelity or the practice of other religions such as Judaism – though these religions could have their own heresies, such as the Sadducees.[30] Another key element of heresy was its collective dimension; most heretics had fallen into their persistent errors through following a leader.[31] Espina then used the earliest heresies in the history of the Church to provide a typology of errors – the Nicolaites erred in their ceremonies; Faustus the Manichee erred in Scripture by condemning the Old Testament; the Greeks erred against the Church by denying the Holy Spirit proceeded from the Father and from the Son; the Sabellians erred against the articles of the faith by denying the Incarnation and the Trinity; the Manicheans and Arians erred against the sacraments of the Church by the denying the Eucharist and suffrages for the dead.[32]

Having offered a definition of heresy, Espina sets out a list of fourteen contemporary heresies, before exploring them in detail and refuting them. These heresies can be grouped broadly under four headings: errors concerning the requisites for entry into the Christian community (such as the necessity or otherwise of circumcision); the mechanisms to atone for sin, during a person's lifetime and after their death (whether Confession is necessary and how it should be performed, whether indulgences are efficacious, whether Purgatory exists); the authority and power of the clergy (including whether priests can command obedience and whether the efficacy of the sacraments is affected by the morality of the

---

[28] *Fortalitium*, II, consideratio v, fol. 50^{r-v}.
[29] *Fortalitium*, II, considerationes i–iii, fols 47^v–48^v.
[30] *Fortalitium*, II, consideratio i, fol. 47^v.
[31] *Fortalitium*, II, consideratio iii, [articulus] 6, fol. 49^r.
[32] *Fortalitium*, II, consideratio iv, fol. 49^r.

celebrant); the existence of fate and the inevitability of certain types of sin (astrological beliefs).[33]

Though Espina's list of contemporary heresies was extensive, it was not exhaustive. The most notable omission was the heresy in Durango. There in the 1440s, a millennarist movement had arisen under the leadership of the Observant Franciscan preacher Alonso de Mella. His followers were accused not simply of holding property in common but also holding women in common and of rejecting ecclesiastical authority and sacramental religion. By the 1460s, this movement had been stamped out by the authorities and Mella had fled to Granada, where he was eventually murdered. This had been a notorious episode: before appearing in Durango, Mella had been condemned by the Pope and imprisoned in Italy and he was the brother of Juan de Mella, bishop of Zamora, who had been elevated to the cardinalate in 1456.[34] This omission can probably be explained by Espina's desire to gloss over an episode that was not only embarrassing but would also undermine Observant Franciscan claims to be at the forefront of the fight against heresy.[35]

Espina's discussion of contemporary heresies opened with two he linked explicitly to *conversos* – the belief that no one could be saved without circumcision of the flesh and the denial of the truth of the Gospel of Christ.[36] Belief in the efficacy of circumcision arose, Espina claimed, only among those who came from Judaism and while he did not make denial of the Gospel of Christ an

---

[33] Full list of heresies in *Fortalitium*, II, consideratio vi, fol. 50^v. These heresies overlap with the typology provided in consideration iv; there are errors of ritual (practice of circumcision), Scripture (denial of the Gospel), against the Church (denial of priestly authority), against the articles of the faith (denial of the afterlife) and against the sacraments (denial of auricular confession).

[34] McKendrick, pp. 66–77. On the Durango heretics, see also Juan Bautista Avalle-Arce, 'Los herejes de Durango', in *Homenaje a Rodríguez-Moñino: estudios de erudición que le ofrecen sus amigos o discípulos hispanistas norteamericanos*, 2 vols (Madrid: Castalia, 1966), II, 39–55; and, for a possible relationship between this movement and the Toledan rebellion, Round, 'La rebelión toledana', pp. 442–43. Though note that the existence of the heresy of the Free Spirit is no longer accepted, see Robert Lerner, *The Heresy of the Free Spirit in the Later Middle Ages* (Berkeley: University of California Press, 1972), pp. 1–34.

[35] Pastore, *Il vangelo*, p. 35.

[36] *Fortalitium*, II, consideratio vi, haeresis 1, fols 50^v–55^r; haeresis 2, fols 55^r–56^r. On this section of *Fortalitium fidei*, see McKendrick, pp. 162–73.

exclusively *converso* heresy, the material he explored related only to New Christians.[37] Espina also discussed numerous other heresies under the heading of circumcision, all of which he linked explicitly to *conversos*. Drawing on a *pesquisa* from Toledo – which had, he claims, come into his hands – Espina provided a catalogue of twenty-two heresies and crimes of which *conversos* had been found guilty.[38] First, they circumcised their sons; second, they denied the Eucharist; third, they kept oil lamps in the synagogues; fourth, they kept the Jewish Sabbath and worked secretly on Sundays; fifth, they took oaths and made contracts following Jewish practices; sixth, they claimed there was nothing else to life than being born and dying; seventh, that when in danger they invoked Adonai rather than Christ or the Virgin; eighth, they claimed Mary not to be a virgin but a sinner; ninth, they slaughtered and ate a lamb on Shrove Tuesday; tenth, they avoided being present in Church when the Host was elevated; eleventh, they pretended their children had been baptised at home under danger of death, to avoid the sacrament in church; twelfth, they performed Jewish ceremonies for the dead; thirteenth, they married within forbidden degrees without seeking dispensation; fourteenth, they took children to synagogues to teach them; fifteenth, they derided the sacrament of baptism; sixteenth, they practiced usury; seventeenth, they were unconcerned about excommunication or absolution; eighteenth, they rarely attended Mass or the Divine Offices or sought confession; nineteenth, they claimed confession to be harmful; twentieth, they were idolaters; twenty-first, they held astrological beliefs; twenty-second, *converso* priests sold hosts to Jews and infidels.[39]

To this lengthy list from Toledo, Espina added further examples deriving from his own personal experience and other information he had received. Drawing on a *pesquisa* conducted by Bishop Pedro of Palencia in 1458, Espina outlined the crimes of a *converso* barber from Frómista, Fernando Sánchez. He had publicly denied the divinity of Christ and claimed only to believe in the God who had

---

[37] *Fortalitium*, II, consideratio vi, haeresis 1, fol. 50^v: 'in hiis solum oritur qui de Iudaismo venerunt'.

[38] *Fortalitium*, II, consideratio vi, haeresis 1, fols. 52^r: 'Quandam pesquipiam [*sic*] que casu venit a manus meas. Et que facta fuit contra hanc gentem in ciuitati Toleti'. On the use of the *pesquisa*, see Meyuhas Ginio, *La forteresse*, p. 125.

[39] *Fortalitium*, II, consideratio vi, haeresis 1, fols 52^r–53^r.

created the universe. Espina had been sent the *pesquisa* by the bishop in order to determine Sánchez's punishment and had recommended imprisonment but after popular outcry this was commuted to ten years exile. When in Segovia in 1459, Espina had been told by an alguacil that numerous *conversos* had attended the synagogue for prayers during the Feast of Tabernacles, dressing and behaving as if Jews.[40] Earlier, in 1458 Espina had preached a series of sermons in Medina del Campo after learning of a community of *conversos* who denied the Gospel of Christ. After his preaching, Espina was told that in addition to denial of the Gospel, at least thirty men had undergone circumcision in preparation for an emigration to North Africa that would allow them to live openly as Jews.[41]

Espina's concatenation of *converso* crimes underlined the extent of the problem that faced Castile. They were, he stated, a 'raging plague' that sought to destroy the faith of Christ.[42] As his examples showed, everywhere he travelled in the kingdom he encountered heretical New Christians, some displaying their errors openly, others acting in secret. The *pesquisa* from Toledo demonstrated such errors not to be those of isolated individuals or the actions of genuine, if misguided, Christians but of crypto-Jews. *Conversos* were fully integrated into Jewish ritual life, from the cradle to the grave, existing as a parallel society to the Old Christian majority. Their approach to Christianity was at best lukewarm and duplicitous and at worst actively hostile, they engaged with the Sacraments only when compelled to do so and even then half-heartedly. As their practice of usury demonstrated, they saw Old

---

[40] *Fortalitium*, II, consideratio vi, haeresis 1, fol. 53[r-v].

[41] *Fortalitium*, II, consideratio vi, haeresis 1, fol. 51[v]; and see also haeresis 2, fol. 55[r]. According to Espina, the leader of this group was a *converso* cleric who had lived in Flanders. On this group, see Mario Esposito, 'Une secte d'hérétiques à Medina del Campo en 1459: d'après le *Fortalicium fidei* d'Alphonse de Spina', *Revue d'histoire ecclésiastique*, 32 (1936), 350–60; Yitzak Baer, *Die Juden im christlichen Spanien*, 2 vols (Berlin: Akademie-Verlag, 1929–36), II, 428; idem, *A History of the Jews*, II, 285. On circumcision as the first requirement for *conversos*' full entry into Jewish communities outside Spain during the sixteenth and seventeenth centuries, see Leonard B. Glick, *Marked in Your Flesh: Circumcision from Ancient Judea to Modern America* (New York: Oxford University Press, 2005), pp. 78–79.

[42] *Fortalitium*, II, consideratio vi, haeresis 1, fol. 53[v]: 'Ideo cum hec pestis rabida conetur ex toto subuertere legem Christi'.

Christians as their enemies and a people to be exploited.[43] Espina's invocation of *converso* insincerity was socially corrosive, placing New Christians in an almost inescapable bind. Any perceived lack of enthusiasm for Christianity – such as an apparent lack of reverence during the Mass or a supposedly incomplete confession – could be construed as evidence of their judaizing. Once it had been established that *conversos* were devious and duplicitous and masters of dissimulation, even protestations of religious sincerity could have the same effect.[44]

The specific examples explored by Espina underlined that *conversos* were the worst of heretics, that knowledge of their errors was widespread, and that their beliefs were heterodox even amongst Jews. When discussing the twentieth error listed by the Toledo *pesquisa*, Espina related the testimony of an unnamed lodger of a *converso* couple. This husband and wife owned a stone reredos containing four wooden idols that they would venerate in secret, extinguishing candles, burning incense and praying in Arabic and in French.[45] Exploring the twenty-first error, Espina asserted that *conversos* were worse heretics than Arians or anyone else who erred against the faith of Christ.[46] He then provided particular detail about the case of a certain Diego Gómez, as recounted in the testimony of one Álvaro Fernández. Gómez had claimed there to be secret scriptures, written in Hebrew, that only the learned had access to. These texts contained the answers to the great mysteries of the faith – the Trinity, the Incarnation, and the Eucharist – and

---

[43] *Fortalitium*, II, consideratio vi, haeresis 1, fol. 52ʳ: 'quod dant publice ad usuras antiquis Christianis in lege Christi dicendo quod dicti Christiani sunt sui inimici et legis. Et ideo non peccant dando ad usuram eis ymmo quod cum hoc faciant lucrantur indulgencias.'

[44] On the idea of reputation as social capital, see Thelma S. Fenster and Daniel Lord Smail, 'Introduction', in *Fama: The Politics of Talk and Reputation in Medieval Europe*, ed. by Thelma S. Fenster and Daniel Lord Smail (Ithaca: Cornell University Press, 2003), pp. 1–11.

[45] *Fortalitium*, II, consideratio vi, haeresis 1, fol. 52ᵛ. McKendrick, p. 168, notes that 'all in all, this description of idol worship in Toledo appears as a distorted mirror-image of normal Christian rites and practices [...]. An analysis of this particular one [fantasy] reveals something of the growing religious and social chasm between Old and New Christians in post-1449 Toledo'.

[46] *Fortalitium*, II, consideratio vi, haeresis 1, fol. 52ᵛ: 'quod sunt peiores heretici quam Arriani et quicumque alii qui contra legem Christi errauerunt.' For a full account of Diego Gómez's case, see fols 52ᵛ–53ʳ.

demonstrated Jesus had possessed the spirit of Mercury, while Muhammad had the spirit of Mars and Abraham that of Saturn. Gómez also claimed that Christ had caused an earthquake at the time of his death through magic and that the Eucharist was round because it was a sacrifice to the sun. Fernández had said these things were against both the law of Christ and of the Jews and that he had wanted to have nothing to do with Gómez. The witness then concluded that he would sooner believe the oath of Saracen – a people proverbial for their untrustworthiness – than that of a *converso* and while there were a few good New Christians, the vast majority were soothsayers, magicians, and believers in evil things.[47] The cases of both the *converso* couple and of Gómez demonstrated that New Christians were not only judaizers but also deeply flawed in their observance of Mosaic Law and the precepts of Judaism. Just as numerous of the Israelites in the Old Testament had been guilty of idolatry and sorcery, so *conversos* fell into the same sins as their forebears.[48]

Having dealt with heresies concerning the circumcision of the flesh and the denial of the Gospel of Christ, Espina moved on to consider twelve other contemporary heresies.[49] Though Espina on occasion links particular heresies to a single specific group – such as the Waldensians's denial of priestly authority – more often he writes of a number of groups being guilty of a particular heresy or else gives no indication of who exactly was at fault.[50] In number of cases, he suggests that Jews, or certain groups amongst them, share in these heretical beliefs. When discussing those heretics who deny the existence of an afterlife, Espina notes such was believed by the Epicureans but also, as Acts of the Apostles made clear, by the Sadducees.[51] Similarly, when exploring astrological beliefs, Espina

---

[47] *Fortalitium*, II, consideratio vi, haeresis 1, fol. 53ʳ: 'Dixit eciam predictus testis quod tantum cognoscebat de predicta gente quod plus crederet vni Sarraceno qui iuraret sibi in lege sua quam vni conuerso qui iuraret sibi super Sancta Dei Evangelia, et quod boni inter eos sunt pauci et pro maiori parte sunt augures, sortientes, creditores malarum rerum.'

[48] On Espina's discussion of idolatry in the Old Testament, see Chapter 4, p. 90.

[49] *Fortalitium*, II, consideratio vi, haereses 3–14, fols 56ʳ–66ʳ.

[50] Waldensians: *Fortalitium*, II, consideratio vi, haeresis 7, fol. 58ʳ.

[51] *Fortalitium*, II, consideratio vi, haeresis 13, fol. 61ᵛ: 'Huius peruerse et dampnate opinionis fuerunt Saducei qui, quia credebant quod anime non erant immortales, negauerunt resurrectionem sicut patet Actuum 24. Hec eciam dampnata opinio istis temporibus eciam in multis malis Christianis'.

stated that the Talmud confirmed the heretical view that the stars determined the fate and character of a person.[52] The connections between certain of the heretical beliefs explored by Espina and the Jews may be strengthened if, as has been suggested, there was a significant current of materialist Averroism in Castilian Judaism that manifested itself in a denial of the soul and the afterlife.[53]

Espina's reasons for drawing connections between some heresies and the Jews go beyond the simple establishing of a genealogy or typology of error. By expanding the range of behaviours and beliefs that could be associated with Judaism, Espina sought to demonstrate that many of the errors of which Castilian *conversos* had been accused were not simply heresy but were judaizing heresy. Even if *conversos* did not return to the observance of Mosaic Law, their beliefs and practices still could be constructed to be indicative of their Jewish origins. Though many throughout medieval Europe might express doubts about the miracles of Christ or subscribe to the principles of religious universalism, when *conversos* did so, Espina was suggesting, they were engaging in judaizing.[54] Moreover,

> Other contemporary sources that censure *conversos* speak of their faithlessness and lack of belief in the afterlife. For example, a *requerimiento* sent to Enrique IV by a league of rebellious nobles in 1464 demanded the king change the composition of his court, ejecting those Christians by name who claimed there was no afterlife and whose rise to prominence was the cause of corruption in the kingdom: 'infieles enemigos de nuestra santa fe católica é otras aunque cristianos por nombre, muy sospechosos en la fe, en especial que creen é dicen é afirman que otro mundo non aya si non nascer é morir como bestias', *Memorias de don Enrique*, pp. 327–34 (p. 328). On this source, see Marie-Claude Gerbet, *Las noblezas españolas en la Edad Media: siglos XI–XV*, trans. by María José García Vera (Madrid: Alianza Editorial, 1997), pp. 291–94; and Luis Suárez Fernández, *Enrique IV de Castilla: la difamación como arma política* (Barcelona: Ariel, 2001), pp. 289–90.

[52] *Fortalitium*, II, consideratio vi, haeresis 14, fol. 64ᵛ.

[53] Francisco Márquez Villanueva, '"Nasçer e morir como bestias" (criptoaverroísmo y criptojudaísmo)', in *De la España judeoconversa: doce estudios*, Serie General Universitaria, 57 (Barcelona: Edicions Bellaterra, 2006), pp. 203–27 (pp. 207–8) [first pub. in *Los judaizantes en Europa y la literatura castellana del Siglo de Oro*, ed. by Fernando Díaz Esteban (Madrid: Letrúmero, 1994), pp. 273–93].

[54] For some comments on religious error among non-*conversos*, see John Edwards, 'Religious Faith and Doubt in Late Medieval Spain: Soria *circa* 1450–1500', *P&P*, 120 (1988), 3–25 (pp. 6, 13–16). On the 'shared sacred landscape' of Old and New Christians, see John Edwards, 'Elijah and the Inquisition: Messianic Prophecy among *Conversos* in Spain, *c*. 1500', *Nottingham Mediaeval Studies*, 28 (1984), 79–94 (p. 93).

as Espina demonstrated in his discussion of fleshly circumcision, such judaizing amounted to the conscious rejection of Christ.

Against the Circumcision of the Flesh

Of the heresies threatening the contemporary Castilian Church, Espina devotes most attention to the practice of fleshly circumcision. As has been seen, it was the first contemporary heretical practice explored by Espina and numerous other practices and beliefs were subsumed within its discussion. Drawing on eyewitness testimonies and hearsay, Espina stressed that this most profound heresy was widespread among Castilian *conversos* and spanned several generations.[55] He writes with grave concern about the circumcision of infants, detailing a number of the excuses parents gave to explain their young sons' lack of foreskins – they would, for example, claim that children had been born without one or had suffered accidents that required its surgical removal.[56] Even more worrying for Espina was the circumcision of adults, such as had occurred in Medina del Campo in 1459.

Medieval Christianity had come to regard the practice of circumcision as the defining marker of Jewish identity, alongside literal observance of the Law of Moses. The *Siete Partidas*, for example, defined a Jew legally as 'aquel que cree e tiene la ley de Moysen segund suena la letra della e que se circuncida e faze las otras cosas que manda essa su ley.'[57] Although within the Iberian context, circumcision was also practiced by Muslims and was seen likewise as a marker of their identity, Espina had relatively little to say about this ritual within Islam. Instead, he discussed circumcision almost exclusively in the context of Judaism or judaizers, linking it with Jews or with those Christians 'qui de iudaismo venerunt' and associating it with a conscious rejection of Christ and

---

[55] *Fortalitium*, II, consideratio vi, haeresis 1, fols 50ᵛ–55ʳ. On Espina's treatment of circumcision, see particularly, McKendrick, pp. 162–65.

[56] *Fortalitium*, II, consideratio vi, haeresis 1, fol. 51ᵛ.

[57] Dwayne E. Carpenter, *Alfonso X and the Jews: An Edition and Commentary on 'Siete Partidas' 7.24 "De los judíos"*, University of California Publications in Modern Philology, 115 (Berkeley, 1986), 7.24.1.4–6, p. 28. See also Dahan, p. 65. For a discussion of medieval Christian views of circumcision which regarded it as the physical and symbolical manifestation of the 'impossibility of Jewish integration', see Glick, *Marked in Your Flesh*, pp. 86–90 (quotation at p. 86).

his Law.⁵⁸ In contrast to discussions by pro-*converso* authors of individual New Christians falling into error or more widespread awareness of the problems of ignorance due to inadequate pastoral care and religious instruction, Espina cast the issue as a simple choice between heresy and orthodoxy.⁵⁹

For Espina, the problem of fleshly circumcision was central to his characterization of *conversos* and his discussion of it allowed him to invoke a variety of themes. First and foremost, circumcision functioned as a clear and unambiguous sign of Judaism. Thus, Espina claimed the practice among *conversos* was evidence of their wish to observe the Law of Moses after receiving baptism.⁶⁰ His discussion also emphasized the extent of the problem of judaizing. Circumcision was not restricted to the older generation of converts, instead new judaizers were being raised across Castile, thus perpetuating the problem into the foreseeable future unless remedies were found. Circumcision was also of importance to Espina because it served as a physical marker of an interior disposition. It was not mere error but a sign of a disposition that was entirely opposed to Christianity. Rather than being sincere converts, the sizeable group of *conversos* who practiced circumcision chose to reject baptismal regeneration and instead to share in the lineage of perfidious and faithless Jews.

Espina dealt first with claims made by some *conversos* that circumcision of the flesh was a requisite for salvation. He concluded that while carnal circumcision was of no use to Christians, spiritual circumcision was an obligation.⁶¹ He built his rejection of fleshly circumcision primarily around extracts from two letters by Paul that discussed the disputes between opponents and advocates of the practice amongst Christians: Galatians (particularly 4.31–

---

⁵⁸ *Fortalitium*, II, consideratio vi, haeresis 1, fol. 50ᵛ. See also McKendrick, pp. 162–63. On circumcision in Islam see Echevarria, *The Fortress of Faith*, p. 162.

⁵⁹ Torquemada had insisted that there was no heresy among *conversos* in Toledo, only instances of individual error, *Tractatus*, i, 6, 136. On defective pastoral care and religious instruction, see Márquez Villanueva, 'Sobre el concepto de judaizante', pp. 107–9.

⁶⁰ *Fortalitium*, II, consideratio vi, haeresis 1, fol. 51ʳ. Espina, having insisted that circumcision and Mosaic Law were separate, was here responding to what he perceived as the Jewish elision of the two.

⁶¹ *Fortalitium.*, II, consideratio vi, haeresis 1, fol. 50ᵛ: 'Prima est quod erroneum est Christiano vti circumcisione carnali. Secunda est quod neccesarium est Christiano vti circumcisione spirituali'.

5.6) and Titus (particularly 1.10–16). This section is one of the very few in *Fortalitium fidei* where Espina did not rely on earlier polemical work to construct his argument. Instead, he supplemented Scriptural quotation and allusion with extracts from the *Glossa ordinaria* and with accounts of events in Castile.

At the heart of the Pauline argument was the idea that salvation could come only through faith in Christ and not through the keeping of Mosaic Law.[62] Following Galatians 6.15, Espina asserted the regenerative power of baptism, explaining how Christians became new men through the sacrament.[63] Having undertaken this essential step towards salvation, those Christians who practiced circumcision turned their backs on their new, regenerated selves in favour of their former state. The gravity of this error was compounded because after the coming of Christ circumcision was no longer valid; for someone who had acquired a new life in Christ to undertake a superseded and empty ritual in the hope of achieving salvation was an even greater failure.[64] Employing a series of Pauline metaphors, Espina argued that a Christian undergoing fleshly circumcision was akin to a freeman becoming a serf, for it was the rejection of the spiritual freedom granted by Christ and the acceptance of the yoke of Mosaic Law. Moreover, as circumcision had been given as a sign of the coming of the Messiah – a theme Espina had already laid out in Book I – undergoing this ritual amounted to the denial that Jesus was the Christ. After the Incarnation and the Passion, circumcision was no longer a token of the Abrahamic Covenant but a practice abhorrent to God and a sin as grave as idolatry. Though such applied to the Jews, who blasphemed and incurred God's wrath through their obdurate

---

[62] On Paul's arguments about circumcision, see Delbert Burkett, *An Introduction to the New Testament and the Origins of Christianity* (Cambridge: Cambridge University Press, 2002), pp. 303–4, and Nirenberg, *Anti-Judaism*, pp. 55–59. For wider disputes in the Early Church between Jews and Gentiles about the obligation or otherwise for Christians to observe Mosaic Law, see Joseph H. Lynch, *Early Christianity: A Brief History* (New York: Oxford University Press, 2010), pp. 40–41, 49–50, and bibliography therein.

[63] *Fortalitium*, II, consideratio vi, haeresis 1, fol. 50ᵛ: 'Qui vere Christianus est factus est noua creatura per baptismum patet Ad Galathas ultima. Si ergo redeat ad circumcisionem carnalem efficitur vetus creatura cum accipiat sacramentum inueteratum quid iam cessauit'.

[64] *Fortalitium*, II, consideratio vi, haeresis i, fol. 50ᵛ: 'Item qui vtitur sacramento quid nichil valet errat, sed Christianus qui utitur circumcisione carnali vtitur sacramento quid nichil valet ergo valde errat maior'.

practice of circumcision, it applied all the more so to New Christians who were reneging on the faith they had professed in baptism. Thus the Christian who practiced circumcision erred more greatly than the Jew who did so.[65]

Circumcised Christians did not just err in belief: Espina was clear that circumcision was an external indication of interior disposition. He underlined the Pauline admonition that in Christ neither circumcision nor the foreskin had any value (Gal. 5.6). Neither could, by themselves, bring about salvation; this came only from faith in Christ. Expanding on Paul's words, Espina quoted the *Glossa* on the need for this faith to be accompanied by charity and love.[66] Seeking salvation not through good works and faith in Christ but through the empty ritual of fleshly circumcision was thus a conscious rejection of the fundamental values of Christian life.[67] Such was further emphasized in Espina's discussion of the Pauline equation of Judaism and slavery and Christianity and freedom, and in his restatement of the Apostle's insistence that the Galatians reject circumcision and Mosaic Law as a yoke that cannot bring salvation. Again, Espina used the *Glossa* to expand on Paul's ideas, identifying slavery with servitude to sin and freedom with citizenship of the heavenly Jerusalem.[68] Thus a Christian who rejected freedom in favour of circumcision also surrendered his place in the fortress of faith.

---

[65] *Fortalitium*, II, consideratio vi, haeresis 1, fol. 51ʳ: 'quia si iudeus uteris circumcisione est blasphemus et in continua ira et odio dei [...], ergo multo forcius erunt blasphemi et in continua ira et odio dei, quicumque christiani vtentes circumcisione et tanto grauius peccant quam iudei.'

[66] *Fortalitium*, II, consideratio 6, haeresis i, fol. 50ᵛ: 'Et iterum Ad Galathas 5: "In Christo Ihesu neque circumcisio aliquid valet neque prepucium sed fides que per dilectionem operatur" super quo dicit Glosa: "fides non utique ociosa, quia fides sine operibus non saluat". Sed que operatur per caritatem dicitur et proprium opus fidei ipsa dilectio est. Sine dilectione fides inanis est, fides cum dilectione Christiani est.'

[67] Such ideas had a long history within Christian exegesis. For example, Bede compared those Christians who believed that alms-giving without a change of heart was sufficient to achieve salvation to the Jews who thought that sacrifices and offerings without justice, mercy, and faith were able to please God, *In primam partem Samuhelis*, in *PL*, 91, cols 499–714d (col. 599d).

[68] *Fortalitium*, II, consideratio vi, haeresis 1, fol. 51ʳ: '"Itaque fratres mei non sumus filii ancille sed libere qua libertate Christus nos liberauit." Super quo dicit Glossa "non sumus filii ancille quia non sumus serui peccati uel legis; sed libere, scilicet, Iherusalem celestis qui est populus nouus regni celorum"'.

Espina claimed that the *conversos* of Castile who underwent circumcision were even greater heretics than the Cretan advocates of this practice censured so strongly by Paul in his letter to Titus.[69] Espina adapted and abbreviated sections of this letter to pile invective against the circumcising *conversos*, accusing them of being:

> inobedientes, vaniloqui, seductores, universos domos subvertentes, docentes que non oportet, mendaces, crudeles, gulosi, non sani in fide, intendentes iudaicis fabuli, avertentes se a veritate, confitentes se nosse Deum, factis negantes, abhominabiles incredibiles, ad omne opus bonum reprobi cuius verba ad litteram sunt'.[70]

By borrowing the words of the Epistle to Titus, Espina was invoking directly the authority of Paul for his assertion that judaizing affected directly the moral character of *conversos*. Faithlessness, mendacity, and cruelty were not mere accusations made against *conversos* by Old Christians, they were the inescapable consequences of New Christians embracing circumcision.

To the now sinful and redundant fleshly circumcision, Espina contrasted the salubrious spiritual circumcision that was required of all Christians. Spiritual circumcision affected not only the interior of the believer – their ideas and desires – but also their exterior behaviour and habits.[71] Espina proposed four reasons for the faithful to practice spiritual circumcision. Firstly, to avoid corruption, removing sin from the heart to prevent the endangering of the soul. Secondly, to purge sin in order to bear fruit in the Church and in eternal life. Thirdly, as a marker of identity, distinguishing the true Christian as a person of God. Fourthly, as a means of achieving a fitting station in Paradise, just as the polished stones are placed in the best and most prominent place in a building, so the

---

[69] *Fortalitium*, II, consideratio vi, haeresis 1, fol. 51ᵛ: 'Isti tales Christiani utentes circumcisione inimici Dei et magis heretici sunt illi de quibus Paulus ad Tytum in primo capitulo enumerat 15 condiciones pessimas'.

[70] *Fortalitium*, II, consideratio vi, haeresis 1, fol. 51ᵛ.

[71] *Fortalitium*, II, consideratio vi, haeresis 1, fol. 54ʳ: 'Debemus ergo nos circumcidere interius et exterius. Interius quantum ad cogniciones et desideria, et exterius quantum ad singula membra et opera. Hec est circumcisio viciorum quam neccesse est quod faciamus'. For a general discussion of the relationship between interior disposition and external behaviour, see Janet Coleman, 'Negotiating the Medieval in the Modern: European Citizenship and Statecraft', *Transactions of the Royal Historical Society*, 22 (2012), 75–93 (p. 87).

spiritually circumcised Christian will take their rightful position in the Heavenly Jerusalem.[72]

Espina adduced a number of passages from the Old Testament in support both of the need for spiritual circumcision, writing of the necessity to circumcise the ears, mouth, heart, and body, and of the requirement to interpret references to circumcision spiritually.[73] This pairing of the contrast between fleshly and spiritual circumcision with the distinction, albeit implicit, between fleshly and spiritual reading underlines the essentially Jewish character of circumcising *conversos* as well as further emphasising carnal circumcision to be an external marker of internal defects. Though he does not make the link explicit, Espina's treatment of the blindness of Jews and their inability and refusal to read their Scriptures spiritually impacts upon his presentation of *conversos*. Just like adherence to Mosaic Law and rejection of Christ, fleshly circumcision was the result of faulty hermeneutics, where *conversos* were mistaking a spiritual injunction for a literal one.

Genealogy and Descent

What part, if any, did descent and genealogy play in the sins and heresies of the *conversos*, was there a genealogical dimension to the perfidy of New Christians? For the Toledo rebels and their ideologues, the answer had been a qualified yes. Though their pronouncements did not amount to a fully developed doctrine of purity of blood, they allowed genealogy and descent a significant role in determining the worth and character of an individual – particularly their suitability for public life and office. Old Christians were eminently suited to such role, whereas New Christians were from the outset subject to the gravest suspicions. Pro-*converso* authors, by contrast, generally denied the possibility of the inheritance of negative characteristics, stressing the regenerative power of the baptismal sacrament.[74] Cartagena, however, allowed for the inheritance of positive characteristics – bravery, honour, and nobility – and suggested such qualities, having remained latent during centuries of Jewish infidelity, could be activated in *conversos* following baptism.[75] Those who rejected baptism, whether through

---

[72] *Fortalitium*, II, consideratio vi, haeresis 1, fols 54ʳ–55ʳ.
[73] *Fortalitium*, II, consideratio vi, haeresis 1, fol. 54ᵛ.
[74] See Chapter 2, pp. 41–45.
[75] *Defensorium*, II, theorema 4, in particular xiv–xviii, 195–211.

apostasy or refusal to embrace Christianity, brought their own past sins and the sins of their ancestors down upon them.[76]

Given the importance that questions of genealogy had played in existing discussions of the status and qualities of *conversos*, Espina said very little in Book II about the issue of inheritance. By insisting on the essentially Jewish nature of heretical *conversos*, he implied that all he had written about the Jews in Book I and all he would go on to write in Book III could apply equally to New Christians. Thus *conversos* were of the perfidious seed of Ishmael and Esau: not only did they come, self-evidently, from the line of Jews who had rejected Christ but their defective observance of the precepts of Judaism – their idolatry and sorcery – showed their kinship with the faithless Jews of the Old Testament. For Espina, however, descent was not solely fleshly but could have a spiritual dimension. Christians, he was clear, were the spiritual heirs of Isaac and Jacob and of the line of virtuous Old Testament figures.[77] Given that Espina allowed for the possibility, however limited and remote, of sincere conversion from Judaism to Christianity, some *conversos* could potentially move from the perfidious lineage of Ishmael to the blessed lineage of Isaac.

If some *conversos* might join the virtuous seed of Abraham, the greater majority travelled willingly and consciously in the opposite direction, rejecting the light of Christianity and returning to the blindness of Judaism. Like Cartagena, Espina proposed a model of latent or potential inheritance, activated through the behaviour of the individual. By judaizing, particularly by practicing fleshly circumcision, *conversos* embraced the literal and defective readings of the Jews, rejoining the lineage of Ishmael and Esau. As Espina made clear in Book III, faulty reading and the embracing of false texts could also activate even more debased ancestries – the demonic line of Adam and Lilith and the monstrous one of Adam and the beasts.[78] In this context, Espina's accusation, drawn from the Epistle to Titus, that *conversos* heeded Jewish fables gained greater weight. Such fables may have been about the need for

---

[76] *Defensorium*, II, theorema 1, vi, 109.

[77] See Chapter 4, p. 95. For the two lines of Abrahamic descent, see *Fortalitium*, I, consideratio iii, articulus 2, fol. 17^r; Israel's idolatry: consideratio iii, articulus 4, fol. 28^r.

[78] See Chapter 4, p. 100. On debased genealogies: *Fortalitium*, III, consideratio ii, fols 73^r.

fleshly circumcision but Espina's words could also imply the fantastical stories of the Talmud.

Inheritance was not wholly determinative of behaviour and moral worth – it needed to be actualised in the individual believer. Espina made clear that nurture and culture played a part in this process. In Book III, he endorsed the forcible removal of children from Jewish and even *converso* parents in order to allow them to be raised as good Christians. Likewise, New Christians were to be kept separate from Jews to avoid bad influences and religious contamination. Even forced conversion could eventually bring positive results. Although such converts themselves were unlikely to become sincere and faithful Christians, in time their descendants might be.

Though a genealogical element can be understood in Espina's treatment of New Christians, nonetheless descent remained a secondary concern within Book II. The heresy of *conversos* was manifest and there existed appropriate remedies to deal with it – if only such remedies would be enforced. Exploring the origins or causes of such heresy was of lesser importance to Espina's argument than the demonstration of its prevalence and the underlining of the threat that it posed.[79] Book II was less a theorization of the nature of heresy and more a call to arms.

The Establishment of an Inquisition

Towards the close of his discussion of the circumcising heresy, Espina reiterated the gravity of the danger it posed to Castile and urged the ecclesiastical and secular powers to take steps to extirpate it. At the end of Book II, he returned to the dangers posed by unchecked heresy. The smallest amount of corruption was sufficient to endanger the whole body of the faithful: Arius, he noted, had been only a single spark in Alexandria but his heresy had spread like a fire throughout the world.[80] The reference to Arius was not incidental – Espina had already noted *conversos* to be worse heretics than Arians, indeed, to be the very worst heretics. If all heresies were a danger to the faith, nevertheless he was clear that the threat from judaizing *conversos* was particularly grave and pressing – a theme he would return to in Book III.

---

[79] *Fortalitium*, II, consideratio vi, haeresis 1, fol. 51^v.

[80] *Fortalitium*, II, consideratio xii, [articulus] 15, fol. 70^r: 'Arrius erum in Alexandria vna scintilla fuit sed quoniam non statim oppressa est totum orbem eius flamma depopulata est.'

Having demonstrated the urgent need for action, in the final six considerations of Book II, Espina outlined his proposed solution. The Church had an obligation to correct those in error – heretics should be given the chance to recant and to revise their beliefs, only if they were recalcitrant ought they to be handed over to the secular arm.[81] Disputation with heretics and infidels was licit, provided it was done to root out error and did not risk imperilling the faith of the audience.[82] To detect heresy, an inquisition was needed. Earlier in the Book, Espina had demonstrated the effectiveness of legal measures and inquisitorial procedures such as *pesquisas* in uncovering judaizing heresy in Toledo and elsewhere, what he now proposed was a more systematic, more regularised and more wide-ranging institution.

The model of inquisition Espina set out corresponded in its essentials to that detailed in the decree of the Council of Vienne of 1311–12, *Multorum querela*. The inquisition was to be staffed either by bishops or specially appointed inquisitors, with the two working independently of each other, except in matters of torture where the consent of both was needed. At least once a year, those accused of heresy were to be investigated and if they confessed and recanted would receive relatively light penalties. Those who persistently relapsed into heresy were to be excommunicated, stripped of property and deprived of any offices held – an exclusion that continued for the next two generations. Those who confessed to heresy were expected to name accomplices or other heretics they knew of and, in general, Espina envisaged a network of informers embracing the whole Christian community.[83] Espina was, in effect, proposing to turn Castile into a surveillance society, where the responsibility for the policing of orthodoxy rested on the entire population.[84]

---

[81] *Fortalitium*, II, consideratio viii, fol. 67^v, and consideratio xii, fol. 70^r.

[82] *Fortalitium*, II, consideratio ix, fols 67^v–68^r.

[83] *Fortalitium*, II, considerationes x–xii, fols 68^r–70^r. This discussion follows closely Pastore, *Il vangelo*, pp. 13–16. See also Alisa Meyuhas Ginio, 'The Fortress of Faith – At the End of the West: Alonso de Espina and His *Fortalitium Fidei*', in *Contra Iudaeos: Ancient and Medieval Polemics between Christians and Jews*, ed. by Ora Limour and Guy G. Stroumsa, Texts and Studies in Medieval and Early Modern Judaism, 10 (Tübingen: Mohr, 1996), pp. 215–37, (pp. 229–30).

[84] Such a notion was also characteristic of friars' understanding of corporate Christian life. Paton, *Preaching Friars*, p. 127 observes: 'Members of

Despite suggestions in the scholarship to the contrary, Espina was not offering here the blueprint for the Spanish Inquisition.[85] Firstly, though Espina was clear that judaizing *conversos* were the most significant problem, his inquisition was designed to stamp out everything he determined to be heresy. Secondly, what he was proposing was the implementation of the standard organization of the medieval papal inquisition. Moreover, what Espina set out in Book II was effectively what he and the Franciscans had lobbied Enrique IV for in 1460, asking that he set up an inquisition akin to the one operating in France – there was nothing novel in the proposals set out in *Fortalitium fidei*.[86] Such is confirmed by the position adopted by pro-*converso* authors and by the long-standing Church policy on the matter. Inquisition had long been adopted as the key means of extirpating heresy and the Council of Basle in the mid-fifteenth century had decreed specifically it to be the appropriate method for dealing with judaizing heresy among converts from Judaism.[87] Both Cartagena and Torquemada had attended this council and their writings indicate that they believed inquisition to be a suitable means to address the religious problems facing Castile. Additionally, Oropesa had acted as an inquisitor in Toledo at the behest of Archbishop Carrillo.[88]

Where Espina differed in his approach from his pro-*converso* contemporaries was in the scope of the inquisition he proposed and the severity of its actions. While Espina insisted that the gravest and most urgent danger came from judaizing *conversos* and that it was upon these that the full force of the inquisition should fall, Oropesa

congregations at sermons [in Siena] are even explicitly exhorted to act as watch-dogs on each other's consciences and to correct each other's faults.'

[85] For example, see Haim Beinart, *Conversos on Trial: The Inquisition in Ciudad Real*, trans. by Yael Guiladi, Hispania Judaica, 3 (Jerusalem: Magnes Press, 1981), p. 19; and Amy I. Aronson-Friedman and Gregory B. Kaplan, 'Editors' Introduction', in *Marginal Voices: Studies in Converso Literature of Medieval and Golden Age Spain*, ed. by Amy I. Aronson-Friedman and Gregory B. Kaplan, The Medieval and Early Modern Iberian World, 46 (Leiden: Brill, 2012), pp. 1–17 (p. 8).

[86] Sigüenza, *Historia*, I, 431: 'y que eso mismo sobre los herejes se haga inquisicion en este reino según como se hace en Francia y en otros muchos reinos y provincias de cristianos'

[87] Carlos Gilly, *Spanien und der Basler Buchdruck bis 1600: ein Querschnitt durch die spanische Geistesgeschichte aus der Sicht einer europäischen Buchdruckerstadt* (Basel: Helbing & Lichtenhahn, 1985), p. 42.

[88] See Chapter 2, p. 40.

had conducted his inquest along broader lines. He had investigated and found error among Old and New Christian alike, seeking to address social tensions between the two factions and apportioning blame to both sides.[89] Torquemada and Cartagena had far less to say about the operation of any inquisition but their assertions that the discriminatory and divisive actions of Old Christians were the more serious heresy suggests that they, too, envisaged an inquest closer to that carried out by Oropesa.[90] In addition, Espina's outlook appears less corrective and more punitive. Alongside his statement in Book III about the vast conflagrations that would occur if an inquisition took place in Castile, can be placed his assertion in Book II that if a heresy is spreading through a region it is better that the heretics are exterminated by the inquisition without delay.[91] Given what Espina had already written concerning the spread and prevalence of *converso* heresy in Castile, the implication would have been clear.

Though differences existed, Espina and pro-*converso* authors were offering, effectively, the same answer to the problem of judaizing New Christians. Indeed, it is noteworthy that the only person seeking something akin to the Spanish Inquisition was Enrique IV. In 1460, he wrote to Pope Pius II requesting that he establish an inquisition in Castile but specifying that inquisitors should be royal appointees. In essence, Enrique was seeking the establishment of a national inquisition, where the king rather than the pope or others in the Church could control the enforcement of religious orthodoxy. Such was presumably intended to allow Enrique to retain a degree of control over the politically and socially divisive issue of *conversos* as well as ensuring that inquisitors would be attuned to his own policies.[92] As the incident of

---

[89] See Pastore, *Il vangelo*, p. 19, who notes that 'l'Inquisizione voluta da Oropesa potesse davvero essere vista come una possibile "otra Inquisición", l'alternativa, nel 1461 ancora vincente, a quella creata vent'anni più tardi.'

[90] Discrimination of *conversos* as heresy: *Defensorium*, II, theorema 4, xxxiv, 266–67; *Tractatus*, ii, 2, 139–40; 4–7, 144–48; i, 4, 134.

[91] *Fortalitium*, II, consideratio xii, [articulus]11, fol. 69ᵛ: 'si aliqui sint heretici qui sic defendunt falsitatem sententie sue ut in terra multitudinem faciant et conuenticulorum segregaciones vel ecclesie conturbationes cogitent tunc absque alia dilatione vel inquisitione exterminandi sunt.'

[92] Pastore, *Il vangelo*, p. 27. The very first bull for the inquisition in Spain, but virtually unknown even at the time (neither Espina nor Oropesa knew of its existence), was issued on 20 November 1451. It gave the bishop of Osma and

Hernando de la Plaza and the foreskins would have demonstrated to the king, the threat of violence and rabble rousing surrounding the *converso* problem was acute. If all parties agreed that the intrinsically oppressive and violent institution of inquisition was the solution, nevertheless the Observant Franciscans and Espina represented a politically dangerous extreme in the heated atmosphere of Castile in the 1460s.[93]

Espina's status as architect of the Spanish Inquisition and proponent of the expulsion of the Jews thus comes less from his own writings and more from the subsequent historiography of late medieval Castile. By the end of the sixteenth century, Luis de Páramo, inquisitor and author of *De origine et progressu officii Sanctae Inquisitionis*, was constructing an over-arching narrative of the fifteenth century in Spain in which all events led inexorably to the establishment of the Spanish Inquisition. For Páramo, Espina had identified correctly the cause of the problems facing Castile – the heresy of the *conversos* and the continuing presence of the Jews – and had proposed the appropriate remedies but only two decades later had the political power existed, in the person of the Catholic Monarchs, to enact them. Once Páramo had intertwined the ideas of Espina with the initiatives of Fernando and Isabel, the differences between them proved increasingly hard to distinguish.[94] The contents of *Fortalitium fidei* were read less in the light of what their author had intended and more in the light of later royal policy, less in the light of the context of the 1460s and more in the light of the context of 1480s and 1490s.

*

Though *conversos* were, in canonical terms, heretics – Christians lapsing into error – for Espina they were clearly a part of the Jewish problem and, indeed, the most troubling part of that problem. Joining ongoing and intense debate about the nature, extent, and implications of judaizing, Espina placed himself firmly on the side

---

the vicar of the bishopric of Salamanca authority as inquisitors for the apostasy of New Christians, p. 26 n63. See also Nieto Soria, pp. 214–19.

[93] On the notion of the legitimacy of coercing individuals in matters of faith, see for example Janet Coleman, 'Citizenship and the Language of Statecraft', in *Finding Europe: Discourses on Margins, Communities, Images ca. 13th–ca. 18th Centuries*, ed. by Anthony Molho, Diogo Ramada Curto and Niki Koniordos (New York: Berghahn, 2007), pp. 223–52 (particularly, pp. 238–44).

[94] Pastore, *Il vangelo*, p. 25.

of the Toledan rebels and other anti-*converso* groups and even extended their ideas. For Espina, judaizing meant *conversos* fully and consciously returning to the observance of Mosaic Law and other Jewish practices, mostly notably circumcision. Not only did such establish their status as faithless reprobates but also entailed the explicit rejection of Christ, abandoning the true spiritual reading of Scripture and returning to a fleshly, literal one. By doing so they shared in the perfidious and damaged ancestry of Ishmael and, perhaps, even the monstrous and demonic descent of the Jews, reserved for those who had chosen to believe the fables of the Talmud.

In contrast to other writers on the *converso* problem, Espina had little to say about genealogical determinism. While he did discuss such matters, his attention in Book II was focused far more on the extent and prevalence of judaizing heresy – the extirpation of this error was the most pressing issue, whether or not it had a genealogical component. In line with the other parties in the dispute, Espina saw inquisition as the appropriate means of dealing with heresy, and with the judaizing heresy in particular, and, though he does not state this explicitly, it seems likely that Espina envisaged the Franciscans at the heart of this new inquisition. Where he differed from his contemporaries was in his vision of the character of this institution – by its very nature, inquisition was repressive and authoritarian but, even for its time, Espina's version was particularly punitive and unforgiving

CONCLUSION

It is easy to construct an over-arching narrative of the rise of persecution in late medieval Castile. The forced conversions of 1391, Ferrer's campaigns in 1411–12, the rebellions of 1449, the establishment of the Inquisition in 1480, and the expulsion of the Jews in 1492 all fit smoothly into a story of the progressive decline of toleration and the growth of oppression and discrimination. Espina, too, sits neatly in the sequence, an ideologue of violence and intolerance pushing Castile further down the path of repressive religious uniformity. Such a narrative, while compelling, should be resisted. As with all such accounts, it privileges homogeneity over complexity, adding direction and destination to discrete events and to ad hoc royal policies. At the same time, it marginalizes dissenting or divergent positions within a society and risks giving particular views a prominence and authority they may have lacked at the time.

As Espina's biography demonstrates, by the late 1450s he and the other members of his Order were competing at court to control the future direction of royal religious policy. What started as an alliance with Alonso de Oropesa and the Hieronymites turned quickly into rivalry, as each Order put forward subtly but significantly different proposals for action. Thus, as he was writing *Fortalitium fidei*, Espina was engaged in a serious debate about the nature of the religious problems facing Castile and the appropriate solutions for them. It was, moreover, a debate that he was losing. If the mutual antagonism between Espina and Oropesa has long been recognized, a close reading of *Fortalitium fidei* makes clear that Espina was also directing his work at other figures within the ecclesiastical hierarchy. To Alonso de Cartagena's walls of faith, constantly constructed and shored-up by the true believers, Espina counterposed his eternal and unchanging fortress of faith. To Juan de Torquemada's vision of isolated New Christian error, Espina opposed generations of heretical judaizers, undermining the kingdom and threatening the Christian faithful.

If the differences between Espina and his opponents were significant, the scope of their arguments and the range of their proof texts were surprisingly narrow. The *converso* controversy was, in essence, a debate about the meaning of a small number of concepts and the significance of a limited selection of scriptural and legal passages. Had Christ fulfilled or superseded Mosaic Law, had the Apostle Paul been concerned most with circumcising judaizers or with those who would fracture the unity of Christianity? Who were the true heirs of Abraham by the virtuous line of Isaac and Jacob, who the perfidious seed of Ishmael and Esau? A minor shift in emphasis or in reading could yield radically different positions with profound implications for the status of minority groups in Castile. Thus for Espina, *conversos* remained in essence and in character Jews and the problem of New Christians was part of a continuum that also embraced the Jewish problem – one could not be solved without solving the other. The outlook of Cartagena and Torquemada was very different: *conversos* were Christians and any problems arose less from their errors than from the hatreds and divisive policies of Old Christians. If Oropesa's position was in some respects closer to that of Espina, seeing the Jews ultimately as the most culpable of all, nonetheless he sought also to apportion blame to Old and New Christians alike. All parties agreed on the need for an inquisition but, again, their visions of this institution diverged in important respects.

Though Espina was responding to contemporary debates in Castile he was operating, too, in a well-defined tradition of mendicant anti-Semitism. Jews were a polluting presence and their neutralization was the essential step on the path to a reformed Christian society that could capture, in some small way, the essence of the Heavenly Jerusalem that was to come. Espina was, however, not simply the slavish copyist of the leading figures of mendicant theology, he drew on the tradition in a creative way to establish his own distinctive position. Although he invoked the Jewish island of Duns Scotus, he rejected the Subtle Doctor's more positive vision of the Mosaic Law. If he took from Thomas Aquinas the possibility of salvation through natural law, nevertheless he rejected the Angelic Doctor's notion of the Jews' privileged access to moral understanding prior to the Incarnation. Within the narrow scope afforded to him by the tradition of medieval theology, Espina picked the path most hostile to Jews and to Judaism.

What part, then, did Espina play in the development of religious persecution in late medieval Spain? What was the role of *Fortalitium fidei* in the decline of toleration and the ending of coexistence? Was Espina the architect of purity of blood and the

Spanish Inquisition? It is but a small step from a model of latent inheritance and hermeneutically activated perfidy to one of purity of blood and corrupt lineage; a small step, too, from an inquisition established to root out heretics, the most dangerous of whom were judaizing New Christians, to an inquisition established with the express purpose of uncovering the crimes of *conversos*. There is equally little distance between calls to kill or expel the worst amongst the Jews and the violent expulsion of entire Jewish communities. Small steps and little distances, but significant ones nonetheless. Espina's remedies for the religious problems that faced Castile are no more palatable than those measures adopted by the Catholic Monarchs but the two should not be conflated. That Espina's intervention in the *converso* debate moved things closer to 1480 and 1492 is true only in retrospect. This, in the end, may be the real significance of *Fortalitium fidei*. Its importance lies less in what Espina actually proposed and more in the subsequent fortunes of his text. It could be read in the decades and centuries after its production not as responding to the very particular religious climate of the 1450s and 1460s or as replying to a series of pro-*converso* texts but as a precocious description of the Spain of the Catholic Monarchs.

BIBLIOGRAPHY

Manuscripts

[Alonso de Espina], *Fortalitium fidei*, El Burgo de Osma, Biblioteca de la Catedral, códice 154.

[Alonso de Espina], 'Sermones de Reverendi Magistri de Spina de penis Inferni', El Burgo de Osma, Biblioteca de la Catedral, códice 26, fols 100^r–115^v.

Primary Sources and Secondary Literature

Abulafia, Anna Sapir, *Christians and Jews in the Twelfth-Century Renaissance* (New York: Routledge, 1995).

Alain de Lille, *Summa de arte praedicatoria*, in *PL*, 110, cols 109–97.

Alonso de Cartagena, *Defensorium unitatis christianae (Tratado en favor de los judíos conversos)*, ed. by Manuel Alonso (Madrid: CSIC, Instituto Arias Montano, Escuela de Estudios Hebraicos, 1943).

Alonso de Cartagena y el 'Defensorium unitatis christianae': introducción histórica, traducción y notas, trans. by Guillermo Verdín-Díaz (Oviedo: Universidad de Oviedo, Servicio de Publicaciones, 1992).

[Alonso de Espina], *Fortalitium fidei*, [Strasbourg: Jean Mentelin, 1471].

Alonso de Oropesa, *Luz para conocimiento de los gentiles*, ed. and trans. by Luis A. Díaz y Díaz (Madrid: Universidad Pontificia de Salamanca, Fundación Universitaria Española, 1979).

Amador de los Ríos, José, *Historia social, política y religiosa de los judíos de España y Portugal*, 3 vols (Madrid: Imprenta de T. Fortanet, 1876).

Amran, Rica, 'Calumnias y falsificación histórica: dos casos de correspondencia apócrifa relacionadas con judíos hispanos durante el medioevo', *Cahiers de linguistique hispanique médiévale*, 29 (2006), 317–26.

Ancient Christian Commentary on Scripture, New Testament VIII: *Galatians, Ephesians, Philippians*, ed. by Mark J. Edwards (Downers Grove: InterVarsity Press, 1999).

Anidjar, Gil, 'Lines of Blood: *Limpieza de Sangre* As Political Theology', in *Blood in History and Blood Histories*, ed. by Mariacarla Gadebusch Bondio, Micrologus' Library, 13 (Florence: SISMEL/Edizioni del Galluzzo, 2005), pp. 119–36.

Aronson-Friedman, Amy I., and Gregory B. Kaplan, 'Editors' Introduction', in *Marginal Voices: Studies in Converso Literature of Medieval and Golden Age Spain*, ed. by Amy Aronson-Friedman and Gregory B. Kaplan, The Medieval and Early Modern Iberian World, 46 (Leiden: Brill, 2012), pp. 1–17.

Augustine of Hippo, *De civitate Dei*, ed. by B. Dombart and A. Kalb, 2 vols, CCSL, 47–48 (Turnhout: Brepols, 1955).

—, *De Genesi ad litteram*, ed. by J. Zycha, Corpus Scriptorum Ecclesiasticorum Latinorum, 28.1 (Vienna: Tempsky, 1894).

—, *Enarrationes in Psalmos*, ed. by E. Dekkers and J. Fraipont, 3 vols, CCSL, 38–40 (Turnhout: Brepols, 1956).

Avalle-Arce, Juan Bautista, 'Los herejes de Durango', in *Homenaje a Rodríguez-Moñino: estudios de erudición que le ofrecen sus amigos o discípulos hispanistas norteamericanos*, 2 vols (Madrid: Castalia, 1966), II, 39–55.

Bachrach, Bernard S., *Early Medieval Jewish Policy in Western Europe* (Minneapolis: University of Minnesota Press, 1977).

Baer, Yitzak, *A History of the Jews in Christian Spain*, trans. by Louis Schoffman, 2nd edn, 2 vols (Philadelphia: Jewish Publication Society, 1992).

—, *Die Juden im christlichen Spanien*, 2 vols (Berlin: Akademie-Verlag, 1929–36).

Bale, Anthony, *Feeling Persecuted: Christians, Jews and Images of Violence in the Middle Ages* (London: Reaktion, 2010).

Beceiro Pita, Isabel, 'La conciencia de los antepasados y la gloria del linaje en la Castilla bajomedieval', in *Relaciones de poder, de producción y parentesco en la Edad Media y Moderna: aproximación a su estudio*, ed. by Reyna Pastor, Biblioteca de la Historia, 1 (Madrid: CSIC, 1990), pp. 329–49.

—, and Ricardo Córdoba de la Llave, *Parentesco, poder y mentalidad: la nobleza castellana, siglos XII–XV* (Madrid: CSIC, 1990).

Bede, *In primam partem Samuhelis*, in *PL*, 91, cols 499–714d.
Beinart, Haim, *Conversos on Trial: The Inquisition in Ciudad Real*, trans. by Yael Guiladi, Hispania Judaica, 3 (Jerusalem: Magnes Press, 1981).
Beltrán de Heredia, V., 'Las bulas de Nicolás V acerca de los conversos de Castilla', *Sefarad*, 21 (1961), 22–47.
Benito Ruano, Eloy, *Los orígenes del problema converso*, Clave Historial, 31, rev. edn (Madrid: Real Academia de la Historia, 2001).
—, *Toledo en el siglo XV: vida política*, Escuela de Estudios Medievales: Estudios, 35 (Madrid: CSIC, Escuela de Estudios Medievales, 1961).
Bethencourt, Francisco, *The Inquisition: A Global History, 1478–1834* (Cambridge: Cambridge University Press, 2009).
Biale, David, *Blood and Belief: The Circulation of a Symbol between Jews and Christians* (Berkeley: University of California Press, 2007).
Boyd, Carolyn P., *Historia Patria: Politics, History, and National Identity in Spain, 1875–1975* (Princeton: Princeton University Press, 1997).
Boyden, James M., '"Fortune Has Stripped You of your Splendour": Favourites and their Fates in Fifteenth- and Sixteenth-Century Spain', in *The World of the Favourite*, ed. by J. H. Elliott and L. W. B. Brockliss (New Haven: Yale University Press, 1999), pp. 26–37.
Buell, Denise Kimber, 'Early Christian Universalism and Modern Forms of Racism', in *The Origins of Racism in the West*, ed. by Miriam Eliav-Feldon, Benjamin Isaac and Joseph Ziegler (Cambridge: Cambridge University Press, 2009), pp. 109–31.
Burkett, Delbert, *An Introduction to the New Testament and the Origins of Christianity* (Cambridge: Cambridge University Press, 2002).
Bynum, Caroline Walker, *Wonderful Blood: Theology and Practice in Late Medieval Northern Germany and Beyond* (Philadelphia: University of Pennsylvania Press, 2007).
Cantera, Francisco, 'Fernando de Pulgar y los conversos', *Sefarad*, 4 (1944), 295–348.

Cañizares-Esguerra, Jorge, 'Demons, Stars, and the Imagination: The Early Modern Body in the Tropics', in *The Origins of Racism in the West*, ed. by Miriam Eliav-Feldon, Benjamin Isaac and Joseph Ziegler (Cambridge: Cambridge University Press, 2009), pp. 313–25.

Carpenter, Dwayne E., *Alfonso X and the Jews: An Edition and Commentary on 'Siete Partidas' 7.24 "De los judíos"*, University of California Publications in Modern Philology, 115 (Berkeley: University of California Press, 1986).

Cátedra, Pedro M., 'La modificación del discurso con fines de invectiva: el sermón', *Atalaya*, 5 (1994), 101–21.

—, *Sermón sociedad y literatura en la Edad Media: San Vicente Ferrer en Castilla (1411–1412), estudio bibliográfico, literario y edición de los textos inéditos* (Valladolid: Junta de Castilla y León, Consejería de Cultura y Turismo, 1994).

Cavallero, Constanza, 'Miles Christi: la construcción del ethos en el *Fortalitium fidei* de Alonso de Espina (Castilla, siglo XV)', *Estudios de Historia de España*, 13 (2011), 149–98.

Charisma and Religious Authority: Jewish, Christian, and Muslim Preaching, 1200–1500, ed. by Katherine L. Jansen and Miri Rubin, Europa Sacra, 4 (Turnhout: Brepols, 2010).

Chazan, Robert, *Daggers of Faith: Thirteenth-Century Christian Missionizing and Jewish Response* (Berkeley: University of California Press, 1989).

—, *Fashioning Jewish Identity in Medieval Western Christendom* (Cambridge: Cambridge University Press, 2004).

—, 'Medieval Anti-Semitism', in *History and Hate: The Dimensions of Anti-Semitism*, ed. by David Berger (Philadelphia: Jewish Publication Society, 1986), pp. 49–65.

—, *Reassessing Jewish Life in Medieval Europe* (Cambridge: Cambridge University Press, 2010).

Christian Attitudes toward the Jews in the Middle Ages: A Casebook, ed. by Michael Frasetto (New York: Routledge, 2007).

Coates, Geraldine, *Treacherous Foundations: Betrayal and Collective Identity in Early Medieval Spanish Epic, Chronicle, and Drama*, Colección Támesis, A281 (Woodbridge: Tamesis, 2009).

Cohen, Jeremy, *Christ Killers: The Jews and the Passion from the Bible to the Big Screen* (New York: Oxford University Press, 2007).

—, *The Friars and the Jews: The Evolution of Medieval Anti-Judaism* (Ithaca: Cornell University Press, 1982).

—, *Living Letters of the Law: Ideas of the Jew in Medieval Christianity* (Berkeley: University of California Press, 1999).

—, 'The Mystery of Israel's Salvation: Romans 11.25–26 in Patristic and Medieval Exegesis', *Harvard Theological Review*, 98 (2005), 247–81.

Cohen, Mark R., 'Anti-Jewish Violence and the Place of the Jews in Christendom and in Islam: A Paradigm', in *Religious Violence between Christians and Jews: Medieval Roots, Modern Perspectives*, ed. by Anna Sapir Abulafia (Basingstoke: Palgrave, 2002), pp. 107–37.

—, *Under Crescent and Cross: The Jews in the Middle Ages* (Princeton: Princeton University Press, 1994).

Cohn, Samuel K., 'The Black Death and the Burning of the Jews', *P&P*, 196 (2007), 3–36.

Coleman, Janet, 'Citizenship and the Language of Statecraft', in *Finding Europe: Discourses on Margins, Communities, Images ca. 13th–ca. 18th Centuries*, ed. by Anthony Molho, Diogo Ramada Curto and Niki Koniordos (New York: Berghahn, 2007), pp. 223–52.

—, 'Negotiating the Medieval in the Modern: European Citizenship and Statecraft', *Transactions of the Royal Historical Society*, 22 (2012), 75–93.

Concilios visigóticos e hispano-romanos, ed. by José Vives (Barcelona: CSIC, Instituto Enrique Flórez, 1963).

Contreras Jiménez, María Eugenia, 'Diego Arias Dávila en la tradición y en la historia', *Anuario de Estudios Medievales*, 15 (1985), 475–95.

The Conversos and Moriscos of Late Medieval Spain and Beyond, I: *Departures and Change*, ed. by Kevin Ingram, Studies in Medieval and Reformation Traditions, 141 (Leiden: Brill, 2009).

Cowling, David, *Building the Text: Architecture as Metaphor in Late Medieval and Early Modern France*, (Oxford: Clarendon Press, 1998).

Crónica de don Álvaro de Luna, condestable de Castilla, maestre de Santiago, ed. by Juan de Mata Carriazo, Colección de Crónicas Españolas, 2 (Madrid: Espasa-Calpe, 1940).

Crónica del rey don Enrique el Cuarto, in *Crónicas de los reyes de Castilla desde don Alfonso el Sabio hasta los Católicos don Fernando y doña Isabel*, ed. by Cayetano Rosell, 3 vols, Biblioteca de Autores Españoles, 66, 68, 70 (Madrid: M. Rivadeneyra, 1875–78), III, 3–222.

Crónica del sereníssimo rey don Juan el Segundo deste nombre, in *Crónicas de los reyes de Castilla desde don Alfonso el Sabio hasta los Católicos don Fernando y doña Isabel*, ed. by Cayetano Rosell, 3 vols, Biblioteca de Autores Españoles, 66, 68, 70 (Madrid: M. Rivadeneyra, 1875–78), II, 273–695.

Dahan, Gilbert, *Les Intellectuels chrétiens et les juifs au Moyen Âge* (Paris: Cerf, 1999).

Debby, Nirit Ben-Aryeh, *Renaissance Florence in the Rhetoric of Two Popular Preachers: Giovanni Dominici (1356–1419) and Bernardino da Siena (1380–1444)*, Late Medieval and Early Modern Studies, 4 (Turnhout: Brepols, 2001).

Dedieu, Jean Pierre, '¿Pecado original o pecado social? Reflexiones en torno a la constitución y a la definición del grupo judeo-converso en Castilla', *Manuscrits*, 10 (1992), 61–76.

Despina, Marie, 'Las acusaciones de crimen ritual en España', *El Olivo*, 9 (1979), 48–70.

Díaz de Montalvo, Alonso, *La causa conversa*, ed. by Matilde Conde Salazar and others (Madrid: Aben Ezra Ediciones, 2008).

Díaz y Díaz, Luis A., 'Introducción', in Alonso de Oropesa, *Luz para conocimiento de los gentiles*, ed. and trans. by Luis A. Díaz y Díaz (Madrid: Universidad Pontificia de Salamanca, Fundación Universitaria Española, 1979), pp. 7–57.

Dictionnaire de théologie catholique contenant l'exposé des doctrines de la théologie catholique leurs preuves et leur histoire, ed. by A. Vacant, E. Mangenot and É. Amann, 14 vols (Paris: Letouzey et Ané, 1909–41).

Echevarría, Ana, 'Catalina of Lancaster, the Castilian Monarchy and Coexistence', in *Medieval Spain: Culture, Conflict and Coexistence, Studies in Honour of Angus MacKay*, ed. by Roger Collins and Anthony Goodman (Basingstoke: Palgrave Macmillan, 2002), pp. 79–122.

—, 'Enrique IV de Castilla, un rey cruzado', *Espacio, Tiempo y Forma. Serie III, Historia Medieval*, 17 (2004), 143–56.

—, *The Fortress of Faith: The Attitude towards Muslims in Fifteenth Century Spain*, Medieval Iberian Peninsula: Texts and Studies, 12 (Leiden: Brill, 1999).

Edwards, John, 'The *Conversos*: A Theological Approach', *BHS*, 62 (1985), 39–49.

—, 'Elijah and the Inquisition: Messianic Prophecy among *Conversos* in Spain, c. 1500', *Nottingham Mediaeval Studies*, 28 (1984), 79–94.

—, 'Fifteenth-Century Franciscan Reform and the Spanish *Conversos*: The Case of Fray Alonso de Espina', in *Monastic Studies: The Continuity of Tradition*, ed. by Judith Loades (Bangor: Headstart History, 1990), pp. 203–10.

—, 'The *Judeoconversos* in the Urban Life of Córdoba', in *Villes et sociétés urbaines au Moyen Âge: hommage à M. le professeur Jacques Heers*, Cultures et civilisations médiévales, 11 (Paris: Presses de l'Université de Paris-Sorbonne, 1994), pp. 287–97.

—, 'New Light on the *Converso* Debate? The Jewish Christianity of Alfonso de Cartagena and Juan de Torquemada', in *Cross, Crescent and Conversion: Studies on Medieval Spain and Christendom in Memory of Richard Fletcher*, ed. by Simon Barton and Peter Linehan, The Medieval Mediterranean, 73 (Leiden: Brill, 2008) pp. 311–26.

—, 'La prehistoria de los estatutos de "limpieza de sangre"', in *Xudeus e conversos na historia: actas do congreso internacional, Ribadavia 14–17 de outubro de 1991*, ed. by Carlos Barros, 2 vols (Santiago de Compostela: Editorial de la Historia, 1994), I, 351–57.

—, 'Religious Faith and Doubt in Late Medieval Spain: Soria *circa* 1450–1500', *P&P*, 120 (1988), 3–25.

Ehrman, Bart D., *Lost Christianities: The Battles for Scripture and the Faiths We Never Knew* (New York: Oxford University Press, 2003).

Elukin, Jonathan M., 'From Jew to Christian? Conversion and Immutability in Medieval Europe', in *Varieties of Religious Conversion in the Middle Ages*, ed. by James Muldoon (Gainesville: University Press of Florida, 1997), pp. 171–89.

Esposito, Mario, 'Une secte d'hérétiques à Medina del Campo en 1459: d'après le *Fortalicium fidei* d'Alphonse de Spina', *Revue d'histoire ecclésiastique*, 32 (1936), 350–60.

Estow, Clara, *Pedro the Cruel of Castile, 1350–1369* (Leiden: Brill, 1995).

Fenster, Thelma S., and Daniel Lord Smail, 'Introduction', in *Fama: The Politics of Talk and Reputation in Medieval Europe*, ed. by Thelma S. Fenster and Daniel Lord Smail (Ithaca: Cornell University Press, 2003), pp. 1–11.

Fernández Gallardo, Luis, *Alonso de Cartagena (1385–1456): una biografía política en la Castilla del siglo XV* (Valladolid: Junta de Castilla y León, Consejería de Educación y Cultura, 2002).

—, 'Alonso de Cartagena: iglesia, política y cultura en la Castilla del siglo XV', 6 vols (unpublished doctoral thesis, Universidad Complutense de Madrid, 1998).

Fita, Fidel, 'La judería de Segovia: documentos inéditos', *Boletín de la Real Academia de la Historia*, 9 (1886), 344–89.

Fredricksen, Paula, *Augustine and the Jews: A Christian Defense of Jews and Judaism* (New York: Doubleday, 2008).

—, *From Jesus to Christ: The Origins of the New Testament Images of Jesus*, 2nd edn (New Haven: Yale Nota Bene, 2000).

Friars and Jews in the Middle Ages and Renaissance, ed. by Steven J. McMichael and Susan Myers, The Medieval Franciscans, 2 (Leiden: Brill, 2004).

Gager, John, *The Origins of Anti-Semitism: Attitudes toward Judaism in Pagan and Christian Antiquity* (Oxford: Oxford University Press, 1985).

Gerbet, Marie-Claude, *Las noblezas españolas en la Edad Media: siglos XI–XV*, trans. by María José García Vera (Madrid: Alianza Editorial, 1997).

Gerli, E. Michael, 'The *Converso* Condition: New Approaches to an Old Question', in *Medieval Iberia: Changing Societies and Cultures in Contact and Transition*, ed. by Ivy A. Corfis and Ray Harris-Northall, Colección Támesis, A247 (Woodbridge: Tamesis, 2007), pp. 3–15.

Gilly, Carlos, *Spanien und der Basler Buchdruck bis 1600: ein Querschnitt durch die spanische Geistesgeschichte aus der Sicht einer europäischen Buchdruckerstadt* (Basel: Helbing & Lichtenhahn, 1985).

Gitlitz, David M., 'Forum: Letter on "Inflecting the *Converso* Voice"', *La Corónica*, 25 (Spring, 1997), 163–66.

Glick, Leonard B., *Abraham's Heirs: Jews and Christians in Medieval Europe* (Syracuse: Syracuse University Press, 1999).

—, *Marked in Your Flesh: Circumcision from Ancient Judea to Modern America* (New York: Oxford University Press, 2005).

Goldenberg, David M., *The Curse of Ham: Race and Slavery in Early Judaism, Christianity, and Islam* (Princeton: Princeton University Press, 2003).

Gonzaga, Francesco, *De origine seraphicae religionis franciscanae eiusque progressibus, de regularis observanciae institutione, forma administrationis ac legibus, admirabilique eius propagatione* (Rome: [n. pub.], 1587).

González Rolán, Tomás, and Pilar Saquero Suárez-Somonte, 'Introducción', in *De la 'Sentencia-Estatuto' de Pero Sarmiento a la 'Instrucción' del Relator: estudio introductorio, edición crítica y notas de los textos contrarios y favorables a los judeoconversos a raíz de la rebelión de Toledo de 1449*, ed. by Tomás González Rolán and Pilar Saquero Suárez-Somonte (Madrid: Aben Ezra Ediciones, 2012), pp. xvii–cxvii.

Goñi Gaztambide, José, *Historia de la bula de la cruzada en España*, Victoriensia, 4 (Vitoria: Editorial del Seminario, 1958).

Gow, Andrew C., *The Red Jews: Antisemitism in an Apocalyptic Age 1200–1600* (Leiden: Brill, 1995).

Grayzel, Solomon, 'The Papal Bull *Sicut Judeis*', in *Studies and Essays in Honor of Abraham A. Neuman*, ed. by Meir Ben-Horin, Bernard D. Weinryb, and Solomon Zeitlin (Leiden: Brill, 1962), pp. 243–80.

Guadalajara Medina, José, *Las profecías del anticristo en la Edad Media* (Madrid: Gredos, 1996).

Hain, Ludwig, *Repertorium bibliographicum in quo libri omnes ab arte typographica inventa usque ad annum MD*, 4 vols (Stuttgart: Cotta, 1826–38).

Harris, Jennifer, 'Enduring Covenant in the Christian Middle Ages', *Journal of Ecumenical Studies*, 44 (2009), 563–86.

Henderson, John B., 'The Multiplicity, Duality, and Unity of Heresies', in *Strategies of Medieval Communal Identity: Judaism, Christianity and Islam*, ed. by Wout J. van Bekkum and Paul M. Cobb, Mediaevalia Groningana New Series, 5 (Paris: Peeters, 2004), pp. 11–27.

Hernández Franco, Juan, *Sangre limpia, sangre española: el debate sobre los estatutos de limpieza (siglos XV–XVII)* (Madrid: Cátedra, 2011).

L'hérédité entre Moyen Âge et époque moderne: perspectives historiques, ed. by Maaike van der Lugt and Charles de Miramon, Micrologus' Library, 27 (Florence: SISMEL/Edizioni del Galluzzo per la Fondazione Ezio Franceschini, 2008).

Herrero Hernández, Cándida, 'Literatura latina de controversia religiosa en la Castilla del siglo XV: una aproximación a su tipología', in *Estudios de latín medieval hispánico: actas del V Congreso Internacional de Latín Medieval Hispánico, Barcelona, 7–10 de septiembre de 2009*, ed. by José Martínez Gázquez, Óscar de la Cruz Palma and Cándida Herrero Hernández (Florence: SISMEL/Edizioni del Galluzzo, 2011), pp. 425–41.

Highfield, Roger, 'Christians, Jews and Muslims in the Same Society: The Fall of *Convivencia* in Medieval Spain', in *Religious Motivation: Biographical and Sociological Problems for the Church Historian*, ed. by Derek Baker, Studies in Church History, 15 (Oxford: Published for the Ecclesiastical History Society by Basil Blackwell, 1978), pp. 121–46.

Hood, John Y. B., *Aquinas and the Jews* (Philadelphia: University of Pennsylvania Press, 1995).

Index alphabetico digestus ordine, in quo recesentur codices manuscripti latini, qui in huius regiae bibliothecae armariis sive tabulariis per pluteos seu sectiones distributi asservantur, in Guillermo Antolín,

Catálogo de códices latinos de la Real Biblioteca del Escorial, 5 vols (Madrid: Imprenta Helénica, 1910–23), V, 331–487.

Inflecting the Converso Voice: Critical Cluster, ed. by Gregory S. Hutcheson, *La Corónica*, 25 (Fall, 1996), 3–68.

Izbicki, Thomas M., 'Juan de Torquemada's Defense of the *Conversos*', *Catholic Historical Review*, 85 (1999), 195–207.

—, 'The Possibility of Dialogue with Islam in the Fifteenth Century', in *Nicholas of Cusa in Search of God and Wisdom: Essays in Honour of Morichi Watanabe by the American Cusanus Society*, ed. by Gerald Christianson and Thomas M. Izbicki, Studies in the History of Christian Thought, 45 (Leiden: Brill, 1991), pp. 175–83.

Jonin, Michel, 'De la pureté de foi vers la pureté de sang: les ambiguïtés orthodoxes d'un plaidoyer *pro converso*', in *L'hérédité entre Moyen Âge et époque moderne: perspectives historiques*, ed. by Maaike van der Lugt and Charles de Miramon, Micrologus' Library, 27 (Florence: SISMEL/Edizioni del Galluzzo per la Fondazione Ezio Franceschini, 2008), pp. 83–102.

Kamen, Henry, 'Limpieza and the Ghost of Américo Castro: Racism as a Tool of Literary Analysis', *Hispanic Review*, 64 (1996), 19–29.

—, *The Spanish Inquisition: An Historical Revision* (London: Weidenfeld & Nicolson, 1997).

Kaplan, Gregory B., *The Evolution of 'Converso' Literature: The Writings of the Converted Jews of Medieval Spain* (Gainesville: University Press of Florida, 2002).

—, 'The Inception of *Limpieza de Sangre* (Purity of Blood) and Its Impact in Medieval and Golden Age Spain', in *Marginal Voices: Studies in Converso Literature of Medieval and Golden Age Spain*, ed. by Amy Aronson-Friedman and Gregory B. Kaplan, The Medieval and Early Modern Iberian World, 46 (Leiden: Brill, 2012), pp. 19–41.

King, P. D., *Law and Society in the Visigothic Kingdom* (Cambridge: University Press, 1972).

Kurtz, Barbara E., 'Diego de San Pedro's *Cárcel de Amor* and the Tradition of the Allegorical Edifice', *Journal of Hispanic Philology*, 8 (1984), 123–38.

Ladero Quesada, Miguel Ángel, *Las guerras de Granada en el siglo XV* (Barcelona: Ariel, 2002).

Langmuir, Gavin I., 'Peter the Venerable: Defense against Doubts', in *Toward a Definition of Antisemitism* (Berkeley: University of California Press, 1990), pp. 197–208, 382–84.

—, 'The Transformation of Anti-Judaism', in *Toward a Definition of Antisemitism* (Berkeley: University of California Press, 1990), pp. 63–99, 362–65.

Late Medieval Jewish Identities: Iberia and Beyond, ed. by Carmen Caballero-Navas and Esperanza Alonso (New York: Palgrave Macmillan, 2010).

Lawrance, Jeremy, 'Alfonso de Cartagena y los conversos', in *Actas del Primer Congreso Anglo-Hispano*, II: *Literatura*, ed. by Alan Deyermond and Ralph Penny (Madrid: Castalia, 1993), pp. 103–20.

—, 'Homily and Harangue in Medieval Spain: The Sermon and Crowds', in *Hacia una poética del sermón*, ed. by Rebeca Sanmartín Bastida, Barry Taylor and Rosa Vidal Doval (= *Revista de Poética Medieval*, 24 (2010)), pp. 147–84.

—, 'Representations of Violence in 15th-Century Spanish Literature', in *Late Medieval Spanish Studies in Honour of Dorothy Sherman Severin*, ed. by Joseph T. Snow and Roger Wright (= *BHS*, 68 (2009)), pp. 95–103.

Lea, Henry Charles, *A History of the Inquisition of Spain*, 4 vols (London: Macmillan, 1906–07).

Lejarza, Fidel de, and Ángel Uribe, 'Introducción a los orígenes de la Observancia en España: las reformas en los siglos XIV y XV', *AIA*, 17 (1957), 17–660.

Lerner, Robert E., *The Feast of Saint Abraham: Medieval Millenarians and the Jews* (Philadelphia: University of Pennsylvania Press, 2001).

—, *The Heresy of the Free Spirit in the Later Middle Ages* (Berkeley: University of California Press, 1972).

Lipton, Sara, *Images of Intolerance: The Representation of Jews and Judaism in the Bible moralisée* (Berkeley: University of California Press, 1999).

Llamedo González, Juan José, 'Juan de Torquemada: apuntes sobre su vida, su obra y su pensamiento', in *Tratado contra los madianitas e ismaelitas, de Juan de Torquemada (Contra la discriminación conversa)*, ed. by Carlos del Valle R. (Madrid: Aben Ezra Ediciones, 2002), pp. 87–118.

López, Atanasio, 'Confesores de la familia real de Castilla', *AIA*, 31 (1929), 5–75.

Lubac, Henri de, *Exégèse médiéval: les quatre sens de l'Écriture*, 4 vols (Paris: Aubier, 1959–64).

Lynch, Joseph H., *Early Christianity: A Brief History* (New York: Oxford University Press, 2010).

MacKay, Angus, 'The Hispanic-*Converso* Predicament', *Transactions of the Royal Historical Society*, 35 (1985), 159–79.

—, 'Popular Movements and Pogroms in Fifteenth-Century Castile', *P&P*, 55 (1972), 33–67.

—, 'Religion, Culture, and Ideology on the Late Medieval Castilian-Granadan Frontier', in *Medieval Frontier Societies*, ed. by Robert Bartlett and Angus MacKay (Oxford: Clarendon Press, 1989), pp. 217–43.

Mansi, Joannes Dominicus, *Sacrorum conciliorum nova et amplissima collectio*, 31 vols (Florence: Antonium Zatta, 1759–98).

Marginal Voices: Studies in Converso Literature of Medieval and Golden Age Spain, ed. by Amy Aronson-Friedman and Gregory B. Kaplan, The Medieval and Early Modern Iberian World, 46 (Leiden: Brill, 2012).

Markus, Robert, *The End of Ancient Christianity* (Cambridge: Cambridge University Press, 1990).

—, *Saeculum: History and Society in the Theology of St Augustine* (Cambridge: University Press, 1970).

Márquez Villanueva, Francisco, 'Conversos y cargos concejiles en el siglo XV', in *De la España judeoconversa: doce estudios*, Serie General Universitaria, 57 (Barcelona: Edicions Bellaterra, 2006), pp. 137–74 (first pub. in *Revista de Archivos, Bibliotecas y Museos*, 63 (1957), 503–540).

—, '"Nasçer e morir como bestias" (criptoaverroísmo y criptojudaísmo)', in *De la España judeoconversa: doce estudios*, Serie General Universitaria, 57 (Barcelona: Edicions Bellaterra, 2006), pp. 203–27 (first pub. in *Los judaizantes en Europa y la literatura castellana del Siglo de Oro*, ed. by Fernando Díaz Esteban (Madrid: Letrúmero, 1994), pp. 273–93).

—, 'El problema de los conversos: cuatro puntos cardinales', in *De la España judeoconversa: doce estudios*, Serie General Universitaria, 57 (Barcelona: Edicions Bellaterra, 2006), pp. 43–74 (first pub. as 'The Converso Problem: An Assessment', in *Collected Studies in Honour of Américo Castro's Eightieth Year*, ed. M. P. Hornick (Oxford: Lincombe Lodge Research Library, 1965), pp. 317–333).

—, 'Sobre el concepto de judaizante', in *De la España judeoconversa: doce estudios*, Serie General Universitaria, 57 (Barcelona: Edicions Bellaterra, 2006), pp. 95–114 (first pub. in *'Encuentros' and 'Desencuentros': Spanish Jewish Cultural Interaction through History*, ed. by Carlos Carrete Parrondo and others (Tel Aviv: University Publishing Projects, 2000), pp. 519–42).

Martínez Casado, Ángel, *Lope de Barrientos: un intelectual en la corte de Juan II* (Salamanca: Editorial San Esteban, 1994).

McKendrick, Geraldine, 'The Franciscan Order in Castile, *c.* 1440–*c.* 1560' (unpublished doctoral thesis, University of Edinburgh, 1987).

McMichael, Steven J., 'Alonso de Espina on the Mosaic Law', in *Friars and Jews in the Middle Ages and Renaissance*, ed. by Steven J. McMichael and Susan Myers, The Medieval Franciscans, 2 (Leiden: Brill, 2004), pp. 199–223.

—, 'The End of the World, Antichrist, and the Final Conversion of the Jews in the *Fortalitium fidei* of Friar Alonso de Espina (d. 1464)', *Medieval Encounters*, 12 (2006), 224–73.

—, 'Friar Alonso de Espina, Prayer, and Medieval Jewish, Muslim and Christian Polemical Literature', in *Franciscans at Prayer*, ed. by Timothy J. Johnson, The Medieval Franciscans, 4 (Leiden: Brill, 2007), pp. 271–304.

—, 'The Sources for Alonso de Espina's Messianic Argument against the Jews in the *Fortalitium Fidei*', in *Iberia and the Mediterranean World of the Middle Ages: Studies in Honor of Robert I. Burns S.J.*, ed. by Larry J. Simon, 2 vols (Leiden: Brill, 1995–96) I, 72–95.

—, *Was Jesus of Nazareth the Messiah? Alphonso de Espina's Argument against the Jews in the 'Fortalitium Fidei' (c. 1464)*,

South Florida Studies in the History of Judaism, 96 (Atlanta: Scholars Press, 1994).

Melammed, Renée Levine, 'Identities in Flux: Iberian *Conversos* at Home and Abroad', in *Late Medieval Jewish Identities: Iberia and Beyond*, ed. by Carmen Caballero-Navas and Esperanza Alonso (New York: Palgrave Macmillan, 2010), pp. 43–53.

Memorial contra los conversos [*'Apelaçión y suplicaçión' de Marcos García de Mora*] in *De la 'Sentencia-Estatuto' de Pero Sarmiento a la 'Instrucción' del Relator: estudio introductorio, edición crítica y notas de los textos contrarios y favorables a los judeoconversos a raíz de la rebelión de Toledo de 1449*, ed. by Tomás González Rolán and Pilar Saquero Suárez-Somonte (Madrid: Aben Ezra Ediciones, 2012), pp. 193–242.

Memorial de diversas hazañas: crónica de Enrique IV, ordenada por Mosén Diego de Valera, ed. by Juan de Mata Carriazo, Colección de Crónicas Españolas, 4 (Madrid: Espasa-Caple, 1941).

Memorias de don Enrique IV de Castilla: contiene la colección diplomática del mismo rey compuesta y ordenada por la Real Academia de la Historia, 2 vols (Madrid: Real Academia de la Historia, 1835–1913).

Mendoza, Íñigo López de, *Doctrinal de privados fecho a la muerte del maestre de Santiago don Álvaro de Luna, donde se introduçe al autor fablando en nombre del maestre*, in *Poesía crítica y satírica del siglo XV*, ed. by Julio Rodríguez Puértolas, Clásicos Castalia, 114 (Madrid: Castalia, 1989), pp. 154–67.

Menéndez Pidal de Navascués, Faustino, *Heráldica medieval española* (Madrid: Hidalguía, 1982).

Meyer, Ann R., *Medieval Allegory and the Building of the New Jerusalem* (Cambridge: Brewer, 2003).

Meyerson, Mark D., 'Forum: Letter on "Inflecting the *Converso* Voice"', *La Corónica*, 25 (Spring, 1997), 179–182.

Meyuhas Ginio, Alisa, 'El concepto de "perfidia judaica" de la época visigoda en la perspectiva castellana del siglo XV', *Helmántica*, 46 (1995), 299–311.

—, 'The *Conversos* and the Magic Arts in Alonso de Espina's *Fortalitium Fidei*', *Mediterranean Historical Review*, 5 (1990), 169–82.

—, *De bello iudaeorum: Fray Alonso de Espina y su 'Fortalitium fidei'*, FIRC, 8 (Salamanca: Universidad Pontificia de Salamanca, 1998).

—, *La forteresse de la foi: la vision du monde d'Alonso de Espina, moine espagnol (?–1466)* (Paris: Cerf, 1998).

—, 'The Fortress of Faith – At the End of the West: Alonso de Espina and His *Fortalitium Fidei*', in *Contra Iudaeos: Ancient and Medieval Polemics between Christians and Jews*, ed. by Ora Limour and Guy G. Stroumsa, Texts and Studies in Medieval and Early Modern Judaism, 10 (Tübingen: Mohr, 1996), pp. 215–37.

Milhou, Alain, *Colón y su mentalidad mesiánica en el ambiente franciscanista español*, Cuadernos Colombinos, 11 (Valladolid: Casa-Museo de Colón, Seminario Americanista de la Universidad de Valladolid, 1983).

Mitre Fernández, Emilio, *Los judíos de Castilla en tiempo de Enrique III: el pogrom de 1391*, Estudios de Historia Medieval, 3 (Valladolid: Universidad de Valladolid, 1994).

Monsalvo Antón, José María, 'Algunas consideraciones sobre el ideario antijudío contenido en el *Liber III* del *Fortalitium fidei* de Alonso de Espina', *Aragón en la Edad Media*, 14–15 (1999), 1061–87.

—, 'Mentalidad antijudía en la Castilla medieval: cultura clerical y cultura popular en la gestación y difusión de un ideario medieval', in *Xudeos e conversos na historia: actas do congreso internacional, Ribadavia 14–17 de outubro de 1991*, ed. by Carlos Barros, 2 vols (Santiago de Compostela: Editorial de la Historia, 1994), I, 21–84.

—, *Teoría y evolución de un conflicto social: el antisemitismo en la Corona de Castilla en la Baja Edad Media* (Madrid: Siglo Veintiuno de España Editores, 1985).

Montes Romero-Camacho, Isabel, 'El *problema converso*: una aproximación historiográfica (1998–2008)', *Medievalismo*, 18 (2008), 109–247.

Moore, R. I., *The Formation of a Persecuting Society: Power and Deviance in Western Europe, 950–1250* (Oxford: Basil Blackwell, 1987).

Moorman, John, *A History of the Franciscan Order: From its Origins to the Year 1517* (Oxford: Clarendon Press, 1968).

Mormando, Franco, *The Preacher's Demons: Bernardino of Siena and the Social Underworld of Early Renaissance Italy* (Chicago: University of Chicago Press, 1999).

Netanyahu, B., 'Alonso de Espina: Was He a New Christian?', in *Toward the Inquisition: Essays on Jewish and Converso History in Late Medieval Spain* (Ithaca: Cornell University Press, 1997), pp. 43–75, 213–31 (first publ. in *Proceedings of the American Academy for Jewish Research*, 43 (1976), 107–65).

—, *The Origins of the Inquisition in Fifteenth Century Spain*, 2nd edn (New York: The New York Review of Books, 2001).

Nickson, Tom, 'The First Murder: Picturing Polemic c. 1391', in *The Hebrew Bible in Fifteenth-Century Spain: Exegesis, Literature, Philosophy, and the Arts*, ed. by Jonathan Decter and Arturo Prats, Études sur le Judaïsme Médiéval, 54 (Leiden: Brill, 2012), pp. 41–59, 279–81.

—, 'Reframing the Bible: Genesis and Exodus on Toledo Cathedral's Fourteenth-Century Choir Screen', *Gesta*, 50 (2011), 71–89.

Nieto Soria, José Manuel, 'Enrique IV de Castilla y el pontificado (1454–1474)', *En la España Medieval*, 19 (1996), 167–238.

Nirenberg, David, *Anti-Judaism: The Western Tradition* (New York: Norton, 2013).

—, *Communities of Violence: Persecution of Minorities in the Middle Ages* (Princeton: Princeton University Press, 1996).

—, 'Deviant Politics and Jewish Love: Alfonso VIII and the Jewess of Toledo', *Jewish History*, 21 (2007), 15–41.

—, 'Enmity and Assimilation: Jews, Christians, and Converts in Medieval Spain', *Common Knowledge*, 9 (2003), 137–55.

—, 'Figures of Thought and Figures of Flesh: "Jews" and "Judaism" in Late-Medieval Spanish Poetry and Politics', *Speculum*, 81 (2006), 398–426.

—, 'Mass Conversion and Genealogical Mentalities: Jews and Christians in Fifteenth-Century Spain', *P&P*, 174 (2002), 3–41.

—, 'Review of Bruce Rosenstock, *New Men: 'Conversos', Christian Theology, and Society in Fifteenth-Century Castile*, Papers of the Medieval Hispanic Research Seminar, 39 (London: Department of Hispanic Studies, Queen Mary, University of London, 2002)', *Speculum*, 80 (2005), 315–17.

—, 'Une société face à l'alterité: juifs et chrétiens dans la Péninsule Ibérique 1391–1449', *Annales. Histoire, Sciences Sociales*, 62 (2007), 755–90.

—, 'Was There Race before Modernity? The Example of "Jewish" Blood in Late Medieval Spain', in *The Origins of Racism in the West*, ed. by Miriam Eliav-Feldon, Benjamin Isaac and Joseph Ziegler (Cambridge: Cambridge University Press, 2009), pp. 232–64.

Norman, Corrie E., 'The Social History of Preaching: Italy', in *Preachers and People in the Reformations and Early Modern Period*, ed. by Larissa Taylor, A New History of the Sermon, 2 (Leiden: Brill, 2001), pp. 125–91.

Ocker, Christopher, 'Contempt for Friars and Contempt for Jews in Late Medieval Germany', in *Friars and Jews in the Middle Ages and Renaissance*, ed. by Steven J. McMichael and Susan Myers, The Medieval Franciscans, 2 (Leiden: Brill, 2004), pp. 119–46.

Olsen, Glenn W., 'Reform after the Pattern of the Primitive Church in the Thought of Salvian of Marseille', *Catholic Historical Review*, 68 (1982), 1–12.

Palencia, Alonso de, *Gesta hispaniensia ex annalibus suorum dierum collecta*, ed. and trans. by Brian Tate and Jeremy Lawrance, 2 vols (Madrid: Real Academia de la Historia, 1998–99).

Pastore, Stefania, *Una herejía española: conversos, alumbrados e inquisición (1449–1559)*, introd. by Ricardo García Cárcel and Adriano Prosperi (Madrid: Marcial Pons, 2010).

—, *Il vangelo e la spada: l'inquisizione di Castiglia e i suoi critici (1460–1598)*, Temi e Testi, 46 (Rome: Edizioni di storia e letteratura, 2003).

Paton, Bernadette, '"Una Città Fatticosa": Dominican Preaching and the Defence of the Republic in Late Medieval Siena', in *City and Countryside in Late Medieval and Renaissance Italy: Essays Presented to Philip Jones*, ed. by Trevor Dean and Chris Wickham (London: Hambledon Press, 1990) pp. 109–23.

—, *Preaching Friars and the Civic Ethos: Siena, 1380–1480*, Westfield Publications in Medieval Studies, 7 (London: Centre for Medieval Studies, Queen Mary and Westfield College, University of London, 1992).

Perea Rodríguez, Óscar, 'Minorías en la España de los Trastámara (II): judíos y conversos', *eHumanista*, 10 (2008), 353–468.

Pereda, Felipe, *Las imágenes de la discordia: política y poética de la imagen sagrada en la España del cuatrocientos* (Madrid: Marcial Pons, 2007).

—, 'La Puerta de los Leones de la Catedral de Toledo: una interpretación en clave litúrgica y funeraria', in *Grabkunst und Sepulkralkultur in Spanien und Portugal/Arte funerario y cultura sepulcral en España y Portugal*, ed. by Barbara Borngässer, Henrik Karge and Bruno Klein, Ars Iberica et Americana, 11 (Frankfurt am Main: Vervuert; Madrid: Iberoamericana, 2006), pp. 155–91.

Pérez Ferreiro, Elvira, 'El tratado de Torquemada y la controversia estatutaria en la decimoquinta centuria', in *Tratado contra los madianitas e ismaelitas, de Juan de Torquemada (Contra la discriminación conversa)*, ed. by Carlos del Valle R. (Madrid: Aben Ezra Ediciones, 2002), pp. 75–85.

Phillips, William D., *Enrique IV and the Crisis of Fifteenth-Century Castile, 1425–1480*, Speculum Anniversary Monographs, 3 (Cambridge, MA: Mediaeval Academy of America, 1978).

Polecritti, Cynthia L., *Preaching Peace in Renaissance Italy: Bernardino of Siena and his Audience* (Washington: Catholic University of America Press, 2000).

Preacher, Sermon, and Audience in the Middle Ages, ed. by Carolyn Muessig, A New History of the Sermon, 3 (Leiden: Brill, 2002).

Preachers and People in the Reformations and Early Modern Period, ed. by Larissa Taylor, A New History of the Sermon, 2 (Leiden: Brill, 2001).

Proceso inquisitorial contra los Arias Dávila segovianos: un enfrentamiento social entre judíos y conversos, ed. by Carlos Carrete Parrondo, FIRC, 3 (Salamanca: Universidad Pontificia de Salamanca; [Granada]: Universidad de Granada, 1986).

Rábade Obradó, María del Pilar, 'Judeoconversos e inquisición', in *Orígenes de la monarquía hispánica: propaganda y legitimación, ca. 1400–1520*, ed. by José Manuel Nieto Soria (Madrid: Dykinson, 1999), pp. 239–72.

Ramos, Rafael, '"Que si a Távara passáis vós serés apedreado por hebreo": una nota a la poesía del Comendador Román', *Hispanic Research Journal*, 10 (2009), 193–205.

Reinhardt, Klaus, and Horacio Santiago-Otero, *Biblioteca bíblica ibérica medieval* (Madrid: CSIC, 1986).

Religious Violence between Christians and Jews: Medieval Roots, Modern Perspectives, ed. by Anna Sapir Abulafia (Basingstoke: Palgrave, 2002).

Robson, Michael, *The Franciscans in the Middle Ages* (Woodbridge: Boydell Press, 2006).

Rodríguez Barral, Paulino, *La imagen del judío en la España medieval: el conflicto entre cristianismo y judaismo en las artes góticas*, Memoria artium, 8 (Bellaterra: Universitat Autònoma de Barcelona, Servei de Publicacións; Barcelona: Publicacions i Edicions de la Universitat de Barcelona, 2008).

Roest, Bert, 'Medieval Franciscan Mission: History and Concept', *Strategies of Medieval Communal Identity: Judaism, Christianity and Islam*, ed. by Wout J. van Bekkum and Paul M. Cobb, Mediaevalia Groningana New Series, 5 (Paris: Peeters, 2004), pp. 137–61.

Rojo Orcajo, Timoteo, *Catálogo descriptivo de los códices que se conservan en la santa iglesia catedral de Burgo de Osma* (Madrid: Tipografía de Archivos, 1929).

Rosenstock, Bruce, 'Against the Pagans: Alonso de Cartagena, Francisco de Vitoria, and *Converso* Political Theology', in *Marginal Voices: Studies in Converso Literature of Medieval and Golden Age Spain*, ed. by Amy Aronson-Friedman and Gregory B. Kaplan, The Medieval and Early Modern Iberian World, 46 (Leiden: Brill, 2012), pp. 117–39.

—, *New Men: 'Conversos', Christian Theology, and Society in Fifteenth-Century Castile*, Papers of the Medieval Hispanic Research Seminar, 39 (London: Department of Hispanic Studies, Queen Mary, University of London, 2002).

Round, Nicholas G., 'Alonso de Espina y Pero Díaz de Toledo: *odium theologicum* y *odium academicus*', in *Actas del X Congreso de la Asociación Internacional de Hispanistas, Barcelona 21–26 de agosto de 1989*, ed. by Antonio Vilanova, 4 vols (Barcelona: PPU, 1992), I, 319–30.

—, *The Greatest Man Uncrowned: A Study of the Fall of Don Álvaro de Luna*, Colección Támesis, A111 (London: Tamesis, 1986).

—, 'Politics, Style and Group Attitudes in the *Instrucción del Relator*', *BHS*, 46 (1969), 289–319.

—, 'La rebelión toledana de 1449: aspectos ideológicos', *Archivum*, 16 (1966), 385–446.

Rubin, Miri, *Gentile Tales: The Narrative Assault on Late Medieval Jews* (New Haven: Yale University Press, 1999).

Ruether, Rosemary Radford, 'The *Adversus Judaeos* Tradition in the Church Fathers: The Exegesis of Christian Anti-Judaism', in *Aspects of Jewish Culture in the Middle Ages: Papers of the Eighth Annual Conference of the Center for Medieval and Early Renaissance Studies, State University of New York at Binghamton, 3–5 May, 1974*, ed. by Paul E. Szarmach (Albany: State University of New York Press, 1979), pp. 27–50.

—, *Faith and Fratricide: The Theological Roots of Anti-Semitism* (New York: Seabury Press, 1974).

Ruiz, Teófilo F., *Spain's Centuries of Crisis, 1300–1474* (Oxford: Blackwell, 2007).

Rusconi, Roberto, 'Antichrist and Antichrists', in *The Encyclopedia of Apocalypticism*, ed. by Bernard McGinn and John J. Colli, 3 vols (New York: Continuum, 1999), II, 287–325.

Sánchez Sánchez, Manuel Ambrosio, 'Predicación y antisemitismo: el caso de San Vicente Ferrer', in *La proyección histórica de España en sus tres culturas: Castilla y León, América y el Mediterráneo*, ed. by Eufemio Lorenzo Sanz, 3 vols (Valladolid: Junta de Castilla y León, Consejería de Cultura y Turismo, 1993) III, 195–203.

Seidenspinner-Nuñez, Dayle, 'Conversion and Subversion: *Converso* Texts in Fifteenth-Century Spain', in *Christians, Muslims, and Jews in Medieval and Early Modern Spain: Interaction and Cultural Change*, ed. by Mark M. Meyerson and Edward D. English, Notre Dame Conferences in Medieval Studies, 8 (Notre Dame: University of Notre Dame Press, 2000), pp. 241–61.

—, 'Prelude to the Inquisition: The Discourse of Persecution, the Toledan Rebellion of 1449, and the Contest for Orthodoxy', in *Strategies of Medieval Communal Identity: Judaism, Christianity and Islam*, ed. by Wout J. van Bekkum and Paul M. Cobb, Mediaevalia Groningana New Series, 5 (Paris: Peeters, 2004), pp. 47–74.

'Sentencia-Estatuto' de Pero Sarmiento, in *De la 'Sentencia-Estatuto' de Pero Sarmiento a la 'Instrucción' del Relator: estudio introductorio, edición crítica y notas de los textos contrarios y favorables a los judeoconversos a raíz de la rebelión de Toledo de 1449*, ed. by Tomás González Rolán and Pilar Saquero Suárez-Somonte (Madrid: Aben Ezra Ediciones, 2012), pp. 20–31

Sermo in die Beati Augustini, in *De la 'Sentencia-Estatuto' de Pero Sarmiento a la 'Instrucción' del Relator: estudio introductorio, edición crítica y notas de los textos contrarios y favorables a los judeoconversos a raíz de la rebelión de Toledo de 1449*, ed. by Tomás González Rolán and Pilar Saquero Suárez-Somonte (Madrid: Aben Ezra Ediciones, 2012), pp. 33–77.

The Sermon, ed. by Bervely Mayne Kienzle, Typologie des Sources du Moyen Âge Occidental, 81–83 (Turnhout: Brepols, 2000).

Los sermones atribuidos a Pedro Marín (B.N.M., Mss. 9433): van añadidas algunas noticias sobre la predicación castellana de san Vicente Ferrer, ed. by Pedro M. Cátedra, Analecta Salmanticensia: Textos Recuperados, 1 (Salamanca: Universidad de Salamanca, 1990).

Serrano, Luciano, *Los conversos don Pablo de Santa María y don Alfonso de Cartagena, obispos de Burgos, gobernantes, diplomáticos y escritores* (Madrid: CSIC, 1942).

Sicroff, Albert A., 'Anticipaciones del erasmismo español en el *Lumen ad revelationem gentium* de Alonso de Oropesa', *Nueva Revista de Filología Hispánica*, 30 (1981), 315–33.

—, *Los estatutos de limpieza de sangre: controversias entre los siglos XV y XVII*, Juan de la Cuesta Hispanic Monographs: Estudios Judeo-Españoles 'Samuel Armistead y Joseph Silverman', 6, 2nd edn (Newark, DE: Juan de la Cuesta, 2010).

Sigüenza, José, *Historia de la orden de San Jerónimo*, rev. by Ángel Weruaga Prieto, Libros Recuperados, 2, 2 vols (Valladolid: Junta de Castilla y León, Consejería de Educación y Cultura, 2000).

Smalley, Beryl, 'The Bible in the Medieval Schools', in *The Cambridge History of the Bible*, II: *The West from the Fathers to the Reformation,* ed. by G.W.H. Lampe (Cambridge: Cambridge University Press, 1969), pp. 197–220.

Simonsohn, Shlomo, *The Apostolic See and the Jews: History*, Studies and Texts, 109 (Toronto: Pontifical Institute of Mediaeval Studies, 1991).

Soifer, Maya, 'Beyond *Convivencia*: Critical Reflections on the Historiography of Interfaith Relations in Christian Spain', *Journal of Medieval Iberian Studies*, 1 (2009), 19–35.

Stocking, Rachel L., 'Early Medieval Christian Identity and Anti-Judaism: The Case of the Visigothic Kingdom', *Religion Compass*, 2 (2008), 642–58 <DOI: 10.1111/j.1749-8171.2008.00087.x>.

Stow, Kenneth, *Alienated Minority: The Jews of Medieval Latin Europe* (Cambridge, MA: Harvard University Press, 1992).

Stuczynski, Claude B., 'Pro-*Converso* Apologetics and Biblical Exegesis', in *The Hebrew Bible in Fifteenth-Century Spain: Exegesis, Literature, Philosophy, and the Arts*, ed. by Jonathan Decter and Arturo Prats, Études sur le Judaïsme Médiéval, 54 (Leiden: Brill, 2012), pp. 151–76.

Suárez Fernández, Luis, *Enrique IV de Castilla: la difamación como arma política* (Barcelona: Ariel, 2001).

Thomas Aquinas, *Summa Theologiae*, in *Corpus Thomisticum*, <http://www.corpusthomisticum.org/sth4066.html> [accessed 6 September 2012].

Trachtenberg, Joshua, *The Devil and the Jews: The Medieval Conception of the Jew and its Relation to Modern Anti-Semitism*, introd. by Mark Saperstein, 2nd edn (Philadelphia: Jewish Publication Society, 2002).

Tratado contra los madianitas e ismaelitas, de Juan de Torquemada (Contra la discriminación conversa), ed. by Carlos del Valle R. (Madrid: Aben Ezra Ediciones, 2002).

Turner, Nancy L., 'Jewish Witness, Forced Conversion, and Island Living', in *Christian Attitudes toward the Jews in the Middle Ages: A Casebook*, ed. by Michael Frasetto (New York: Routledge, 2007), pp. 183–209.

Valle R., Carlos del, 'En los orígenes del problema converso', in *Tratado contra los madianitas e ismaelitas, de Juan de*

Torquemada *(Contra la discriminación conversa)*, ed. by Carlos del Valle R. (Madrid: Aben Ezra Ediciones, 2002), pp. 29–74.

Van Engen, John, 'Christening the Romans', *Traditio*, 52 (1997), 1–45.

Vázquez, Isaac, 'Repertorio de franciscanos españoles graduados en teología durante la Edad Media', in *Repertorio de historia de las ciencias eclesiásticas en España*, 7 vols (Salamanca: Instituto de Historia de la Teología Española, 1967–79), III, 235–320.

Vidal Doval, Rosa, 'La matriz medieval de la disidencia en Castilla: la herejía judaizante y la controversia sobre los conversos', in *Disidencia religiosa en Castilla la Nueva en el siglo XVI*, ed. by Ignacio J. García Pinilla (Ciudad Real: Almud, 2013), pp. 13–28.

—, 'El muro en el Oeste y *La fortaleza de la Fe*: alegorías de la exclusión de minorías en la Castilla del siglo XV', in *Las metamorfosis de la alegoría: discurso y sociedad en la Península Ibérica desde la Edad Media hasta la Edad Contemporánea*, ed. by Rebeca Sanmartín Bastida and Rosa Vidal Doval (Frankfurt am Main: Vervuert; Madrid: Iberoamericana, 2005), pp. 143–68.

—, '"Nos soli sumus christiani": *Conversos* in the Texts of the Toledo Rebellion of 1449', in *Medieval Hispanic Studies in Memory of Alan Deyermond*, ed. by Andrew M. Beresford, Louise M. Haywood and Julian Weiss (Woodbridge: Tamesis, 2013), pp. 215–36.

—, 'Predicación y persuasión: Vicente Ferrer en Castilla, 1411–1412', in *Hacia una poética del sermón*, ed. by Rebeca Sanmartín Bastida, Barry Taylor and Rosa Vidal Doval (= *Revista de Poética Medieval*, 24 (2010)), pp. 225–43.

Vose, Robin, *Dominicans, Muslims and Jews in the Medieval Crown of Aragon* (Cambridge: Cambridge University Press, 2009).

Wadding, Luke, *Annales Minorum seu Trium Ordinum a S. Francisco institutorum*, rev. by José Maria Ribeiro da Fonseca, 2nd edn, 25 vols (Rome: Rochi Bernabò, 1886).

Whitehead, Christiania, 'A Fortress and a Shield: The Representation of the Virgin in the *Château d'amour* of Robert Grosseteste', in *Writing Religious Women: Female Spiritual and Textual Practices in Late Medieval England*, ed. by Denis

Renevey and Christiania Whitehead (Cardiff: University of Wales Press, 2000), pp. 109–31.

—, *Castles of the Mind: A Study of Medieval Architectural Allegory* (Cardiff: University of Wales Press, 2003).

Wills, Garry, *Font of Life: Ambrose, Augustine, and the Mystery of Baptism* (Oxford: Oxford University Press, 2012).

—, *Saint Augustine* (London: Weidenfeld & Nicolson, 1999).

Worcester, Thomas, 'Catholic Sermons', in *Preachers and People in the Reformations and Early Modern Period,* ed. by Larissa Taylor, A New History of the Sermon, 2 (Leiden: Brill, 2001) pp. 3–33.

Yerushalmi, Yosef Hayim, '"Serviteurs des rois et non serviteurs des serviteurs": sur quelques aspects de l'histoire politique des Juifs', *Raisons politiques,* 7 (2002), 19–52 <DOI: 10.3917/rai.007.0019>.

INDEX

Abel 57, 93
Abraham 43, 54, 92, 94–95, 100, 102, 131, 139, 148
Adam 37, 54, 100, 139
allegory 54, 67–69, 75, 110
Alexander the Great 94
Alfonso VIII 107
Alfonso de Valladolid 71
Libro de las batallas del Señor 71
Alonso Carrillo 24, 35, 39n14, 40, 72, 142
Alonso de Cartagena 4, 8, 34, 35, 76
Anacephaleosis 109
biography 36
Defensorium unitatis christianae 8, 34, 36–38, 41–43, 46–49, 53, 54–56, 59–63, 65, 72, 96, 97, 102 n61, 103, 115 n116, 122–24, 138, 139, 142–43, 147–48
Alonso de Espina
biography 21–29
Dialogus de fortuna 30 n100
Fortalitium fidei 19, 29–32
self-representation 20, 75–79
'Sermones de Reverendi Magistri de Spina de penis inferni' 31 n103
Alonso de Mella 127

Alonso de Oropesa 9, 24–25, 34, 76, 83, 86, 96–97, 122, 142–43, 147–48
biography 39–40
Lumen ad revelationem gentium 9, 35, 40–41, 44–45, 46, 51–53, 54, 58–59, 60, 63, 65, 97, 123, 124
Álvaro de Luna 5–7, 22, 30 n100, 123 n18
ancestry 100, 145
Gentile 41–42, 47, 51 n72, 58, 60, 63, 96
Jewish 7, 8 n24, 34, 39, 41–42, 47, 59, 63, 103, 117
Old Christian 25, 43, 46–47
anti-Semitism 11, 14, 16, 18, 28, 34, 100, 107 n82, 122, 148,
Antichrist 73 n27, 85, 94, 98 n48
Arians 126, 130, 140
Augustine of Hippo 17, 45 n43, 69–70, 82–83, 95 n37, 98, 99, 102 nn62–63, 113 n107
Averroism 132

Baer, Yitzak, 11
baptism 2, 3, 8, 35, 37, 41, 47–51, 53, 55, 93, 102, 110–14, 122–23, 28, 134–36, 138–39

Benedict XIII 3
Bernardino of Siena 26, 27 nn90–91, 28, 72, 74 n29, 77, 79 n47, 84, 111 n101
bull of crusade 23, 71
Burgo de Osma, El 31
Burgos 4, 36, 49, 103

Calixtus II 18
Calixtus III 23, 71
Caspian Mountains 94, 114
Castro, Américo 11
Catholic Monarchs 10, 30, 144, 149
City of God 80–83, 86
Christian
   community 2–3, 8, 15, 27 n92, 34, 41, 43–45, 46, 58, 80–83, 106 n78, 126, 141
   equality 35, 39, 41, 44, 49, 53, 65
   identity 41, 47, 137
Church
   as perfect entity 44–45, 52–53, 58, 60, 82–83
   in Castile 1, 33, 36, 44, 76, 83,
   Militant 41, 45 nn42–43, 55, 68, 69, 74, 125
   metaphors for 41–42, 44, 57, 70, 72
   Primitive 81–82
   Triumphant 69
circumcision 43, 50, 53, 54, 92–93, 120, 123–24, 125, 126, 127–29, 133–40, 145
Constantinople 71, 85, 111
conversion 1, 2, 3, 5, 11, 19, 28, 44, 48–49, 56, 59, 61, 65, 76, 79, 85, 88–89, 95 n39, 99, 108–15, 116, 121 n10, 139–40, 148
converso
   debate 5, 14–15, 30, 33–34, 62–63, 64, 120, 147–48
   heresy 24, 46, 50, 53, 87, 119, 120–22, 124–25, 127–31, 133–38, 140–44
   identity 13–14, 41, 62, 63, 120,
   nobility 37, 48–49, 103
   persecution 6, 11, 13, 34, 35, 39, 41, 43, 46, 51, 52, 59–60, 147–48
   problem 2–10, 22 n71, 30, 34, 35, 46, 51, 60, 63, 64, 65, 68, 87, 110, 116, 119, 142, 144–45, 148
   historiography 10–19
   social advancement 5, 10, 110
   theology 59–64
convivencia 1, 11, 15, 81, 114, 148
Córdoba 9
Council of Basle 5 n12, 15, 36, 37, 64, 142
Council of Vienne 141
covenant 62
   Abrahamic 54, 88, 89, 90, 93, 94, 135
   new 88, 90
   covenantal
   continuity 54, 55, 56, 62
   supersession 54, 56, 62, 65, 95
Crusade 23, 71, 76, 81

demons 9, 19, 67–68, 74, 81, 86, 100
Deuteronomy 116–17
Diego Arias Dávila 4, 25
Durango heretics 53, 127,

ecclesiology 9, 59
Edomites 43, 96
England 79, 109–110, 116
Enrique IV 4, 22–24, 30, 40, 71, 84, 131 n51, 142, 143–44
Epistle to Titus 42–43, 45 n40, 47 n47, 120, 123, 135, 137, 139
Epistle to the Galatians 47 n47, 93, 134–36
Epistle to the Hebrews 93
Epistle to the Romans 17, 47 n47, 57, 61–63, 99 n49
Esau 43, 54, 94, 96, 102, 139, 148
eschatology 74, 82 n60, 83, 85, 88
Eucharist 50, 57, 126, 128, 130, 131

Fernán Díaz de Toledo 4, 8
fortress 67–72, 73–74, 80–82, 85–86, 136, 147
France 24, 105 n77, 106 n80, 109, 116, 142
Francis of Mayrone 126
Fuero Juzgo 115

genealogy (see also ancestry) 7, 12, 39, 43, 45, 49, 51, 60, 62, 65, 87, 94–95, 100–3, 122, 138–40, 145
Glossa ordinaria 135–36

Granada 1, 23, 29, 71, 80, 81–82, 127
Guadalupe 40, 45 n40,

heresy 1, 7, 37 n9, 46, 50, 60, 65, 74, 124–33, 143
  judaizing 5, 10, 46, 50, 53, 87, 119, 120–22, 123–24, 132, 133–38, 145
hermeneutics 69, 90 n12, 149
  carnal 98, 101, 102, 103, 105, 111, 138
  spiritual 98, 102
Hernando de la Plaza 24, 144
host desecration 78 n46, 105
Hieronymites 22 n73, 24, 39–40, 147

Iberian Peninsula 1, 11, 15, 29, 31, 49 n58, 71, 73, 89, 95 n39, 102
indulgences 23, 126, 130 n46
inheritance 7, 46–49, 51, 87, 94, 100–2, 138–40, 49
inquisition 46, 59, 116, 122, 124, 141–44, 145
  episcopal 40, 53, 60, 82
  papal 23–24, 53, 80, 141–43
  Spanish 1–2, 10–12, 14, 25, 29, 30, 142–44
Isaac 43, 54, 94–96, 100, 102, 117, 139, 148
Isaiah 17
Ishmael 43, 94, 96, 102, 117, 139, 145, 148
Ishmaelites 96
Islam 64, 71, 74 n30, 116, 133–34

Israel 17, 37, 39–40, 42 n26, 43, 44, 51, 53–59, 60, 61, 63, 95 n39, 99 n49, 103, 117
Lost Tribes of 94, 114

Jacob 17, 43, 54, 93–96, 100, 102, 139, 148
Jerónimo de Santa Fe 71
Contra Iudaeos 71
Jerusalem 41–42, 49 n58, 55, 81, 84, 94, 97, 109, 114, 136, 138
New Jerusalem 59, 72, 82
Jews
    attacks on Christianity 73, 88–89, 103–8
    blasphemy 105
    host desecration 105
    ritual murder 26, 78, 105–6, 109
    usury 105, 106, 112, 128–29
    expulsions 1, 3, 11, 18, 29, 74 n29, 88, 106 n80, 108, 109–10, 114, 117–18, 144, 147, 149
    identity 48 n55, 61, 96, 133
    legislation 3, 24, 64 n125, 86, 88, 108, 109, 114–17
    persecution 2–3, 18, 111, 147
    salvation 17, 61, 74, 88, 89, 134
    Spanish 102–3
    spiritual blindness 17, 88 n6, 97–111, 117, 138, 139

John Duns Scotus 123, 148
Juan II 4, 5, 8, 9, 21, 30 n100, 35, 37 n9, 50, 114, 123 n18,
Juan de Torquemada 4, 8, 34, 35, 37–38, 63, 72, 76
    Tractatus contra madianitas et ismaelitas 4, 8, 34, 38–39, 41, 43–44, 46, 50–52, 53–54, 56–58, 60–63, 65, 96–97, 119, 122–23, 134 n59, 142–43, 147–148.
Judaism 3, 5, 16, 18, 62, 87, 88–108, 112, 115, 116, 119, 120, 122–23, 124 n21, 125, 126, 127, 131, 132, 133–34, 136, 139, 148,
    Biblical 59, 74, 89–97
    rabbinic 59, 74, 87, 97–108
    relationship with Christianity (see also covenant) 53–59, 60–61, 62, 65, 89–90, 95–97, 108
    judaizing (see heresy)

kinship 14, 41, 51, 94, 100 n56, 139

Last Judgment 60, 82–83
law 7, 15, 27, 46, 80, 113, 114, 116
    of Christ 37, 41, 55–56, 58–60, 87 n3, 89–97, 119, 125, 131
    Mosaic 16, 17, 37, 41, 44, 52–56, 58–59, 87 n3,

88, 89–97, 98, 102, 110 n96, 113 n108, 116, 117, 119, 123, 124, 125, 131–38, 145, 148
abolition of 59, 91, 92, 103–4
letrados 37, 109 n91
Leyes de Ayllón 3, 80, 114
Lilith 100, 139
Lope de Barrientos 4, 8, 22 n72
Luis de Páramo 144

Marcos García de Mora 8, 46 n46, 123, 124 n21
Memorial contra los conversos (or *Apelación y suplicación*) 8, 37 n9, 38 n11, 39 n13, 42 n29, 87 n2, 120–21, 123–24,
Medina del Campo 26, 129, 133
Mendicants 18, 26–29, 34, 72, 77, 80, 84, 86, 148
Mcnéndez Pelayo, Marcelino 10–11
millennarism 8 n24, 53, 84, 127
Muslims 9, 19, 25, 43, 68, 70, 73, 74, 76, 79, 80, 81, 83, 86, 121 n10, 133

Name of Jesus 25, 28
natural law 92, 95–96, 148
neophytes 12, 37, 47, 53, 115 n114, 120
Netanyahu, Benzion 11–12
New Christians (see *conversos*)
Nicholas V 8, 35

Observant Franciscans 20, 22, 23–25, 26, 29, 31, 53, 72 n22, 76–77, 85, 124, 127, 144
Origen 62

Pablo de Santamaría (Shelomo ha-Levi) 4, 5 n11, 36
paganizing (see also judaizing) 46
papal bulls
Dum fidei catholicae 24 n78
Humani generis inimicus 8, 38
Nuper siquidem ad aures 8
Si ad reprimendas 8
Sicut Judaeis 18
Vineam soreth 76 n37
Passion of Christ 44, 50, 55, 91, 92, 93, 105 n76, 117, 119, 135,
Patriarchs 95, 96
Paulinism 61, 63
Pedro I 107
Pedro Montoya 102
Pius II 24 n78, 38, 143
polemical texts 12, 14, 30, 73 n23
political theology 35
pollution, social 24–25, 27, 70, 83–84, 148
preachers 20, 23, 26–28, 31, 42, 67, 75–78,
Psalms 18, 51, 67 n1, 69
public opinion 13–14, 26, 29–30
purity of blood (*pureza de sangre*) 2, 7, 8, 10, 12, 14–15, 138, 148–49

Raymond Martí 71, 104
  Pugio fidei 71, 104
reform 20, 26–27, 70, 72, 80–85
Observant 29, 72
Rodrigo 79, 107, 116

Sadducees 103, 126, 131
Sánchez-Albornoz, Claudio 11
Segovia 21 n68, 22, 76, 111, 129
Sentencia-Estatuto de Pero Sarmiento 6–8, 9, 49, 83 n65, 110 n96, 120, 124 n24
sermon 24, 26–27, 31, 38 n10, 70, 75, 77, 78, 79 n47, 129, 141 n84
Siete Partidas 133
Sisenando 115

Talmud 87, 100–1, 104, 112, 132, 140, 145
Távara 106, 107 n82
Thomas Aquinas 87 n3, 92, 113, 148
Toledo 39 n14, 46, 50, 52, 65, 72, 107, 115–16, 122, 125, 134 n59
  inquisition 24–25, 40, 59, 122, 128–30, 141, 142
  revolt 5–9, 35, 36, 52, 60, 83 n65, 87 n2, 109, 110 n96, 123 n18, 124, 125, 138
Torah 110
Tortosa, Disputation 104

Valladolid 26, 70,
Vincent Ferrer 3, 20 n67, 26, 28, 77, 114, 115 n114, 147
Visigothic legislation 109–10, 115, 123, 124 n21

www.ingramcontent.com/pod-product-compliance
Lightning Source LLC
Chambersburg PA
CBHW030236240426
43663CB00037B/1172